The Ideology of the Offensive

A volume in the series

Cornell Studies in Security Affairs

edited by Robert Jervis,
Robert J. Art
Stephen M. Walt

A full list of titles in the series appears at the end of the book.

The Ideology of the Offensive

MILITARY DECISION MAKING AND
THE DISASTERS OF 1914

JACK SNYDER

Cornell University Press

ITHACA AND LONDON

First published 1984 by Cornell University Press
First printing, Cornell Paperbacks, 1989

International Standard Book Number 0-8014-1657-4 (cloth)
International Standard Book Number 0-8014-8244-5(paper)
Library of Congress Catalog Card Number 84-7783
Printed in the United States of America
*Librarians: Library of Congress cataloging information
appears on the last page of the book.*

Cornell University Press strives to use environmentally
responsible suppliers and materials to the fullest extent possible in
the publishing of its books. Such materials include vegetable-based,
low-VOC inks and acid-free papers that are recycled, totally
chlorine-free, or partly composed of nonwood fibers.

1 2 3 4 5 6 7 8 9 10   Cloth printing

4 5 6 7 8 9 10   Paperback printing

Contents

Illustrations

MAPS

FIGURES AND CHARTS

Preface

The disastrous offensives of August 1914 constitute one of history's great unsolved puzzles. Why did the military strategists of Europe's major continental powers choose to defy the inexorable constraints of time, space, and technology, which so heavily favored the defensive? This book explains their strategic doctrines in terms of three components: rational calculation, bias that reflects the influence of parochial interests on perception and policy, and bias that results from the need to simplify complex decisions.

I believe that this perspective provides a persuasive new way of interpreting the events that led to the offensive disasters of 1914. But I also have hopes that it will prove effective when applied to the origins of offensive strategies in other times and other places. Understanding the military's urge to plan for offensive war is of the very greatest urgency, for I believe that offensive strategies in themselves increase the likelihood that wars will be fought.

None of the simple explanations for the epidemic of bad strategy that racked Europe in 1914 is satisfactory. Although France, Germany, and Russia did not favor the status quo, their offensive military plans were designed primarily as protection against conquest by others rather than as instruments of conquest. Offense they erroneously considered the best defense.

It is not true, as some commentators have argued, that the offensives were sound strategy and almost succeeded. The Germans came closest to success, but only because of inadvertent help from an ill-conceived French offensive. Nor is it true that logistical limitations and the strategic implications of defensive firepower were unforeseeable. Numerous military experts had read the operational lessons of the Boer and Russo-Japanese wars more or less correctly, and the war planners themselves often had a good sense of the difficulties that these factors would cause for their offensives. It is also misleading to see the campaigns of August 1914 as the result of some transnational "cult of the offensive"—a military expression of a social Darwinist zeitgeist, Bergsonian *élan vital*, cultural despair, or romantic atavism that characterized the whole epoch. As late as 1910 Russia had an extremely defensive war plan, and France a relatively defensive one.

Historians who have studied the war planning of individual countries offer more helpful insights into the sources of offensive strategies, but even their work entails two main shortcomings. One is the tendency to describe and evaluate rather than to explain. We are told, for example, that Alfred von Schlieffen's errors as a strategist stemmed from his narrow, dogmatic application of traditional German operational principles, but we are not told why German strategists found those principles so attractive and why dogmatization occurred. Similarly, the French historians of the "nation-in-arms school" have shown us that the *offensive à outrance* was somehow linked to the denigration of French reservists and the misreading of German plans, but the polemical aims of these writers distracted them from the analytical goal of disentangling cause and effect.

Historians of single countries have a second shortcoming. They fail to express their insights in general terms, so that their findings might be compared across countries or across time. Absorbed with the idiosyncrasies of their own cases, these historians miss the common thread that explains the offensive bias of all of the European powers—namely, the parochial interests and outlook of military professionals.

The failed offensives of 1914 pose more than a purely historical puzzle. Students of nuclear strategy such as Herman Kahn and Thomas Schelling have often viewed the July Crisis as a parable for our own age, showing how offensive strategies and the belief in a first-strike advantage can lead states to attack preemptively even when their motive is self-defense. More recently, such political scientists as Robert Jervis and George Quester have elaborated on these suggestions, tracing a number of ways in which offensive strategies and force postures make war more likely by promoting a Hobbesian competition for scarce security. These authors have often proceeded as if technology itself were the source of the trouble—that is, war will be more likely when military technology makes attacking easier than defending. This book casts doubt on their view. Strategic instability in 1914 was caused not by military technology, which favored the defender and provided no first-strike advantage, but by offensive war plans that defied technological constraints. The lesson here is that

[10]

doctrines can be destabilizing even when weapons are not, since doctrine may be more responsive to the organizational needs of the military than to the implications of the prevailing weapon technology. This conclusion is supported by recent investigations of strategic planning in various historical settings. Especially notable are Barry Posen's *The Sources of Military Doctrine: France, Britain, and Germany between the World Wars* (Cornell University Press, 1984) and Stephen Van Evera's "The Causes of War" (University of California at Berkeley dissertation, 1984).

Finally, readers interested in the questions raised by this book will also want to consult the summer 1984 issue of *International Security*, which includes an article by Stephen Van Evera on "The Cult of the Offensive and the Origins of the First World War" as well as my own article, "Civil-Military Relations and the Cult of the Offensive, 1914 and 1984." Both stress the role of offensive strategies as a cause of the war, and thus they underscore the importance of understanding the origin of these offensives and the conditions under which offensive bias might recur in our own era.

Hypotheses about the sources of strategic doctrine, which are derived from cognitive and organizational theories of the decision-making process, are outlined in Chapter 1. This introductory chapter also lays out the historical puzzle that is to be explained and discusses the comparative methods that are used to test the three theories. Chapters 2, 4, and 6 explain the adoption of offensive strategies in France, Germany, and Russia, respectively. They respond to a series of standard questions asked of each of the cases. Chapters 3, 5, and 7 are organized chronologically. Each provides detailed evidence supporting the argument advanced in the preceding chapter. The French chapters make extensive use of material from the Archives de la Guerre in Paris. The German chapters rely almost entirely on published sources, which are plentiful because of the widespread interest that the German case has provoked. The Russian chapters were enriched by research in the Lenin Library in Moscow, but the author had no access to Soviet archives. A great deal of the evidence about Russian war planning is taken from works published in the Soviet Union in the 1920s and 1930s. Although this Russian material is available in the United States, it has nonetheless been poorly exploited by Western scholars. The evidence presented in these chapters, even apart from the interpretations offered, should be of considerable interest to historians. The concluding chapter makes comparisons among the cases and discusses the implications of the findings for theories of decision making and international conflict.

[11]

I am grateful for the helpful comments and criticisms received from Michael Brown, Elliot Cohen, Ronald Cole, Roger Haydon, Robert Jervis, Michael Mandelbaum, John Mearsheimer, Steven Miller, Barry Posen, A. L. Ross, Warner Schilling, Nina Tamarkin Snyder, Stephen Van Evera, and Samuel Williamson. Financial and institutional support was received from the Peace Studies Program of Cornell University, the International Research and Exchanges Board, the Hubert Humphrey Fellowship of the U.S. Arms Control and Disarmament Agency, and the Center for International Affairs of Harvard University. Michael and Nicholas Daniloff generously allowed me to make use of General Iurii N. Danilov's unpublished papers.

JACK SNYDER

New York City

The Ideology of the Offensive

[1]

Military Bias and
Offensive Strategy

All of the major continental powers entered World War I with offensive strategies; all suffered huge strategic costs when, predictably, their offensives failed to achieve their ambitious aims. These failed offensives created political and operational difficulties that haunted the states throughout the war. Germany's Schlieffen Plan, for example, helped bring Britain into the war, provoking the protracted naval blockade that the Germans had hoped to avoid. Similarly, the miscarriage of France's Plan 17 allowed Germany to occupy large portions of northeastern France, hindering the operation of the French wartime economy and making more difficult a negotiated settlement on the basis of the status quo ante. Finally, the annihilation of the Russian forces invading East Prussia squandered troops that might have produced decisive results if concentrated on the Austrian front. Each of these countries would thus have been in a better position to secure an acceptable outcome if it had fought the war defensively from the beginning.

The offensive strategies had another, more profound cost: the war might never have occurred had the advantages of the defender been better appreciated. States would have understood that maintaining their security did not require preventive attacks on others. The lure of conquest (in any event a secondary motive for the offensives) would have been diminished if its difficulties had been more clearly recognized.[1]

The adoption of these offensives cannot be explained in terms of a rational strategic calculus. As the Boer and Russo-Japanese wars had foreshadowed, the tactical and logistical technologies of this era strongly favored the defender. In no case did geopolitical considerations decisively outweigh the technological advantages of a defensive strategy. Likewise, aggressive national aims are inadequate as an explanation for deciding upon the ill-fated offensives of 1914. While none of the major continental states could be described as strictly favoring the status quo, the overriding criterion used by top military planners was security, not conquest.

The choice of offensive strategies by the continental powers was primarily the result of organizational biases and doctrinal over-simplifications of professional military planners. Some causes of offensive bias may have been common to all countries. The decisive sources of bias, however, were peculiar to each case, rooted in specific interests, preconceptions, and circumstances.[2]

Of the three largest continental powers, the French chose the least rational strategy. Technology, geography, and the need to coordinate with Russian efforts should all have pushed them strongly toward the defensive, but offensive bias overshadowed these incentives. The source of this bias was the military's organizational interest in preventing the professional army from being turned into a training cadre for a mass army composed of civilian reservists. Since everyone agreed that French reservists were good only for defense, the military fought institutional change by touting the indispensability of the offense. For the same reasons, they discounted the significance of German reservists, an intelligence failure that had near-fatal consequences in August 1914. In the aftermath of the venomous Dreyfus affair, institutional protection became an overwhelming concern for the French military and a powerful source of bias that had no equal in Germany or Russia.

Germany's geopolitical circumstances offered a clear incentive neither for offense nor for defense. Because of Russia's slow mobilization, a rapid German offensive had some chance of beating France and Russia piecemeal, before Russia's full weight could be brought to bear. A quick victory would have been difficult, however, because of the defender's tactical and logistical advantages. On the other hand, a German defensive strategy, based on an impregnable line of fortifications on the short Franco-German border, could not have offered quick victory either, but it would have provided two major advantages. First, if Germany had fought a strictly defensive war, Britain would not have had sufficient motive to join the Franco-Russian war effort. Second, with France checked by a German defense line, Russia would have been easier to deter or defeat.

Yet parochial interests and a parochial outlook would lead the German military to denigrate defensive alternatives. The extraordinary prestige of the German army rested on its historical ability to deliver rapid offensive victories, as it had against Austria in 1866 and France in 1870. Although German strategists recognized that improvements in firepower were making the attacker's task tactically more difficult, they could not accept that a future war would inevitably take the form of an inglorious, unproductive stalemate. At the same time, their professional preoccupation with potential military threats led them to overestimate the inevitability of war with France and Russia. As a result, they underrated the ability of a defensive posture to deter war and overrated the need for a capability to attack preventively. Over time, these offensive predispositions became magnified and dogmatized, as the powerful, centralized General Staff succeeded in inculcating the whole officer corps with a simple, standard offensive doctrine.

Germany's widely anticipated decision to deploy more than four-fifths of its army against France gave Russia a strong incentive to attack the German rear. In the Russian case, the error lay not in the decision to attack but in the decision to attack too soon with too weak a force. The hasty, undermanned advance into East Prussia led to the encirclement and destruction of a Russian force of 100,000 men at Tannenberg. This strategic disaster can be explained partly by intra-military politics and partly by the Russians' psychological need to see the necessary as possible. The General Staff in St. Petersburg, emphasizing their strategic aim of preventing a collapse of the French army, placed the highest priority on an early attack on Germany's rear. However, local commanders in Kiev sought to divert forces for their own offensive, against Austria. The absence of a strong central authority to adjudicate this dispute resulted in a compromise that left commanders on both fronts too weak to carry out their tasks. Nonetheless, the General Staff continued to deem a hasty attack on Germany a strategic necessity. Choosing to see the necessary as possible, they discounted captured German war games that foretold the spectacular German victory at Tannenberg.

In sum, strategic decision making in all three states was similar in that institutional and cognitive biases led to the adoption of unduly offensive strategies. In each case, however, the intensity and the decisive causes of offensive bias differed because of varying external and internal circumstances. Bias was greatest—and most influenced by motivational factors—in France, where grave threats to organizational interests provided an overwhelming incentive to skew strategy and doctrine. Bias was less acute in Germany and Russia, where no single motive for error was quite so compelling. There, the choice of offensive strategy resulted from the interplay of rational plausibility, motivational biases of lesser intensity, and doctrinal oversimplifications.[3]

RATIONALITY AND BIAS IN STRATEGIC ANALYSIS

A rational policymaker may prefer either an offensive or a defensive strategy; the choice depends on goals and on a variety of geopolitical factors. Almost invariably, some degree of bias will influence the assessment of these factors. Generally speaking, we can divide sources of bias in decision making into two groups: the first, biases rooted in the motivations of the decision makers, especially in their parochial interests, and the second, biases that result from decision makers' attempts to simplify and impose a structure on their complex analytical tasks. Both groups of bias can be viewed as cognitive phenomena, skewing the perceptions and choices of individual decision makers; they can also be considered organizational phenomena, shaping the structure, ideology, and standard operating procedures of institutions.[4]

Sometimes decision makers prefer policies because of motives they would rather not admit, even to themselves. In such cases, the need to find an acceptable justification for the policy they prefer will skew perceptions and analysis. "Decision making" will be a process of rationalization rather than of rationality. In strategic policy making, the most pervasive source of motivational bias is the institutional interest of the military.[5] The military tends to favor policies that promote its organizational aims. Since these favored policies must be justified in strategic terms, strategic perceptions and analysis are likely to become skewed whenever organizational interests are at odds with sound strategy.

Rationalization is also likely when the strategist has no acceptable options—that is, when any strategy would almost certainly involve an unacceptable sacrifice of some key value. In practice, decision makers in this situation tend to adopt risky strategies, but in rationalizing this choice, they also tend to overrate the probability that their strategy will succeed. In other words, people see the "necessary" as possible.

Because decision makers need to make complex analytical tasks more manageable, they inevitably use perceptual and analytical shortcuts in devising solutions to problems[6] and thus fall victim to a second group of biases. In military analysis, the most important simplifying device is the strategic doctrine, which imposes a structure on

[18]

the strategic problem and suggests possible solutions. But doctrine, in simplifying reality, introduces biases into strategic analysis.

In most cases, then, the choice between offensive and defensive strategies will be the result of some combination of rational incentives, motivational biases, and doctrinal oversimplifications. In particular circumstances, examined in detail immediately below, one or another of these determinants will dominate the decision makers' choice.

OFFENSE AND DEFENSE: A RATIONAL CALCULUS

A rational strategist's choice of an offensive or a defensive strategy should depend on national aims (i.e., foreign-policy goals), technological and geographical constraints, and the military balance. In 1914 the particular circumstances of each of the European powers produced in each case a different set of rational incentives. France's circumstances should have pointed decisively to defense. In Germany, there were some incentives for offense but probably stronger reasons to remain on the defensive. In the Russian case, Germany's decision to deploy only weak forces in the East virtually forced Russia to mount some kind of attack, but a less hasty offensive would have fared better than the plan that was actually adopted.

National Aims

A state particularly needs an offensive strategy when it seeks to conquer or coerce others. France, Germany, and Russia each had some interest in revising the political status quo in Europe, but in no case did this interest outweigh security as the primary determinant of military strategy.

Historians sometimes assume that the French offensive strategy was dictated by an offensive political aim—regaining the provinces of Alsace and Lorraine, lost to Germany in 1870.[7] The French General Staff certainly did hope that victory in a general European war would "enable the map of Europe to be redrawn," but this hope did not determine the shape of their war plan.[8] Even proponents of a "defensive-offensive" or "counteroffensive" strategy wanted to recapture Alsace-Lorraine, but they argued that this could be done only by capitalizing on the strategic error that Germany would make in attacking France.[9] Meanwhile, proponents of offense did not dispute that operational necessities, not the revanchist urge, should shape

French strategy; they simply had a different view of those necessities.[10]

Germany was also inclined to revise the political status quo in Europe. Although the desire to annex European territory was not particularly strong until the war had already begun, Germany had other, more diffuse revisionist aims that an offensive capability on land in Europe might have served. Germany's "reach for world power," a vague striving for politico-economic influence in a variety of semicolonial enterprises, was hampered by the irremediable inferiority of its fleet relative to Britain's. Consequently, Germany needed an offensive, war-winning capability on the continent to neutralize the political consequences of the naval imbalance. Arguably, the ability to overturn the continental balance would allow Germany to get its way in colonial and sphere-of-influence disputes, not only with France and Russia but also with Britain.[11]

This thesis sounds so logical that it deserves to be true. In fact, however, the General Staff officers who shaped the strategy of the German army were neither so systematic nor so single-minded in the pursuit of German *Weltpolitik*. Each of the three chiefs of staff who worked out Germany's offensive war plans from 1870 to 1914 was primarily preoccupied by the need to secure German survival in a two-front war. As a General Staff memorandum of 1902 put it: "We are not out for conquest, but seek merely to defend what is ours. We shall probably never be the agressor, always the attacked. The swift successes we shall need, however, can be achieved with certainty only when we take the offensive."[12] Even junior General Staff officers, some of whom were avowedly expansionist, were primarily concerned with the threat to German security posed by the encircling Entente. In their view, offense was the best defense. Conveniently, they saw no conflict between a strategy designed for security and a strategy designed for expansion.

Among Russian war planners, those who argued for an offensive against Germany proceeded strictly from considerations of Russian security. Those who argued for an offensive against Austria, however, cited not only military operational reasons but also a political aim, that of clearing the way for Russian hegemony in the Balkans and the Turkish Straits. In this sense, the overcommitted, offensive nature of the plan ultimately adopted, which provided insufficient forces for both offensives, can be partially attributed to the lure of conquest.

Technology and Geography

In strictly operational terms, both attacking and defending confer some advantages and some disadvantages. The attacker's characteristic advantages derive from surprise and the initiative, the defender's from terrain barriers, fortifications, shorter supply lines, and better mobility. The relative weight of these advantages and disadvantages depends on the specific technological and geographical circumstances in which the campaign is to take place. In 1914 technology and geography would combine to reinforce the defender's characteristic advantages and to lessen those of the attacker. These facts were foreshadowed by every war fought between 1860 and 1914, but they were only partially appreciated by European military strategists of the era.

In matters of tactics, the Boer and Russo-Japanese wars drove home the fact that improvements in firepower were making assaults on prepared positions extremely costly. German doctrine had long appreciated the difficulty of frontal attacks and emphasized flank maneuvers to avoid them. To some degree, the French also understood this problem, but they overrated the ability of élan and marginal tactical innovations to overcome it. The Russians also looked on the advantages of the defense as a problem to be overcome, not as an opportunity to be exploited.

In matters of strategic maneuver and logistics, the technologies of 1914 also gave the defender an inherent advantage. Although the railroads allowed the attacker to concentrate a large force on the frontier very quickly, the mobilization and transport of a significant force still took at least a few days and could hardly be kept secret. As long as the defender countermobilized quickly, maintained a reasonable covering force on the frontier, and concentrated forces in a safe area, a disarming first strike in the style of Pearl Harbor could not succeed in 1914. The attacker might still achieve surprise in the location of the attack, but prevailing technologies made it difficult to exploit the advantage that surprise conferred. For example, in August 1914 the French high command consistently misread evidence indicating that a large force was outflanking the French army by way of northern Belgium. The French persisted in this error for more than three weeks after mobilization, when they finally decided to shift their forces by rail to meet the threat to their left flank. These rail redeployments easily recaptured the initiative from the exhausted, ill-supplied Germans, who had had to "maneuver" on foot once they crossed the frontier into Belgium.

The defensive nature of the railroads was demonstrated not only in France but on every front in August 1914. Most spectacularly, the German defenders of East Prussia used the railroads to shuttle between the two wings of a Russian pincer maneuver, easily achieving local superiority despite their inferiority in the theater as a whole.

Even the Russians, defending against an Austrian thrust into Poland, used a rapid redeployment by rail to plug a huge gap that opened up in their front line. In every case, the railroads allowed the defender to outmaneuver the footbound attacker and to recapture the initiative.

In addition to this advantage in transportation, defenders were also able to exploit advantages conferred by water barriers, permanent fortifications, and relatively short supply lines. Even the sheer magnitude of the forces engaged provided a huge advantage to the defender, particularly on the western front. Once a certain density of forces is achieved, defenders can succeed even if they are substantially outnumbered. Adding attackers to a narrow front produces diminishing returns, not victory.[13] The violation of Belgian neutrality more than doubled the length of the western front, however, and reduced this defensive advantage.

War planners did not ignore these operational and logistical advantages of the defender, but they did underrate them. As a result, planners were unduly optimistic about the chances of their own offensive plans and unduly pessimistic about the prospects of defensive alternatives.

The Military Balance

As a rule, the weaker power is usually the defender and the stronger is the attacker. This rule tacitly recognizes the advantages of the defense, and even the European powers followed it before 1914. France adopted a strictly defensive strategy during its period of weakness in the 1870s, and Russia did the same after being weakened by the Russo-Japanese War. When the balance of forces was more equal, however, strategists tended to forget the advantages of the defense.

The anticipated trend of the balance can also influence the choice between offense and defense. In Germany and Russia, for example, strategy was strongly influenced by the anticipation of momentary advantages that could be exploited only by offensive means. These included "windows of opportunity" that would open—and, if not exploited, close—during the anticipated course of the war as well as permanently adverse trends in the military balance that gave an incentive for preventive war.

German strategists believed that Russia's slow mobilization would give them a window of opportunity during the initial weeks of the war. If they did not achieve a decisive early victory over France, they believed, Russian numerical superiority and a British blockade would eventually turn the tide against them. As it turned out, Germany was better equipped than Russia to endure a long war, despite the British blockade. Nonetheless, Germany gambled on its fleeting chance for a rapid decision against France and, as a result, opened a window of opportunity for Russia. Correctly anticipating the Germans' decision to deploy only a week force on the eastern front, the Russians felt themselves doubly compelled to advance very rapidly against Germany. First, the Russian General Staff, fearing that France would succumb without immediate assistance, felt compelled to close the Germans' window of opportunity in the west. Second, the Russians wanted to exploit their own window against Germany by advancing to a stronger, shorter defense line along the River Vistula, which would be easier to hold after the Germans turned their attention to the east. Both the Russians and the Germans were pessimistic about their chances against the others in a long war; consequently, both adopted risky offensives in order to end the war quickly or to improve their prospects in a longer war.

Another reason for the Germans' preference for offense was the preventive strain in their strategic thinking. Ever since 1870, German strategists had been anticipating the day when a revived France and a growing Russia would threaten to outstrip the combined military capability of Germany and Austria. When that time came, as the General Staff argued it had in 1887, an offensive capability would be needed to launch preventive war against one or both potential enemies. On that occasion, the civilian leadership substituted an arms buildup for a preventive war. In the period after 1912, however, the Germans doubted their ability to keep abreast of planned increases in the Russian army. They saw a closing window of opportunity for a preventive war and, not accidentally, had an offensive war plan to carry it out.

At least some of these windows of opportunity really existed, but strategists consistently overrated their importance relative to factors favoring the defense. Because of the defender's great tactical and logistical advantages, it was unrealistic to believe that France could be defeated during the brief opportunity created by Russia's slow mobilization. Even though the French played into the Germans' hands by attacking, their residual defensive capability was still sufficient to prevent a final decision and to reverse the tide. For the same reasons, anticipated improvements in Russian capabilities would not have outstripped Germany and Austria's ability to fight a defensive war successfully. The Russian build-up did threaten the viability of Germany's offensive plan, but only because it was so tenuous in the first place.

Thus a rational calculus can yield an offensive strategy when some or all of the following conditions hold: (1) the state is expansionist, (2) technology either favors the attacker or at least does not strongly favor the defender, (3) geography does not strongly favor the defender, (4) the military balance is favorable, and (5) the anticipated trend of the balance is unfavorable. But in 1914 technology strongly favored the defender, a fact that alone should have outweighed all the countervailing incentives for offense. Consequently, strictly rational calculations cannot explain the strategies that were adopted.

OFFENSIVE BIAS: MOTIVATIONS AND INTERESTS

Policies are sometimes shaped by motives that conflict with the dictates of sound strategy. When such conflict occurs, perceptions and analysis will be skewed so that the decision can be justified as an apparently rational public-policy choice. In strategic policy making before World War I, we can identify two types of such motivated biases: biases caused by the institutional interests of the military, and biases caused by the need to see the necessary as possible.

Institutional Interests

The institutional interests of the military had a pervasive influence on strategic policy, analysis, and perceptions in the period before World War I. In each of the continental powers, parochial interests played some role in biasing strategy in favor of the offense. Some of these parochial biases are of a kind that should always lead any military organization to prefer offense; others favored offense in 1914 but under different conditions might favor defense. Germany offers examples of the former variety, France of the latter.[14]

Offense is difficult and demands large defense budgets. It is also productive—productive in that decisive offensive campaigns produce demonstrable returns on the state's investment in military capability. In the 1880s, for example, Field Marshal Colmar von der Goltz pushed the view that "modern wars have become the nation's way of doing business"—a perspective that made sense only if wars were short, cheap, and hence offensive.[15]

Another dividend of offense is the increased prestige and heightened self-image of the army. The quick, decisive Wars of German Unification turned the Prussian officer corps into demigods, whom the rest of the nation honored and emulated. Offense looks even better to the military when it considers the alternatives. As Barry Posen puts it, offense makes soldiers specialists in victory, defense makes them specialists in attrition, and deterrence makes them specialists in slaughter.[16]

The elder Helmuth von Moltke succinctly stated the universal wish of military commanders: "The politican should fall silent the moment that mobilization begins."[17] This silence is least likely to happen during limited or defensive wars, where the whole point of fighting is to negotiate a diplomatic solution. Then, political considerations—and hence politicians—have to figure in operational decisions. The military is most likely to be allowed operational autonomy when the operational goal is to disarm the adversary quickly and decisively by offensive means. For this reason, the military will seek to force doctrine and planning into this mold.[18]

These motives for offensive bias operate in a wide variety of historical and social settings. More idiosyncratic were the institutional interests that biased the French in favor of the offensive in the years before 1914. Briefly, the military touted the offensive because traditional French military institutions could claim an offensive capability where militia-type institutions could not. In other circumstances, however, these incentives might be reversed. If traditional institutions were best suited for defense and a competing institutional scheme was best suited for offense, the military would be likely to denigrate the offense in order to preserve its "organizational essence."[19] In the 1930s, for example, the preservation of the organizational status quo worked against the offensive doctrine and force postures urged by Charles de Gaulle in France and Heinz Guderian in Germany.[20]

In addition to specifying whether an institutional interest favors offense or defense, the analyst should also specify the strength of the resulting motivation. The general rule is that the motivation for bias will be greatest when three conditions prevail: first, institutional interests are under a severe, immediate threat; second, the interests at stake are fundamental ones, especially self-image and organizational essence;[21] finally, there must be some contradiction between institutional interests and sound strategy. By definition, there is no bias if accurate perceptions and analysis happen to be perfectly compatible with institutional interests.

Decisional Conflict

Conflicts between institutional and strategic interests are not the only source of motivated bias. Psychologists have long speculated that bias may also be caused by other types of "decisional conflicts." These types might include a conflict between the decision maker's preconceptions and evidence showing that they are incorrect, a conflict between the decision maker's aims and evidence showing that they are unattainable, or a trade-off between any two values that the decision maker holds. Some psychologists argue that all of these types of conflicts produce stress, which the decision maker may try to eliminate by denying the existence of the conflict. They hold that the denial is accomplished through some bias in perception or analysis,[22] a hypothesis that helps to explain some of the strategic errors of 1914.

Decisional stress is most painful when circumstances seem to offer no chance of achieving an acceptable outcome. This was the situation facing General Iurii Danilov, the chief operational planner in the Russian General Staff in 1914. Danilov was very skeptical of France's chances against Germany in the opening phase of the war and even more pessimistic about Russia's prospects in a long war against Germany. This evaluation led him to place a high priority on an immediate Russian offensive into East Prussia in order to relieve the pressure on the French. Bureaucratic politics prevented Danilov from allocating sufficient forces to do the job safely and successfully. Rather than abandon or delay his offensive, however, Danilov eliminated his "decisional conflict" by underrating the operational difficulties of the advance into East Prussia. Believing that the hasty attack was necessary, he chose to see it as possible. This inclination to see the necessary as possible favored the offense in the Russian case, but in other circumstances, it might favor the defense. For example, the commander of a beseiged garrison will tend to underrate the offensive capabilities of the opponent if he feels that surrender would be unthinkable.

In summary, some sources of motivated bias should always favor the offense, but others may favor either offense or defense, depending on the circumstances. The strength of the motivation for bias depends on the intensity of the threat to the decision maker's interests, the importance of the interests at stake, and where institutional interests are involved, the degree to which they conflict with sound strategy.

OFFENSIVE BIAS: THE NEED TO SIMPLIFY

Questions of military strategy, like most public-policy problems, entail considerable complexity and uncertainty. Most of the elements of the problem are known in only an approximate way. How strong are the opposing sides? What will the opponent do with his forces? How will new, relatively untested technologies affect the conditions of combat? What will be the likely consequences of various alternative courses of action? Large amounts of information bearing on these questions may be available, but much of it may be contradictory or ambiguous.

To make the complex task of war planning more manageable, the military strategist needs to develop relatively simple but effective techniques for scanning and organizing information about the problem, and for structuring and evaluating the available options. It is primarily military doctrine, a set of beliefs about the nature of war and the keys to success on the battlefield, that performs this function for the military planner. These beliefs provide a framework for organizing information and criteria for evaluating its importance. They also provide a curriculum for the training of new soldiers, a guide for the design of organizational structures, and a criterion for the establishment of standard operating procedures. Thus, doctrine helps to provide a simple, coherent, standardized structure both for strategic thought and for military institutions.

The cognitive and organizational need for simplicity and stable structure also shapes the evolution of doctrinal beliefs. Core assumptions are formed by early experiences or training. These are difficult to change, despite disconfirming evidence or incentives to adopt new beliefs. Discrepant information is either ignored or incorporated into the belief system in a way that minimizes the need to change the system's structure.[23] Vivid, firsthand experiences, personal successes and failures, and events important to the person's state or organization play a disproportionate role in the subsequent learning process.[24] In this way, military doctrines—like any belief system—reflect the need for continuity, ease of recall, and a restricted scope of attention to information.

As the strategist's belief system simplifies and structures the strategic problem, it inevitably introduces elements of bias into perceptions and choices. If new problems do not fit into the categories that the old beliefs establish, they will not be well understood. Those aspects of the problem which lie outside the strategist's inevitably limited scope of attention will be ignored. Beliefs formed on the basis of early training or parochial experiences, however, may not continue to be an appropriate guide for defining the problem.

The case studies of strategic planning before 1914 suggest five sources of bias that involve some form of doctrinal simplification.

Some of these biases always favor the offense; some favor either offense or defense, depending on specific circumstances; others act to intensify whatever biases may already exist.

1. *Focus of attention.* The professional training and duties of soldiers force them to focus on threats to the state's security and on the conflictual side of international relations. Necessarily preoccupied with the prospect of armed conflict, they see war as a pervasive aspect of international life. In their focus on the role of the military in ensuring national security, they forget that other means can also be used toward the same end. For these reasons, the military professional tends to hold a simplified, zero-sum view of international politics and the nature of war. In this kind of Hobbesian world, wars are seen as difficult to avoid and almost impossible to keep limited.

When the hostility of others is taken for granted, prudential calculations are slanted in favor of preventive wars and preemptive strikes. Indeed, as German military officers were fond of arguing, the proper role of diplomacy in a Hobbesian world is to create favorable conditions for launching preventive war. A preventive grand strategy requires an offensive operational doctrine. Defensive plans and doctrines will be considered only after all conceivable offensive schemes have been decisively discredited. Under conditions of uncertainty, such discrediting will of course be difficult, so offensive plans and doctrines will frequently be adopted even if offense is in the operational sense no easier than defense.

The assumption of extreme hostility also favors the notion that decisive, offensive operations are always needed to end wars. If the conflict of interest between the parties is seen as limited, then a decisive victory may not be needed to end the fighting on mutually acceptable terms. In fact, a successful defense may suffice to deny the opponent his objectives. However, when the opponent is believed to be extremely hostile, disarming him completely may seem like the only way to induce him to break off his attacks. For this reason, offensive doctrines and plans are needed, even if defense is easier in an operational sense.

Kenneth Waltz argues that states are socialized to the implications of international anarchy. Because of their professional preoccupations, military professionals become "oversocialized." Seeing war more likely than it really is, they increase its likelihood by adopting offensive plans and buying offensive forces.[25] In this way, the perception that war is inevitable becomes a self-fulfilling prophecy.

2. *Formation of doctrine.* Either from the individual or from the organizational point of view, doctrinal beliefs are inordinately influenced

[28]

by a few formative experiences. Past wars and early training, in particular, establish patterns of thought and organization that are highly resistant to change. As technology and other factors change, however, these old patterns may not remain appropriate. In other words, they constitute a bias. Depending on the lessons imparted by these formative experiences, this bias may favor either offense or defense. From the Wars of Unification, the German army learned to appreciate the great advantages of decisive offensive strategies, even though the lesson was already dubious in 1871 and had become downright dangerous by 1914. In contrast, mainstream opinion in all the European armies drew the inference from World War I that offense had become extremely disadvantageous, a bias that led many to underrate the offensive potential of the modern tank.[26]

3. *Dogmatization of doctrine.* All doctrines are "dogmatic" in the sense that they are simple, narrow, deductive, and resistant to changes, but some are more dogmatic than others. Among individuals, dogmatism is most likely in theoretical, sand-table strategists, who have had little direct experience in managing a war. In organizations, doctrines are likely to become dogmatic when authority is highly centralized and when environmental disruptions, like wars or domestic political changes, are absent. Under these conditions, central military authorities can succeed in inculcating a simple, standard doctrine via war college training, field manuals, institutional structures, and war plans. This process of disseminating a doctrine throughout the organization tends to make a simple doctrine even simpler, because it must be made easily communicable. As a result, dogmatization and standardization make existing biases more extreme, whether they are offensive or defensive.

4. *Economy of calculation.* One of the functions of doctrine is to provide rules of thumb for simplifying complex operational calculations. Logistical calculations can be particularly onerous. In the prewar Russian and German armies, war planning at the highest levels proceeded on the basis of extremely casual assumptions about logistical feasibility. Lower-level logistical planners, responsible for working out the details, were supposed to implement strategy, not evaluate it. In principle, logistical rules of thumb might be optimistic and thus favor the offense, or they might be pessimistic and thus favor the defense. In the Russian and German cases, however, the rule of thumb employed was a friction-free, best-case estimate of marching and supply capabilities.[27]

5. *Reduction of uncertainty.* Posen points out that "taking the offensive, exercising the initiative, is a way of structuring the battle."[28]

Defense, in contrast, is more reactive, less structured, and harder to plan. People in charge of large organizations seek structure—or the illusion of structure. Hence, as Stephen Van Evera deduces, the military will prefer the task that is easier to plan even if it is more difficult to execute successfully. The Russian case provides direct support for this view. Between 1910 and 1912 regional staffs explicitly complained that the General Staff's defensive war plan left their planning problem too unstructured.

In sum, doctrinal simplification invariably introduces some degree of bias into strategic analysis. Some military biases, like the overestimation of the likelihood of war, tend to favor the offense. Other biases, like the inordinate influence of formative experiences, may favor either offense or defense, depending on the specific circumstances. Still other biases, like the organizational need to simplify and standardize doctrine, reinforce whatever bias already exists.

THE SYNTHESIS: ORGANIZATIONAL IDEOLOGY

The selection of an offensive or defensive strategy is determined by the interaction of rational calculation, motivational biases, especially those due to institutional interests, and the cognitive and organizational need for doctrinal simplification. The outcome of the decision-making process will reflect both the content of each of these three determinants and their relative strength.

If all three factors point toward the same strategy, the outcome is clear. If they imply different strategies, however, the outcome will depend on their comparative weights. Rational calculation will weigh most heavily when the supporting evidence is clear and decisive; it will carry less weight when environmental incentives and constraints are ambiguous. Motivated bias will be greatest when central values, especially key parochial interests, are severely threatened. Doctrinal simplification will be greatest when institutions are strong and centralized, when environmental disruptions are absent for a long time, and when the top strategist is what John Steinbruner calls a "theoretical thinker." When one of these determinants is stronger than the other two, it will dominate the choice between an offensive and a defensive strategy. When each of the three carries significant weight, strategy will be a synthesis of rational, motivational, and doctrinal considerations.

In both the French and the German cases, this synthesis was accomplished by means of an organizational ideology, which included beliefs about the nature of war, prescriptions for healthy military institutions, and doctrines for military operations. In essence, the ideology represented a consensus of views on abstract principles, which had practical implications. Eventually, the ideology became institutionalized in field regulations, organizational structures, war plans, and war college curricula.

Organizational ideologies differ in the way they synthesize the rational, motivational, and doctrinal determinants of strategy, according to the differing strength of each of the determinants. Five patterns are noteworthy in the decades before 1914.[29]

In France between 1880 and 1898, the military developed a relatively flexible, undogmatic ideology, centered on a moderately offensive doctrine. It helped to neutralize a moderate threat to traditional institutional arrangements. Although the ideology was unambiguous in its defense of these tenets in the abstract, pragmatism reigned in applying them to the concrete problems of war planning and, to some extent, those of institutional reform.

Later in the same country, between 1905 and the outbreak of war, a more extreme version of the organizational ideology emerged. In the aftermath of the Dreyfus affair and the resulting attacks on traditional military institutions, the French military's organizational ideology evolved in the direction of caricature, with an extreme emphasis on the offensive. Threats to core values and the increasing intrusion of parochial interests into military policy making led to perceptual biases, of which the misreading of German strategic intentions is the most striking example.

Germany between 1870 and 1890 illustrates ideology as a more rational guide to action. The doctrine of the rapid decision by a battle of encirclement simplified planning and satisfied the requirements of organizational self interest, but these functions were not allowed to jeopardize the primary role of doctrine as a guide to success on the battlefield. Field Marshal Helmuth von Moltke strove to create a doctrine that was consistent both with the realities of modern warfare and with his preference for rapid, decisive victories. Whenever these two sets of concerns came clearly into conflict, however, Moltke sacrificed some of his preferences in order to maintain the feasibility of his plans and doctrine.

From 1890 to the start of war, the German organizational ideology evolved into an institutionalized dogma. Moltke's successors did not retain the same balance among the three determinants of the organizational ideology. Alfred von Schlieffen, a narrower and more theoretical thinker than Moltke, bowed to cognitive and institutional

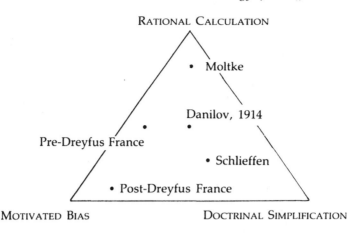

Figure 1. Strategic choice: Balance of determinants.

incentives to dogmatize Moltke's doctrine and used a double standard in evaluating alternative views.

Finally, prewar Russia exemplifies the absence of unified organizational ideology. The development of a unified organizational ideology was prevented by the comparative decentralization of Russian military institutions and by the doctrinal and organizational upheavals that followed the Russo-Japanese War. As a result, the synthesis of rationality, motivated bias, and doctrinal simplification was more ad hoc and less stable than in France and Germany. In August 1914 Danilov's improvised strategy reflected a mixture of analytical realism, motivated optimism, and pessimistic preconceptions. The lack of a structured ideology more hindered than helped effective performance in war. Military organizations that lack a unified doctrine, like the Russian army in 1914, tend to find that the advantages of "keeping an open mind" do not compensate for the lack of a coherent theory of victory.

Intramilitary Politics

Up to this point, I have portrayed strategic planning as a unitary process, not a pluralistic one. In a unitary decision process, plans and doctrines are derived either from the values and perceptions of an individual decision maker or from the shared perspectives of a like-minded group. In the German case, the organizational ideology was sufficiently institutionalized that one can treat German planning in unitary terms. In the French case, however, competing viewpoints vied for influence over strategic planning doctrine. The French war plan in 1914 resulted from the victory of one of these outlooks within the military. This victory allowed General Joseph Joffre, the French chief of staff, to lay down strategic policy according to the predispositions and interests of the people sharing this common view. In this sense, the French plan can also be discussed as the product of a unitary process of decision making.

In the Russian case, however, strategic policy was the product of a pluralistic decision process. No single viewpoint or group within the Russian military could dominate the planning of war. The Russians lacked both a unified, undisputed doctrine and a centralized, universally recognized authority for adjudicating strategic disputes. Under

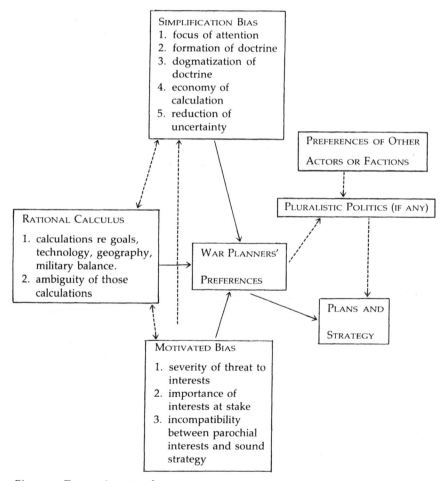

Figure 2. Determinants of strategy.

these circumstances, war plans reflected a political compromise between alternative strategic conceptions. Under the terms of the de facto compromise, the General Staff were allowed their offensive against Germany and the dissenters in the military districts were allowed their offensive against Austria. Pursuing these two offensives diminished the forces available for each one. Consequently, the compromise plan was more overcommitted and more offensive than the initial preference of either faction.[30]

In this sense, the Russian offensives result from the workings of pluralistic politics rather than the interests, predispositions, or simplifications of any particular group. Still, there remains the question of how a plan entailing a dangerous overcommitment of forces could have been seen as an acceptable compromise, and to answer it, biases in the unitary perspectives of the competing groups must be considered.

METHOD OF ANALYSIS

In the case studies, I test, by the method of controlled comparison, causal hypotheses about how strategies were made.[31] Three different kinds of comparison are used: different time periods in the same country, different factions in the same country at the same time, and different countries.

To facilitate comparison, the following sequence of questions will be asked of each of the three cases:

What were the strategic problems and objectives of the planners in each country?

What was the war plan that they devised?

Why did it fail to achieve their objectives?

To what extent was its failure anticipated?

Should the difficulties have been foreseen?

Were there more promising alternatives?

Why were these alternatives rejected or ignored?

Was the evaluation of alternatives biased?

What was the cause of this bias?

The first chapter on each case is organized according to these questions. The longer second chapter, which presents more detailed evidence in support of the argument, is organized chronologically.

The use of these different sorts of comparisons has two purposes. The first is to show that variations in the purported cause (or independent variable) do in fact correlate with variations in the hypothesized outcome (or dependent variable). The second is to establish that these outcomes were caused by the independent variable and not by some third factor.

[34]

Making comparisons between offensive and defensive periods within the same country allows us to hold many variables (e.g., geography, culture) constant. This method eliminates a number of potentially competing causes and identifies those independent variables which changed when the strategy changed. In the French case, for example, increases in offensive thinking corresponded with increases in threats to traditional military institutions, while strategic factors remained relatively constant.

A second useful technique is to compare the views of offensive and defensive factions within a country at a particular time. In this technique, therefore, strategic variables are held perfectly constant. In the French case, for example, factional views on strategy and intelligence correlate with views on institutional reforms. That the institutional viewpoints came first helps to establish institutional preferences as a determinant of strategic preferences and perceptions of threat.

The comparison of two countries occasionally proves useful, but it provides a generally inferior method of testing causal relationships, because so many variables are left uncontrolled. At least in the cases examined in this book, national circumstances differed in so many ways that controlled comparison was extremely difficult.

Methodologists tend to denigrate single-case studies, because they allegedly provide no controls on the operation of the variables. This claim is false. Given the difficulty of finding two cases that are similar in all respects except the variable to be tested, comparisons within cases are likely to be better controlled than comparisons between cases.[32] Additional cases are useful for illustrating additional ways in which variables can be combined, but they are not indispensable for implementing the method of controlled comparison.

Operational Definitions

Were perceptual and analytical errors produced by systematic bias or were they a random result of the inherent difficulty of decision making under uncertainty? Five criteria help us to decide the answer. Three focus on the quality of the decision makers' perceptions and choices.[33] The first is logical consistency. Did the use of evidence and arguments adhere to normal standards of logic and consistency, or were they systematically manipulated to favor a particular set of perceptions and policies? Were offensive and defensive plans judged according to different standards? The second concerns the thoroughness of analysis. Was important information ignored? Were important costs and risks of the preferred strategy overlooked? The third involves the accuracy of perceptions. Did the preferred strategy rely on an inaccurate perception of reality for its justification? Given the information available to the planners, do historians feel that their views were less plausible than alternative interpretations? Did informed contemporary observers share their views?[34]

Two other criteria focus on circumstantial evidence about the reasons for perceptual and analytical errors. First, did inaccuracies, inconsistencies, or omissions tend to support the rationalization of policies promoting institutional interests? Second, were omissions or inaccuracies the result of the rigid application of narrow, inappropriate preconceptions, or were they the result of the inherent ambiguity of the evidence? Generally speaking, systematic bias can be assumed if erroneous perceptions or choices can be explained in terms of institutional interests or preconceptions and if errors consistently favor one strategy over others. In contrast, a decisionmaker's errors can be considered random if they fail to correlate with institutional interests and preconceptions and if some of them tend to support one strategy while others support its reverse.

Practical criteria are also needed to identify and measure the factors that explain the direction and degree of bias. Explanations using such terms as "degree of ambiguity," "strength of interest," and "degree of threat" can all too easily degenerate into tautology unless those factors can be measured independently of the outcomes they purport to explain. Each term presents its own difficulties.

1. *Ambiguity and plausibility.* If there is no ambiguity, only one view is plausible. Ambiguous circumstances are those which permit a broad range of plausible interpretations. Therefore, the greater the ambiguity, the greater the likelihood becomes that erroneous, biased perceptions will be sufficiently plausible to gain acceptance. To determine the degree of ambiguity in a given set of historical circumstances, there is no substitute for close historical analysis. Given the information available to the decision maker, how broad a range of plausible interpretations was consistent with the evidence? How varied were the views of informed, neutral observers?

Nonetheless, scholars do not have to depend entirely on ad hoc historical assessments. It is possible to identify a few kinds of circumstances that tend a priori to entail either a high or a low degree of ambiguity. For example, abstract issues are likely to allow greater freedom for erroneous interpretations than are concrete issues. The truth of this proposition accounts for the two-tiered nature of the lessons drawn from the Russo-Japanese War: concrete lessons about weaponry and tactics were learned fairly accurately, but lessons at the more abstract level were not.

Recent or firsthand evidence tends to be less ambiguous than faded recollections or secondhand evidence. The lessons of 1870, for example, were most clearly understood in the immediate aftermath of the war and became increasingly distorted as time passed. Similarly, those Russian officers who participated in the Russo-Japanese War were much more likely to understand the effects of firepower on the modern battlefield. Ian Hamilton, the British observer in Manchuria, suggests that the revelations of primary experience may fade rapidly, however, when interests are involved: "On the actual day of battle naked truths may be picked up for the asking; by the following morning they have already begun to get into their uniforms."[35]

Most obviously, ambiguity is great when the decision maker lacks important information. As regards military doctrine, ambiguity will be high when the rate of technological change is high and the amount of recent combat experience is small.

2. *The importance of values and interests.* The strength of the motivation to adopt a biased assessment of strategic options is determined in part by the importance of the values and interests that an unbiased assessment would jeopardize. However, there is a danger of calling "central" any value that seems to be causing a misperception.[36] It is necessary, therefore, to devise a practical way of determining which values are the more important.

One solution to the problem is to list in rank order the kinds of values that are typically found to be most important to decision makers—that is, the values that they are most reluctant to sacrifice in trade-off situations.[37] It is frequently said that the decision maker's self-image or sense of identity is the crucial core value. The French and German cases suggest that the observation is probably correct, but this insight serves only to shift the search from typical core values to typical elements of the self-image. In the French case, the most salient elements of self-image were the habits and traditional ideals expressed in the daily life of the professional army's primary social unit, the regiment. In the German case, the most salient elements were quite different: the prestige and self-justification of the military profession as expressed in the doctrine of short, victorious, historically beneficial wars. The factors potentially contributing to the decision maker's self-image can, it appears, be disparate and numerous. An a priori listing would be at best difficult and perhaps not particularly useful.

A second way to determine which of a decision maker's values and beliefs are most important is to apply a direct measurement. For this purpose, the most central values and beliefs are those whose change would imply the greatest change in other values and beliefs. Using this criterion, practitioners of "cognitive mapping" have developed formal procedures for determining which of a decision maker's causal beliefs are most important.[38] To the extent that using this method, different coders produce the same results, it might be adapted to determine the centrality of values as well as beliefs. In practical terms, however, the best proof of centrality is likely to be a conventional historical argument. In the German example, such a case could be made for the centrality of the concept of war as an inevitable and necessary engine of progress. This keystone held together the prestige, self-concept, and operational doctrine of the German military. In the French case, the most important role was played by the concept of the soldier's career as a special calling, requiring a special code of honor and a quasi-monastic separation from civil society. This concept was not only embodied in regimental life but it was also perversely reflected in operational doctrines and intelligence estimates. Significantly, soldiers who did not believe in the concept of a separate military caste were also less likely to value or believe in the rest of the organizational ideology. That is, change in the central value or belief implied a change in all the rest. In these and other cases, the only guarantee that the concept of centrality has not been employed in a circular or arbitrary way is the degree to which the historical argument is convincing.

3. *The degree of threat.* The greater the severity of threats to important institutional values and interests, the greater the motivation becomes for a biased strategic assessment. This explanatory criterion is particularly significant to the French case. Fortunately, increases in the severity of the threat to traditional French military institutions were relatively unambiguous. They are reliably corroborated both by contemporary commentators and by subsequent historical accounts.

4. *Dogmatism.* The criteria for measuring "dogmatism," as applied to Schleiffen, for example, are a resistance to changing central beliefs in the face of disconfirming evidence; a narrowness of approach to problems; an insensitivity to the need for different solutions to fit different circumstances; and a reliance on deductions from theory rather than inferences from evidence. While I shall make no attempt to achieve precise measurement for any of these criteria, they are nonetheless specific enough to permit rough, but reliable, characterizations of the degree of dogmatism.[39] In any event, they should suffice for evaluating the conventional wisdom that Schlieffen as a strategist was more dogmatic than the elder Moltke.

[38]

In addition to these various methodological difficulties, the scope of the analysis and the limitations of the available data are subject to several significant qualifications.

In all three cases, studies focus primarily on the perceptions and choices of military decision makers. This emphasis is not arbitrary. As the cases will demonstrate, civilians rarely played a direct role in military planning, although in Russia the evidence is not conclusive and in France direct interventions did occasionally occur. In all cases, civilians imposed indirect constraints on strategic planning, in the form of military budgets, conscription laws, and the general direction of foreign policy. In arguing the case for alternative strategies, I accept these constraints as givens.

A second, related qualification has to do with causes of offensive bias that were common to all three states. In the main, this book contends that the offensives of 1914 cannot be explained by a pan-European cult of the offensive, rooted in long-term transnational causes. If war had broken out as late as 1910, two of the three powers would have had relatively defensive strategies.[40] This is hardly the stuff of a deeply rooted, transnational cult of the offensive. Nonetheless, two transnational factors should be mentioned. The first might be termed "the 1870 model." The Prussian campaigns of 1866 and 1870 offered European militaries and civilians alike an attractive model of a short, successful, offensive war. Although French and Germans drew immediate tactical lessons from 1870 that stressed the strength of defensive firepower, the surface "lesson" of the war was that rapid, problem-solving offensives were not only feasible but beneficial. In contrast, the 1914–1918 model would weigh heavily on European strategists of the interwar period, even though the development of armored and motorized forces was undermining the relevance of its lessons.

Civilian attitudes toward war constitute the second transnational factor of significance to the period. Because of the prevalence of social Darwinist views throughout Europe, civilians tended to share the military's zero-sum view of international politics. Consequently, the military's plans for fast-moving, decisive, unrestrained operations fitted well with their own thinking. But civilian elites had an even stronger reason not to want to question their military's short-war thinking. European elites tended to see their capitalist socioeconomic order as a fragile edifice that could not survive the strains of a long war of attrition. In a prolonged conflict, economic collapse and revolution would, they believed, be difficult to forestall. For social Darwinists who believed that wars could not be avoided, keeping them short and decisive was the only way to prevent permanent, radical change. As a result, and in comparison with their role in other historical periods, civilians had little inclination to meddle in the war planning of the professional military.[41]

Nevertheless, these transnational, background factors should not be overemphasized. Both were compatible with offensive or defensive strategies, as the historical record shows. At most, they operated as permissive causes of the offensives of 1914, failing to bar offensive inclinations that arose for other reasons.

The final qualification that needs to be made concerns the insufficiency of data in the Russian case. Although the chronology of the Russian planning process is well documented, the motivations for some of the changes in the war plan are not. The explanations presented in memoirs and published documents tend to be superficial. Soviet historiography has not been particularly incisive, and Western scholars have not had access to archival materials on military planning. Consequently, interpretations of Russian decision making cannot be definitive. Data problems in the French and German cases are much less severe. Especially compared to the kind of data that would be available for a contemporary case study of military planning, the historical evidence exhibits few lacunae. In fact, this fullness of evidence is the major advantage of using historical rather than contemporary cases to study the sources of bias in strategic policy making.

Although military technology has changed since 1914, the fundamental workings of the human mind as a problem-solving tool have not. Interests and preconceptions are still sources of bias in the making of military policy. Organizational ideologies still develop, for similar reasons and with similar effects on policy. Of course, lessons drawn from historical cases must be general enough to accommodate changes in the technological or the social setting. As long as this qualification is borne in mind, the following case studies may illuminate the sources of bias in human decision making—both in military contexts and in general.

[2]

France: Offensive Strategy as an Institutional Defense

In the years before the First World War, three problems preoccupied French military planners: the quantitative and qualitative superiority of the German army, the comparatively slow mobilization of the Russian army, and the unknown direction of the German attack in the west. Since these circumstances seem to indicate the need for a defensive, delaying strategy, one might speculate that the offensive French military strategy was shaped by the offensive political aim of recovering Alsace-Lorraine and not by military-operational considerations. In fact, however, the desire to recapture the provinces lost to Germany in 1870 had no major effect on French strategy.

The goal of revanche had been kept alive through the 1880s by Léon Gambetta and other militant republicans who had risen to prominence in the struggle against the German occupation. Even then, however, the revanchist mood had relatively little effect on the pragmatically defensive war plans of the day. By the 1890s the new generation of Frenchmen was even less concerned with patriotic themes. This antipatriotic trend was reversed in 1911, when the Agadir Crisis brought France and Germany to the brink of war. But even the reawakening of French patriotism that followed the Agadir incident was not primarily concerned with the recovery of Alsace and Lorraine. Rather, it was motivated by the desire to prevent what the French saw as additional German encroachments on French sovereignty. For example, the memoirs of General Joseph Joffre, the chief of the General Staff during the creation of Plan 17, do not mention the desire for revanche as a factor in French strategic planning. Instead, Joffre argued that a frontal offensive into Lorraine was needed to "prevent French territory from being invaded and becoming the theatre of the first battles.[1]

In any event, Frenchmen agreed that Alsace-Lorraine could be recovered only as the result of the decisive defeat of the German army. The debate between proponents of offensive strategies and proponents of counteroffensive strategies was not a dispute about war aims. Rather, it was a disagreement about the best way to defeat Germany on the battlefield, whether for offensive or for defensive political reasons.

The anticipated German attack posed several problems for French military planners. The first was the prospect of an unfavorable military balance on the western front. In purely quantitative terms, France managed to field almost as many men on the western front in August 1914 as did Germany. Drawing on a population of more than 67 million, Germany deployed about 1,700,000 soldiers and support personnel for the Marne campaign, while the French population of fewer than 40 million yielded about 1,650,000. Including 125,000 British and 175,000 Belgians, the Allies enjoyed a numerical superiority of about 250,000.[2]

These figures belie the qualitative advantages that Germany gained from a larger population and a larger standing army. Whereas the Germans could reject the less promising half of each year's class of potential conscripts, the French could reject only one-fifth. Yet despite accepting a smaller proportion of each class, the Germans trained a larger number of recruits each year. As a result, the Germans had more trained reservists in the younger age groups. German reservists, assigned either to fill out active units or to form reserve units, were consequently in better physical condition and more recently trained than their French counterparts. Since French reserve units were of poor quality, they were deployed far to the rear and generally did not see action before the end of August 1914. The French were able to match German troop numbers during the Marne campaign only because the German advance brought the battle into the French rear, where French reserve units were being formed.[3]

French planners were not particularly concerned about the superior quality of German reservists, incorrectly believing that reserve units would not play an important role in the decisive initial engagements. They were quite concerned, however, about the numerical disparity between the two countries' active forces. In 1912, for example, the peacetime strength of the German army was 657,000, compared to 519,000 for the French. In 1913 the Reichstag voted to increase the size of the German standing army by yet another 150,000 over three years.[4] This disparity between French and German active duty strengths would have allowed Germany to use fewer reservists in raising its active units to wartime strength. French planners feared not only that this would give the German forces a qualitative advantage but also that it would allow the Germans to mobilize their forces more quickly than the French. In particular, the French worried that German units stationed near the French border would be able to attack the French covering forces in the first week of mobilization, before the arrival of French reservists.

Concern about such an *attaque brusquée* was eliminated in 1913, however, when France adopted a three-year term of military service. By August 1914 this new law had increased the number of French active duty soldiers to 736,000, compared to 725,000 for the Germans.[5] As socialist critics pointed out, this new manpower did not increase the total wartime strength of the French army at all, but it did solve the alleged problem of a German *attaque brusquée*.

The French army also relied on the Russian alliance to mitigate its quantitative and qualitative shortcomings. The Russians, however, needed up to forty days to complete their concentration on the Austro-German frontier. Unless the Russians attacked Germany prematurely, the French would have to face almost the whole German army on their own during the first weeks of war. Assuming that both the French and the Germans launched immediate offensives in Lorraine, a major battle could take place there as early as the sixteenth day of mobilization. For this reason, Joffre and his predecessors lobbied the Russians for an early offensive in the east and helped finance the construction of rail lines needed to speed the Russian concentration. Some strategists in France and Russia saw that the danger to France in the opening days of the war could be lessened not only by a premature Russian offensive in the east but also by French delaying tactics in the west. If the French remained on the defensive, the Germans could not achieve a decisive victory before the bulk of the Russian army was ready. At the very worst, the French would be pushed back to their strong line of fortresses along the Meuse and Moselle rivers. To overcome this barrier, the Germans would have either to mount protracted siege operations against the forts or to outflank them by a time-consuming march through Belgium. Only if the French committed themselves to an immediate, irretrievable offensive would a decisive encounter be possible by the sixteenth day.[6]

This argument was advanced not only by Russian commentators and French critics of Joffre's offensive doctrine but also by General Noël de Castelnau, Joffre's chief deputy in the General Staff during the development of Plan 17. Although a strong partisan of the offensive, Castelnau was less extreme than the younger officers who advocated the *offensive à outrance*—an unrestrained offensive at all times and under all conditions. A few months before the war broke out, Castelnau left the General Staff to take a field command. During these last months of peace, his strategic memoranda argued that the need to coordinate French and Russian operations required the French to adopt a "counteroffensive" strategy, no matter how desirable it might be in principle to seize the initiative at the outset.[7]

Perhaps the most difficult problem facing French war planners was uncertainty about the direction of the German attack. In the decade before the war, French military authorities became increasingly concerned about the possibility that the Germans would attack France through Belgium, to avoid the heavily fortified Franco-German frontier. This idea was supported by inferences drawn from German railroad construction, German military publications, and some captured documents. None of the evidence was absolutely conclusive, however, and none of it revealed the full extent of the German flank march in an unambiguous way.

In the face of this uncertainty, Joffre entertained three hypotheses about the direction of the German advance: an attack from Lorraine only, an attack across the southern tip of Belgium toward the Meuse just north of Verdun, and a feint from Lorraine followed by a delayed advance through Belgium.[8] The French, to the extent that they committed their forces in either direction, risked being outnumbered on the other front if they had guessed wrong about German intentions. Their dilemma was exacerbated by the fact that French civilian authorities would not allow Joffre to enter Belgian territory before the Germans did. Consequently, French forces deployed to meet a possible German march through Belgium would be temporarily out of action if the Germans attacked only in Lorraine.[9]

PLAN 17

By 1914 Joffre believed that France had made great progress toward solving its strategic problems. The three-year law had resolved the quantitative and qualitative problems of the French army, as Joffre understood them. The problem of coordinating the timing of Allied efforts had apparently been solved by the Russians' promise to begin their offensive against Germany on the fifteenth day of mobilization.[10] Joffre believed that his final problem, the unknown direction of the German attack, could be managed by the deployment scheme of Plan 17.

Joffre's plan of operations sought to deal with his uncertainty in

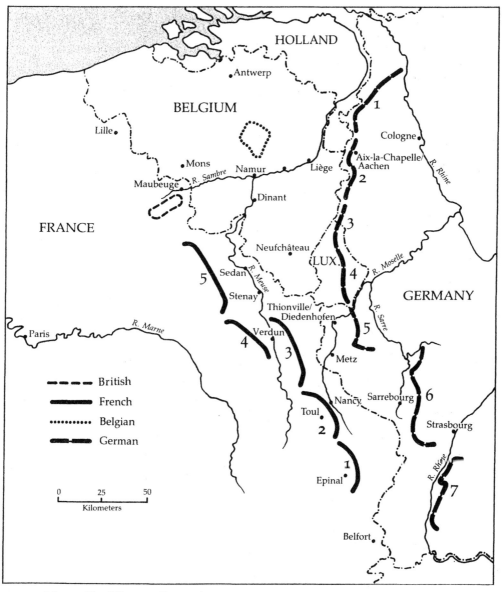

Map 1. The Western Front, August 1914.

two ways. First, Joffre argued that the French should "seize the initiative" and not be "dominated from the start by the enemy's decision." The Germans should be made to respond to French plans, not vice versa. Nonetheless, the direction of the German attack could not be entirely ignored. Joffre's second stipulation was consequently that the deployment of French forces and the direction of the French offensive should be an appropriate response either to a violation of Belgium or an attack from Lorraine.[11]

Consistent with these ideas, Plan 17 deployed the twenty-one corps of the French army in three groups: ten corps in the First and Second armies in Lorraine; five corps in the Fifth Army on the Belgian frontier; and six corps in the Third and Fourth armies behind the pivotal fortress of Verdun. The last group could be faced northward to counter a German violation of southern Belgium or eastward to join an offensive in Lorraine. In any event, Joffre believed, an attack to the north of Metz by the Third and Fourth armies would answer most contingencies, since it would threaten the southern flank of a German advance into Belgium or the northern flank of German operations in Lorraine.[12]

The Failure of Plan 17

Plan 17 failed to prevent the German right wing from advancing to the very outskirts of Paris. Using reserve units in the front lines, the Germans were able to extend their front across northern Belgium, outflanking the French Fifth Army and the British Expeditionary Force and outnumbering them by three to two. Meanwhile, the French frontal attacks toward Lorraine and the Ardennes failed to make any progress. The tide of battle turned in favor of the French only when Joffre broke off those offensives, shifted forces to the French left, and brought reserve units into the battle. All of these measures were antithetical to his original plan of campaign.[13]

Three major errors contributed to the reverses suffered by the French army in August 1914. All of them were in some measure foreseeable and preventable. The first was the intelligence failure. Neither Joffre nor his intelligence bureau came close to predicting the true strength or northerly extension of the German right wing. The source of their error was their refusal to believe that the Germans would use reserve units in the front lines, a misperception that persisted into the fourth week of the campaign.[14] Yet this practice was hardly unforeseeable. French intelligence had obtained German mobilization plans showing that reserve units would be grouped into

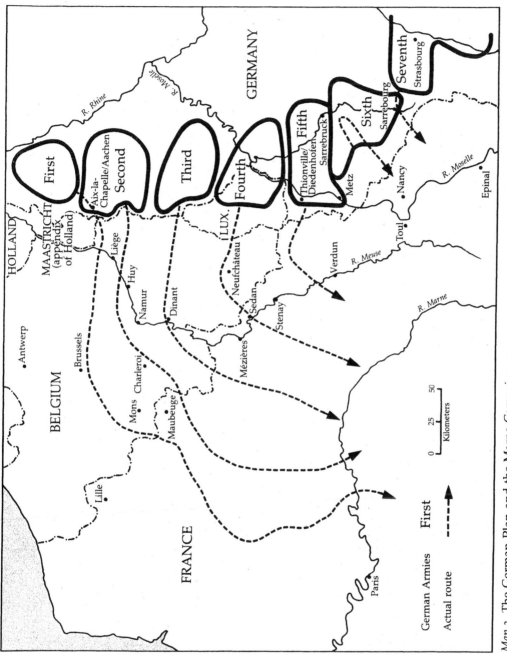

Map 2. The German Plan and the Marne Campaign, 1914.

field corps. Indeed, these plans explicitly stated that "reserve troops are employed in the same way as the active troops."[15]

The second error was the planners' passion for the *offensive à outrance*. The frontal offensives of Plan 17 defied the advantages that modern firepower conferred on the defense. Even more than other military men of the day, Joffre and the advocates of the *offensive à outrance* ignored the tactical lessons of the Boer and Russo-Japanese wars, which demonstrated the difficulty of penetrating defensive positions by means of frontal assaults.

Finally, the planners failed to make better use of French reserve units. By 23 August Joffre had engaged only four of France's 25 reserve divisions.[16] In these units alone, almost 400,000 trained soldiers sat out the opening battles. Although French reservists were older than their German counterparts, they could certainly have occupied a defensive front, where the demands of marching and maneuvering would be minimal. In any case the quality of French reserve units was affected more by the shortcomings of their equipment, leadership, and retraining programs than by any inherent limitations. As Barbara Tuchman has remarked of the pikemen and bowmen of the thirteenth century, "despised as ineffective, they were ineffective because they were despised."[17]

Defensive or Counteroffensive Alternatives

In the years before the war, French soldiers and publicists advanced several defensive or "counteroffensive" schemes that were more promising than Plan 17.

Most French socialists favored a six-month term of universal military service to train reservists for a national militia. This system would have virtually eliminated the traditional standing army, which the socialists execrated because of its role in suppressing the Paris commune in 1871.[18] While the socialists did not hide the political motives behind their militia proposal, they also advanced strategic arguments in its favor. In the 1913 debate on the three-year service law, for example, the socialist parliamentary leader Jean Jaurès argued that the German army intended to use reserve units in the front lines, thereby extending the arc of its advance across northern Belgium. France could only counter such a deployment, Jaurès believed, by making more efficient use of its own reservists. If all of France's trained manpower were used, a continuous defense line could be set up from Switzerland to the English Channel. In a positional defense of this kind, active forces would have little advantage over reservists. Consequently, the money needed to support a large standing army would be better spent on improved equipment for reservists. To rebut the charge that a militia system would be vulnerable to an *attaque brusquée* by the German standing army, Jaurès argued that the French fortress line would protect the militia's concentration in the southern sector of the front, while the marching distance across Belgium would offer sufficient protection in the north.[19]

Within the military, a similar plan was advocated by General Victor Michel, the vice-president of the Supreme War Council and ex officio commander-designate of the French army in the event of war. Michel was one of the "republican" generals who sympathized with civilian critics of traditional military ways and rose to prominence for largely political reasons. An earlier assignment as inspector of reserve forces had led Michel to believe that the reserves could be made into an effective fighting force, ready to take action at the outset of a campaign. Having no prejudices regarding reserve troops, he believed that the Germans would use their reservists in the front lines, attacking through northern Belgium. In 1911 he drew up his "demi-brigade" plan to meet such a threat. Each active regiment would have a reserve regiment annexed to it in wartime, increasing the size of each field corps from 45,000 to 70,000 men. This enlarged front-line army of 1,290,000 men could cover the entire French frontier, deploying 770,000 men on the Belgian border alone.[20]

Many older officers retained a preference for the "counteroffensive" or "defensive-offensive" strategies that had been popularized by General Henri Bonnal in the 1890s. Such strategies held that the French should avoid an irrevocable commitment to an early offensive, waiting instead for flaws to appear in the Germans' plan of attack. Three kinds of arguments supported counteroffensive thinking. First, it was expected that the German army could begin its offensive somewhat sooner than the French could.[21] Consequently, it was considered illusory to think that a French offensive could "seize the initiative" away from the Germans.[22] It was more likely to result in the French being poorly deployed against the German attack. Second, although adherents of the counteroffensive concept were not opposed to offensive operations per se, they believed that the proponents of an indiscriminate offense were foolhardy. Indeed, a well-timed, well-placed counterattack would, they believed, produce a greater effect than a frontal assault.[23] Finally, they pointed out that a counteroffensive could be timed to coincide with the full force of a Russian offensive in the Germans' rear.

Counteroffensive thinkers tended to be more attuned than Joffre was to the dangers of a major German advance through Belgium. For example, Generals Joseph-Simon Gallieni and Charles Lanrezac, commanders of the Fifth Army during Joffre's tenure as chief of the General Staff, suggested shifting four corps from Lorraine to the Fifth Army to parry the German right wing. However, even Gallieni and Lanrezac did not anticipate the full extent of the German sweep through northern Belgium, in part because they did not foresee the major role that the German reserve corps would play. As a result, these advocates of a counteroffensive saw no need to use French reserve units more intensively. If their ideas had been adopted, the French army would have been better positioned but still outnumbered during the opening phase of the campaign.[24]

Explaining the Errors of Plan 17

The errors of Plan 17 stemmed from the French army's organizational ideology, which proclaimed that offensive operations by a cohesive, professional army were the key to success in war. Proponents of this ideology argued that defensive doctrines ruined the morale of the troops and led to a fatal passivity on the part of the commander. "We must always seek to create events, not merely to suffer them," Colonel Ferdinand Foch told his students at the war college. "*Faire la guerre, c'est attaquer.*"[25]

According to the mainstream of French military opinion, the form of military organization best suited to offensive operations was a professional army with a minimum term of service of three years. Offensive maneuvers, it was argued, required tactical skills and automatic discipline that could not be inculcated during a short term of service. The risks and rigors of offensive operations were likewise portrayed as requiring great cohesion and instinctive trust among the members of small units—qualities that could be fostered only through long association. Above all, a successful offensive was seen as depending on the moral superiority of the attacking force. The attackers might suffer heavier losses than the defenders, but they could still win the battle as a result of superior morale. "A battle won is a battle in which one refuses to acknowledge defeat," Foch insisted.[26] In the opinion of most officers raised in the traditions of the French professional army, this kind of moral courage could be developed only through long exposure to the military values of honor, self-sacrifice, and esprit de corps.

Reservists, in contrast, were believed to possess none of these qualities. Thinking about their family responsibilities, reservists would not be as daring and self-sacrificing as celibate professional soldiers. Lacking the cohesion that comes from living and training together, reserve units placed in the front lines would merely dilute the offensive spirit of the active units. For these reasons, increasing the number of troops while decreasing their quality would have fatal consequences.[27]

The principal function of this organizational ideology was to protect the essential features of traditional French military life and institutions. On its face, the French military ideology favored a long-service professional army because long service was a prerequisite for successful offensive operations. In fact, the reverse comes closer to the truth. The offensive was favored largely because it provided a strategic argument against unwanted transformations in traditional military institutions. This is not to argue that military authorities and publicists were cynical in advocating the offensive. On the contrary, they genuinely believed in the strategic advantages of those offensive doctrines which were so convenient from the standpoint of their institutional interests.

Between 1871 and 1905 the normal conscription period was reduced from seven to two years.[28] As a result the rhythm of life in the military's basic social unit, the regiment, was unavoidably altered. Under the long term of service, the tone of regimental life was set by career officers and old soldiers who had become habituated to military routines and values. Long service thoroughly socialized the members of the regiment to military discipline, a sense of hierarchy, and the military ideals of bravery, honor, daring, and esprit de corps. Thus long service insulated the army from the rise of bourgeois, democratic values in the society at large. The shortened term of service ended this isolation. Instead of a club of like-minded old soldiers deferential to authority, the regiment became a training ground for future reservists. Conscripts were frequently hostile to military service and at best indifferent to military ideals. There was no longer a concentration of old-timers high enough to create a "proper" atmosphere for new recruits. With the short term of service, recruits left before they were fully acculturated. Periodic call-ups of unmotivated reservists and civilianized reserve officers further disrupted the old routines. Moreover, as military training became universal, the conditions of military life became a salient issue for parliamentary inquiry. Civilians tended to see regimental life as fostering drunkenness, gambling, and debauchery rather than honor and self-sacrifice. Their pressures for change threatened the traditional right of the military to establish a separate code of conduct based on its own ideals.[29]

[51]

These practical threats to military values were exacerbated by the underlying mistrust between the military and republican politicians. Particularly in the early years of the Third Republic, most military officers were monarchists or Bonapartists. Many were devout Catholics and were incensed by the republican government's anticlerical policies. Conversely, republicans were concerned that the military would support a rightist coup d'etat.

The Dreyfus affair of 1897–98 was a catalyst for this underlying mistrust and difference in values. The military's persistence in a blatant miscarriage of justice against a Jewish General Staff officer accused of espionage seemed to confirm the republicans' worst fears. The military appeared to be a state within a state, subject to no law but its own. Military values of unthinking obedience and blind loyalty seemed irreconcilable with the democratic values of due process, tolerance, equality, and the rule of reason. The rallying of conservatives and monarchists to the side of the military made the officer corps appear the spearhead of a movement to overthrow the Republic. The attacks by the Dreyfusards likewise confirmed the fears of the military. The right of the military to regulate its own internal affairs needed to be actively defended against the interventions of the irresponsible radicals. Not only was autonomy at stake, but the honor and integrity of future wartime commanders were being questioned. This blow at military morale jeopardized the defense of the country; therefore military honor had to be preserved, regardless of the guilt or innocence of Dreyfus.[30]

The Dreyfus affair produced a realignment of French politics, with a center-left government replacing the previous center-right coalition. The new government concluded that the old formula for civil-military entente had been proved a failure. It set out to "republicanize" the French officer corps by direct interference in appointments, promotions, and war college admissions. The network of Masonic lodges was used to check on the political opinions of candidates for promotion. At the same time, the length of service was reduced to two years, officers were told to educate their recruits in nonmilitary subjects, and traditional disciplinary powers were curtailed. Not satisfied even by these changes, socialists like Jaurès urged even shorter terms of military service and more fundamental changes in military institutions.

Under such onerous conditions, the French army needed its organizational ideology to defend itself against further encroachments and, if possible, to regain lost ground. This need contributed directly to the three principal errors of Plan 17.

The French army needed to denigrate its own reserve units. If the army admitted that reserve units could fight successfully alongside active units at the opening of a campaign, then it would find it difficult to argue against even the most extreme proposals for turning the army into a training school for a militia.

The French Military could not afford to perceive the true shape of the German war plan. As Richard Challener has noted, "to buttress their case [against reservists], military writers tried to convince the French people that the German army intended to place no trust in its own reserves."[31] If they admitted that German reserve units could be used in forced-march, offensive operations, they would have a hard time explaining why French reserve units were unfit even for the defensive sectors of the front line. Moreover, if French military planners had accurately perceived German intentions, they would have had to use French reserve units in the front line, in order to avoid a numerical imbalance and to extend the French front to cover the Belgian frontier. In other words, for Joffre to perceive the imminent danger would have been tantamount to admitting that Michel had been right. Finally, in 1913 all of France was preoccupied with the bill to reinstate the three-year term of service. The military was arguing that recent increases in the German standing army had created the danger of a no-warning *attaque brusquée,* which might overwhelm the weak French covering force before the bulk of the active army could be filled out with its complement of reservists. The only solution, the military claimed, was to increase the size of the peacetime *couverture* by expanding the active army by 50 percent. Since military training was already universal, this could be done only by increasing the length of service to three years. A correct view of German intentions would have completely undermined the military's case for the three-year law. The General Staff, recapitulating the tactics of the Dreyfus confrontation, manufactured fake German documents to support their view.[32] The extent to which the army was taken in by its own public relations measures is unclear. But in any case, the atmosphere was hardly conducive to the dispassionate evaluation of intelligence data.

The doctrine of the offensive at all costs helped to protect the military's institutional interests in two ways.[33] It provided an argument against an increased reliance on reserve units in general and against Jaurès's militia scheme in particular. Jaurès himself admitted that French reservists were best suited for defensive operations. Consequently, if people could be convinced that offensive operations were the sine qua non of success on the battlefield, the professional army would be saved.[34] Furthermore, the doctrine of the offensive allowed the French General Staff to play down potentially disturbing intelligence about German intentions. According to Colonel Loyzeaux de Grandmaison, the chief proponent of the *offensive à outrance,* it did not matter if imperfect intelligence failed to predict an enemy's flanking maneuver. Regardless of the enemy's moves, it would still be better to launch a frontal offensive than to compete in "the exaggerated lengthening of the front."[35] Echoing Grandmaison, Joffre's assistants in the General Staff, Henri-Mathias Berthelot and Castelnau, claimed that a sharp French blow against the German center would disrupt the attack of the German right, no matter where its exact location.

EXPLAINING THE INTENSITY OF FRENCH BIAS

The need to protect institutional interests and traditions explains the general direction of the biases of the French military ideology. In order to explain the intensity of those biases, however, a broader range of factors must be considered.

First, the degree of threat to traditional military values and interests varied greatly between 1870 and 1914. During the 1870s the term of service remained quite long and there was little pressure to reduce it significantly.[36] During the 1880s and 1890s the threat to traditional military institutions was greater, but still moderate. The period of service was shortened to three years, but otherwise the prestige and autonomy of the military were not seriously challenged. After the Dreyfus affair, however, the degree of threat reached what from the military point of view were crisis proportions. The term of service was reduced to two years, and almost all of the traditional practices of the old professional army were called into question.

These variations in the degree of threat correlate closely with the intensity of the military's bias in the areas of military organization, operational doctrine, and war planning. In the 1870s tactical doctrines tended to be defensive, and moderate institutional changes were accepted as a necessary consequence of the defeat of 1870. In response to civilian pressures for military reform in the 1880s and 1890s, biases in favor of the offensive and against reservists increased. The military was not yet threatened in a fundamental way by these moderate pressures, so the resulting biases had only a moderate effect on war planning and decisions about force posture. As Douglas Porch remarks, "The stronger the regular army, the more faith officers placed in the usefulness of reservists."[37] The serious challenges to the professional army after 1898 gave rise to much stronger biases in questions of military doctrine and organization. This trend affected war planning only after 1911, when Joffre replaced Michel as commander-designate. In the preceding years, top military authorities had been chosen largely on the basis of their amenability to institutional reforms. One consequence was to limit the ability of figures espousing the emerging offensive, antireservist doctrine to shape plans and policy.

The degree to which organizational biases influenced war planning was also affected by the degree of ambiguity of the strategic problems facing French planners. Between 1888 and 1893, for example, Germany planned quite openly to increase the number of reservists in its front-line armies. As a result, the French war minister, Charles de Freycinet, wrote to the chief of the General Staff, Marie-François de Miribel, that "we cannot remain faced with such an increase in forces without taking similar measures."[38] Under the circumstances, Miribel had to agree. In contrast, German plans to intensify the use of reservists in later years were secret. Evidence of this intention was available, but it was sufficiently ambiguous to allow French institutional biases to shape their perceptions.

The stability of doctrinal predispositions had a mixed effect on the intensity of the French military's strategic biases. On the one hand, preconceptions may have had a moderating effect, because they resisted change despite increases in the level of threat to military interests. For example, older officers, schooled in the counteroffensive concepts of the 1890s, could not accept the more extreme formulations of such "Young Turks" as Grandmaison. On the other hand, preconceptions had an exacerbating effect when they coincided with motivational biases. For example, the habitual French preference for strength in depth rather than extended linear formations helps to explain the intelligence failure. Because the French did not appreciate the value of a flanking maneuver through northern Belgium, they found it easy to underestimate its likelihood.

Of these three factors, the changing level of threat to military interests played the most important role in shaping the development of the French military ideology. Other factors are important, however, in explaining lags in the effect of threats on doctrine and policy. For example, the stability of individuals' doctrinal beliefs helps to explain why the *offensive à outrance* only gradually took hold in the aftermath of the Dreyfus crisis and the reformist André ministry. Civilian control of top military appointments likewise helps to explain why the offensive doctrine did not affect war planning until 1911, when civilian threats to military autonomy were less acute. Before 1911 the military had perhaps a greater incentive to develop a self-protective doctrine but insufficient opportunity to implement it.[39]

The following chapter will show in more detail the link between increasingly offensive doctrines and increased threats to the institutional interests of the French military. It will also trace the connections among the intelligence failure, the denigration of reservists, and the *offensive à outrance*, demonstrating that the use of strategy to protect the military's organizational interests was the taproot of all of the errors of Plan 17.

[3]

France: Du Picq, Dreyfus, and the Errors of Plan 17

Between 1870 and 1898 the French military began to develop an organizational ideology centered on the vision of offensive operations carried out by a cohesive, professional army. This ideology helped to protect traditional military values and interests against proponents of a shortened term of military service. Since the threat to these interests was relatively moderate before 1898, the resulting ideological bias was also moderate.

Ideological bias was greatest in abstract questions of operational doctrine and least in questions of concrete policy, such as war planning. This disparity occurred presumably because doctrine is the more public and the more closely related to the socialization of new members of the organization. It is therefore the key to the development of a self-protective organizational ideology.

ARDANT DU PICQ AS MILITARY IDEOLOGIST

Even before the Franco-Prussian War, the rise of the nation-in-arms concept was spurring the development of an organizational ideology that would protect the traditional military way of life. Colonel Charles Ardant du Picq provided the most striking and influential statement of this ideology. Written shortly before his death in the 1870 campaign, his *Etudes sur le combat* had a great effect on subsequent French military thinkers, most notably Georges Gilbert, Ferdinand Foch, and Loyzeaux de Grandmaison.[1]

Ardant du Picq was preoccupied with the role of fear in battle and how to overcome it. Fear is a natural human emotion, he believed, which can only be overcome by ingrained discipline and by the absolute confidence in one's comrades-in-arms that comes only from long personal association. These qualities can be best achieved in professional armies with a long term of service, during which proper attitudes and esprit de corps can be inculcated.

> A wise organization insures that the personnel of combat groups changes as little as possible, so that comrades in peacetime maneuvers shall be comrades in war. From living together, and obeying the same chiefs, from commanding the same men, from sharing fatigue and rest, from cooperation among men who quickly understand each other in the execution of warlike movements, may be bred brotherhood, professional knowledge, sentiment, above all unity. The duty of obedience, the right of imposing discipline and the impossibility of escaping from it, would naturally follow.[2]

Moreover, he argued, mutual confidence and unit cohesion are the most important elements of victory, far outweighing mere numerical superiority. In fact, greater numbers will be counterproductive if they entail decreased cohesion. "What good is an army of two hundred thousand men of whom only one-half really fight, while the other one hundred thousand disappear in a hundred ways? Better to have one hundred thousand who can be counted upon." Naturally, reserve units mobilized only in wartime have the least cohesion. "Troops, no matter how well drilled, who are assembled haphazard into companies and battalions will never have, have never had, that entire unity which is born of mutual acquaintanceship."[3]

The element of the offensive is not as prominent in Ardant du Picq's writings as it would become under later ideologists. Nonetheless, his discussion of the moral factor in war provides one of the key arguments used in the later development of the offensive ideology. The main advantages of the defensive are, he says, merely material. From the more important moral standpoint, the defense is likely to be unnerved by the apparent confidence of the attacker. "When confidence is placed in superiority of material means, valuable as they are against an enemy at a distance, it may be betrayed by the actions of the enemy. If he closes with you in spite of your superiority in means of destruction, the morale of the enemy mounts with the loss of your confidence. His morale dominates yours. You flee. Entrenched troops give way in this manner."[4]

Several factors may have shaped Ardant du Picq's outlook: the traditional army emphasis on regimental esprit, his personal, heroic ethic, and his combat experience in Syria and Algeria, where French organizational cohesion consistently triumphed over superior numbers.[5] At least in part, however, *Etudes sur le combat* must be seen as a response to the debate on universal military training that arose in France after the Prussian victory at Sadowa in 1866. In that campaign, the large number of reservists trained under Prussia's three-year service increased the numerical strength of the standing army without detracting from its quality. The French suddenly awoke to the fact that the Prussian nation-in-arms dwarfed the French professional army. A few military reformers, encouraged by Napoleon III, sought to incorporate some of the Prussian institutions into the French military system. In Parliament, the dominant bourgeois factions interested themselves in these ideas primarily as a means for reducing the length of service for conscripts. Radicals hoped that a more "democratic" army would be less likely to intervene in domestic politics on the side of reaction. The compromise that resulted from this incompatible mixture of motives produced a set of reserve institutions that posed little political threat and little burden of service. They also had little military value.[6]

It must be admitted, however, that even a well-designed reform would have encountered great resistance from professional soldiers. Raoul Girardet, the foremost sociologist of the French military, compares service in the old army to life in a monastic order. The closed society of the regiment was kept isolated from civilian contact by frequent changes in locale. Transfers between regiments were rare. Like the monastic ethic, the military ethic operated on a moral plane different from that of civilian, bourgeois values. The idea of the nation-in-arms and its concomitant, a short term of service, was bound to disrupt the established life and spirit of the regiment. They would jeopardize the army's prime social values, comradery, and habitual respect for officers' authority.[7]

Ardant du Picq's attacks on "the theory of the big battalions" and his defense of the close-knit regimental unit can only be understood in this context.[8] Nonetheless, he should not be construed as a reactionary. In arguing against the importance of numerical superiority at Sadowa, he was willing to admit that a shorter term of service may not necessarily yield disaster: "The Prussians conquered at Sadowa with [well-trained] soldiers, united, accustomed to discipline. Such soldiers can be made in three or four years now, for the material training of the soldier is not indeed so difficult."[9] This willingness to accept moderate changes in the interests of military efficiency would characterize French military attitudes even more strongly after the 1870 defeat.

THE PREDOMINANCE OF THE DEFENSIVE IN THE 1870S

In the decade after the Franco-Prussian War, French strategic and tactical thinking was strongly defensive in character. The strategic defensive can be attributed primarily to France's weakness with respect to Germany and the impossibility of attacking until the army was rebuilt.[10] It thus reveals more about circumstances than about inclinations. The defensive trend at the tactical and operational levels, however, is noteworthy for two reasons.

First, it shows that later French offensive views were *not* derived from the experiences of the Franco-Prussian War. The defensive trend in French tactical doctrine was originally based on the lessons of the Austro-Prussian War of 1866, which had demonstrated the defensive advantages of modern firepower.[11] The campaign of 1870 did nothing to change this assessment. Although commentators on the 1870 campaign did criticize French commanders for excessive passivity,[12] doctrinal writings continued to stress the effects of firepower, the need for cover, and the impossibility of close-order tactics. In retrospect, General Charles de Gaulle would praise the field regulations of 1875 as realistic and flexible compared to the more doctrinaire offensive regulations of later periods. He attributed the difference to the fact that the lessons of the Franco-Prussian War were still vivid in the minds of the officers who drafted the 1875 document.[13] Later commentators who stressed the offensive lessons of the 1870 campaign, on the other hand, were basing their views on selective and fading perceptions of what the war was really like.[14]

Second, the defensive tendencies of the 1870s coincided with a period in which military interests were little threatened. To put the doctrinal trends of the 1870s into a political and organizational context, it should be recalled that the republican government after the suppression of the Paris commune was quite conservative. President Louis Thiers favored the professional army as a bastion of the status quo against the revolutionaries; large numbers of armed reservists would threaten the social order. Nonetheless, the Prussians' cost-effective reserve system had clear and undeniable advantages. The French army had been greatly outnumbered in 1870, because the Prussians had mobilized the large number of civilian reservists they had created by means of universal three-year training. The costs of increasing the French standing army to match German numbers would have been prohibitive. Consequently, the Parliament adopted a two-tiered system in which some conscripts would be obliged to serve five years and others would serve a year or less. This change seems on its face to be a major one, but traditionalist generals like Auguste Alexandre Ducrot knew that they would be allowed to "economize to the greatest possible extent on the six-month soldiers in order to save as much as possible for the career soldiers."[15] As David Ralston points out, "In 1872 . . . the specter of a really radical reform of the army was not even raised. No one advocated the resurrection of the nation in arms or the abolition of the standing army as certain republicans had before 1870."[16]

In this nonthreatening environment, the military had little need for self-protective ideologies. In fact, some of the younger, more progressive officers wanted the French army to go further in emulating the Prussians. Particularly interesting in this period are the writings of Jules-Louis Lewal, a young officer who later rose to prominence as a minister of war and an authoritative spokesman on military doctrine and organization. In 1872 Lewal launched a campaign against traditionalist biases in the army. He contended that the development of firepower had tipped the balance between numerical superiority and troop quality in favor of sheer weight of numbers. "Personal valor no longer finds the same latitude for employment as formerly. Consequently, it has become less important. The initiative, intelligence, and élan of the troops are effaced before the colossal power of the machine." In other words, the reservist-oriented system of shorter but universal terms of service was quantitatively necessary and qualitatively acceptable. However, Lewal cautioned, large numbers should not be confused with untrained multitudes. Even if modern soldiers are basically machine-handling robots, they need to be trained to become proficient robots.[17]

Lewal would change his message by the turn of the century. From attacking the traditionalism of his colleagues and praising the benefits of the nation-in-arms, he turned to defending the professional soldier against militia proponents. It was not so much that Lewal's ideas had changed as that the times had changed. In 1872 the danger lay in failing to adopt the organizational changes needed to compete with the German enemy. Later, the overriding danger would become the fundamental changes demanded by the army's enemies within France. Coincident with this shift in his writings on organization, Lewal would also come to place greater emphasis on the offensive than he had in the 1870s.[18]

Some historians allege that, during this period, institutional reasons for military traditionalism were reinforced by changes in the social origins and political opinions of the officer corps in the 1870s. After 1870, they have held, the proportion of noblemen among new officers increased significantly, making the army less democratic at the same time that French society was becoming more democratic and more bourgeois.[19] Although recent research suggests that the percentage of aristocratic officers did not increase, the evidence about officers' opinions is harder to dismiss. In 1878, for example, republican politicians who feared a military coup in support of President Edme Patrice de MacMahon (a conservative former marshal) and against the Parliament collected data on officers' political views. They found a concentration of antirepublican sentiment at the two extremes of the military hierarchy, among young lieutenants and among older generals who had risen to prominence under the previous regime.[20] Though the picture of an antirepublican army should not be overdrawn, this general perception tended to reinforce the military's purely institutional worries and helped to create the civil-military polarization catalyzed by the Dreyfus affair.

INSTITUTIONAL THREAT AND DOCTRINAL RESPONSE IN THE 1880s

During the 1880s governmental and parliamentary opinion increasingly favored a reduction and equalization of military service. Although the military's feelings about these changes were mixed, most officers favored the status quo. As the threat to existing military institutions grew, French military doctrine increasingly emphasized the offensive and the need for a professional standing army to carry it out. This doctrinal trend found expression in field regulations and war college curricula, as well as in the writings of military publicists. Nonetheless, the military at this stage was hardly operating with a siege mentality. The army continued to improve, materially and organizationally, with the willing support of the republican government. The offensive trend did not become dogmatized, and some doctrinal excesses were corrected within the military itself.

Following a constitutional showdown with the republican-dominated Parliament, Marshal MacMahon resigned the presidency in 1879, opening the way to a fuller democratization of French political life. Pressure to shorten the length of military service began almost immediately. In the 1881 election, about 275 candidates were pledged to reform the conscription laws. Following the republican electoral victory of that year, a parliamentary commission set out to study various conscription proposals. The Chamber of Deputies passed a three-year service bill in 1884, but the measure did not become law until 1889 because of Senate opposition and disagreement over specific features of the bill.[21]

The military authorities made clear their uneasiness about this trend. In 1881 the members of the reorganized Supreme War Council were told by the war minister, a professional officer, that they should act as "the guardian of the traditions of the army, its guarantee against ill-considered and precipitous innovations."[22] For the most part, they fulfilled this charge. The *Spectateur militaire* reported in 1882 that the long term of service was favored by a majority of the Supreme War Council and by virtually all the corps commanders. General Antoine-Eugène Chanzy, the commander-in-chief-designate, held that the current system was adequate and should not be changed while the international situation remained threatening.[23] The council members, while admitting that the technical training of an infantryman could be accomplished in three years, insisted that a longer period was necessary to inculcate the indispensable military esprit.[24] Marshal François Canrobert argued that French recruits could not be compared to German recruits in this regard: "If the Germans have a good army with the three-year service, that is due to the respect for authority with which they are imbued from infancy. Respect, the basis of discipline, does not exist in France; we need therefore a longer term of service."[25] Finally, both Chanzy and Canrobert raised the specter of a slippery slope toward a militia. Tactically, they disagreed with General Jean-Baptiste Billot, who argued that the military should submit a three-year bill to preempt more radical proposals.[26] It is noteworthy that Billot was one of the "republican generals" who had risen to prominence in the 1871 campaign of popular national resistance improvised by the republicans Léon Gambetta and Charles de Freycinet. Chanzy and Canrobert belonged to an earlier generation, more rooted in the traditions of the professional army.

Also beginning around 1880, tactical preferences, particularly among young officers, increasingly inclined toward the offensive. The moderately defensive field regulations of 1875 came under attack. The *Journal des sciences militaires* proclaimed that "what we are demanding is the return to our national tradition of the offensive and the repudiation of a timorous tactic that softens our soldiers and takes away all their élan."[27] The new field regulations of 1884 placed greater emphasis on the offensive and on close-order formations. They were inspired in part by the Russian tactician M. I. Dragomirov, famous for the maxim, "The bullet is a stupid fellow, but the bayonet is a true friend."[28]

In the same year, Lucien Cardot, a war college professor and ad-

[63]

mirer of Dragomirov, began to popularize the teachings of Karl von Clausewitz. In his lectures, Cardot interpreted Clausewitz as an apologist for the offensive. Dallas Irvine paraphrases Cardot's rendering of Clausewitz in the following way: "War must be an utmost exertion of force, and especially of moral force, for the complete destruction of the enemy's armed resistance, and to this end the offensive should be undertaken whenever practicable and in its simplest, most direct, and most vigorous form."[29] This interpretation of Clausewitz was (to be generous) one-sided, underemphasizing his distinction between "absolute war" and "real war" and ignoring his belief that the defensive is the stronger form of war. Nonetheless, it provided intellectual justification for the offensive instincts of young officers, like Foch, who attended Cardot's lectures.

This proselytizing led to the adoption in 1887 of yet another set of field regulations, which stressed the offensive even more than the 1884 version had done. According to the new regulations, "an infantry that is brave and energetically commanded can march under the most violent fire, even against well-defended trenches, and seize the position." They also urged an increase in the density of the attack.[30]

The higher military authorities soon acted to correct this extreme document. The mid-1880s saw technological developments—smokeless powder and rifles with an improved rate of fire—that made massed assaults less feasible than ever. General Billot told the Supreme War Council that the new regulations sought to bring back the Austrians' suicidal bayonet attacks of 1859 and 1866. Serious officers, he said, considered the regulations as so much "theater." The strongest critics of the 1887 regulations were Billot, one of the most moderate council members on the reserve and three-year service issues, and Freycinet, the civilian war minister who was personally overseeing the upgrading of the reserves' role.[31] Many of the other council members agreed with them about tactical realities, if not about institutional arrangements. By 1895 the regulations of 1887 had been superceded by a somewhat more balanced document.

Toward the end of the 1880s the link between the *armée de métier* and the offensive was made explicit in a series of articles by Captain Gilbert, who had a major influence on both Foch and Grandmaison.[32] Gilbert contended that "the offensive doubles the energy of the troops at the same time that it concentrates the thoughts of the commander on a single objective, in the form of a simple idea, incessantly pursued." In contrast, the defending army must be oriented *à tous azimuths*, never knowing the direction of the attack. "A defensive, set-piece battle is a battle lost."[33]

Gilbert argued that only active units could participate directly in the offensive. Reservists are not accustomed to arms, not in shape for marching, and lack "esprit de corps." They are older, and "youth is the age of sacrifices generously consented." Finally, reservists will not be as daring, because they have families and positions to lose. Consequently, a small, professional force should deliver the initial shock that destroys the enemy's field army. Reservists should guard lines of communications, participate in siege and mop-up operations, and replace casualties. Mixing active and reserve units together in combat would only tie the mobile elite to a dead weight. "The principle of the simultaneity of the employment of forces should be applied only to forces of the same type," Gilbert wrote, responding to Freycinet's proposal to form reserve corps for front-line use.[34]

Gilbert's views led him to interpret developments in the German army rather one-sidedly. He claimed that the German army law of 1888, which among other things attempted to organize reserve units as a potential part of the field army, had falsely "lured" the French toward the "mirage" of huge armies. According to Gilbert, the Germans knew perfectly well that there must be a division of labor between active and reserve units, with the former winning the battles and the latter serving as occupation troops. Unlike French proponents of a greater role for reserve units, he saw the 1888 German law as "accentuating the separation, misunderstood by us, of the troops of the first and second line." He wrote that "in 1870, our neighbors defeated us by the numerical superiority of their reserves. This time, they plan to surprise us by the suddenness [*brusquerie*] of an attack conducted exclusively, at the beginning, with the permanent effectives."[35] Gilbert's interpretations in this regard were both extreme and inaccurate. German war plans always envisioned a fairly active role for the divisions formed out of the younger classes of reservists, despite differences of opinion within Germany on their proper role. Moreover, German capabilities of the period did not justify the *attaque brusquée* that Gilbert feared.[36] In short, although Gilbert was occasionally an insightful and objective commentator, his judgment was frequently influenced by his ideological agenda.[37]

Although the need to justify the professional army is probably not the only reason for the rise of offensive thinking in the 1880s, one frequently cited alternative explanation can definitely be ruled out: that is, the "lessons" of military history. In this period, preferred doctrine ruled history, not vice versa. Indeed, some of the interpretations that contemporary analysts offered of the Franco-Prussian War were particularly perverse. General Louis-Adolphe Maillard, one of the leading figures at the war college, recounted the disastrous frontal attack of the Prussian Guards at St. Privat but claimed that the guards' huge losses occurred because they failed to press the attack with sufficient determination: "Do not stop, that's the formula!" Failures of will and implementation were the culprits, not the frontal attack itself.[38] Similarly, one of the livelier tactical disputes of the 1880s involved the offense enthusiast Cardot (who set out to reinterpret the Franco-Prussian War in light of the teachings of "Clausewitz") and the more defensive-minded Barthélmy Palat (a historian who wrote a multivolume history of the war based on definitive primary research).[39] The Russo-Turkish War of 1877–78 was also creatively interpreted. The failure of Russian attacks against Turkish trenches at Plevna was blamed on insufficient élan,[40] and typically, the Turks were criticized for the passivity of their defense rather than praised for checking the advance of superior forces.

Despite the offensive biases of most war college professors and military writers, French planners of the 1880s were hardly doctrinaire advocates of the offensive. As strategic railroads and army organization gradually improved, the General Staff grew more confident and moved French deployments closer to the frontier. Nonetheless, the French armies would venture no more than a "defensive offensive," since the Germans, it was believed, would be able to complete their mobilization first and seize the initiative. Plan 8 of 1887 expressed this vision in a mature form. It deployed four active armies in forward positions in Lorraine and three reserve armies fairly far to the rear.[41]

The intelligence estimate for Plan 8 similarly showed none of the biases that appeared in Gilbert's essays. Reserve divisions "of the line" (i.e., formed from comparatively young classes of reservists) were included in the total number of battalions that Germany would have available for the decisive battle in Lorraine. This French intelligence estimate is consistent with an earlier one, which contended that "The reserve troops are destined to march with the field army and are mobilized almost as rapidly as the latter. According to the German mobilization plan, active regiments terminate their mobilization on the fifth day and reserve troops on the seventh. There is thus reason to believe that the reserves will cross the frontier very close behind the active troops." A German *attaque brusquée* was explicitly deemed unlikely.[42]

In short, offensive doctrines during the 1880s increased in popularity among French officers, coinciding with an increased concern about the threat to traditional military institutions. However, military institutions continued on balance to prosper, and offensive, antireservist ideas did not become dogmatized. Although publicists like Gilbert allowed their preoccupation with institutional issues to cloud their strategic judgments and intelligence estimates, responsible military authorities were not significantly affected by ideological biases.

REALISM AND SELF-INTEREST IN THE 1890S

The passage of the three-year law in 1889 posed anew the questions of how the military would adapt to forced change. While increasing the number of trained reservists, the new law also increased the size of the standing army by reducing the number of exemptions. Thus the military could have chosen to ignore the large pool of reservists and, as in the past, tailor its budgets and war plans to the needs of the standing army. However, the war minister, Freycinet, urged the formation of new reserve divisions and corps capable of operating as part of the field army.

Surprisingly, the General Staff and the Supreme War Council were not unduly opposed to such ideas. It certainly helped that the military trusted Freycinet, who had taken the military viewpoint in questions of staff organization and matériel.[43] The main reason for the military's interest in maximum exploitation of reserve manpower, however, was the increase in the size of the German army. Between 1887 and 1893 the Germans had increased their peacetime forces and greatly enlarged their potential pool of reserve manpower by adopting a two-year term of service for the infantry. The Germans demonstrated their intention to exploit the manpower bonanza of the two-year system by adding a "demi-battalion" to each active regiment. In peacetime, this fourth battalion would be half the size of the other three; but upon mobilization, reservists would bring it to full strength. Moreover, French intelligence continued to believe that German reserve divisions would participate in the opening battles.[44] Finally, the French still had to reckon with the possibility of fighting the Germans and the Italians simultaneously. Thus, despite the modest increase in the French standing army in 1889, the French active corps could still have been seriously outnumbered in a European war.

These bare facts forced the French military authorities to give the full use of trained manpower priority over traditional institutional interests. Ironically, Freycinet's principal collaborator was the chief of the General Staff, General Marie-François de Miribel, considered by most republicans to be a dangerous reactionary. But as France's chief war planner, Miribel held primary responsibility for dealing with the problem of numerical inferiority, and this problem proved more potent than his political views in determining his attitude toward the reservists.

At first, Miribel simply formed a reserve corps in each of the districts that formed an active corps. Seeking a better solution for the long run, the Supreme War Council began to discuss a wide variety of options for incorporating more reservists into the field army. All the proposals had a common drawback, however, in that they required the cannibalizing of officers and matériel from active units in order to establish an infrastructure for reserve and mixed units. The council members regretted the decision, but most of them understood that strategic exigencies required it. One scheme or another, they hoped, could minimize the damage. Operational commanders, on the other hand, viewed the problem differently. To them, the numerical balance between France and Germany was a remote abstraction, whereas the gutting of their existing system of organization was tangible. Under pressure from corps commanders, council proposals increasingly favored the retention of personnel and hardware by active units at the expense of reserve and mixed formations. The distinction between first- and second-line troops that Freycinet had hoped to erase was reestablished. At the level of implementation, operational commanders further shortchanged the new formations. Although the nonsoldier Freycinet claimed that the reserve units looked just as fit as the active forces, council members returned from inspection tours convinced that the reforms were failing.[45]

Fortunately, the problem of potential inferiority vanished almost as quickly as it had appeared. With the active encouragement of the French General Staff, the French and Russian governments established in 1892 an entente against the Triple Alliance (of Germany, Austria, and Italy) and in 1894 a full military defense pact. These agreements diminished the incentives favoring radical measures to incorporate greater numbers of reservists into the front-line forces. Even lesser measures were mostly abandoned when the Germans announced the termination of their demi-battalion experiment. They grouped the active cadres of these fourth battalions into new active corps and relegated the reservists formerly assigned to them to reserve units. At the same time, German War Minister Paul Bronsart von Schellendorf told the Reichstag that reserve divisions would be used strictly for siege, garrison, and lines of communication duties at the beginning of a war. Only later could they be used on the battlefield.[46]

However, Bronsart's remarks did not reflect the views of the chief of the German General Staff, General Schlieffen. The change in German reserve policy resulted from the influence on the kaiser of traditionalist military men, who feared that an enlarged army would bring the middle classes into the Junker officer corps and urban socialists into the lower ranks. Alfred Schlieffen, however, was more concerned with the need to find sufficient forces for a two-front war than with the Junkers' private agenda. Like Miribel, Schlieffen was willing to try any organizational innovation that might ease his strategic problems. Although the policy of the kaiser and the Junker traditionalists meant that the army would not fully exploit Germany's trained manpower in its force structure, Schlieffen still planned to make active use of the reserve divisions that were available.[47]

To some extent, French military intelligence seems to have understood this distinction:

> It is known, of course, that in principle the Germany military authorities consider reserve divisions as not available for participation in the initial battles at the beginning of the war, but one may suppose that, in the case of a war on two fronts, the Germans envision the possibility of using some of these divisions in the eastern theater of operations, where the first encounter will take place significantly later than in the west.[48]

Nonetheless, the French General Staff felt able by 1898 to draw up a new war plan that clearly marked French reserve units as second-echelon forces. The addition of a "demi-battalion" of reservists to each active regiment partially offset the reduction of the field army that this redefinition of reservists entailed. Although organizational interests influenced this decision, the French actions were not based on dogmatic bias. Rather, all the observable indicators of German policy conveniently permitted the French to abandon the troublesome reserve policies initiated under Freycinet. The more egregious errors only came later, when the German army reemphasized the role of reserve forces and the embattled French military failed to attune its intelligence estimates to the new reality.

After the Dreyfus watershed, the French military would look back on the 1890s as a golden age. The military had considerable power to arrange its own affairs and, after the alliance with Russia, felt confident of its ability to carry out its strategic mission. Professional soldiers had, moreover, worked out a satisfactory modus vivendi with popular demand for a shortened term of service. Of course, press skirmishes between military ideologists and militia advocates continued, but they remained a distant danger, too hypothetical to skew policy decisions. Just as Miribel had been realistic enough to entertain Freycinet's proposals for countering the Germans' numerical advantage, so too a spirit of realism and moderation dominated strategic and tactical thought. While most military commentators retained a general preference for the offensive, practical policies were quite moderate. War plans continued to be based on "defensive-offensive" assumptions, and field regulations became less stridently offensive than those of the 1880s.[49]

SUBJUGATION AND REASSERTION, 1898–1911

In the years following the Dreyfus affair, the French military faced serious threats to its organizational autonomy and traditions, its doctrinal preference for the offensive, and its traditional formula for parrying a German invasion. It is no exaggeration to say that the morale of the officer corps was crushed by the politically motivated reforms of the André ministry, which attacked the personal dignity of the officer and soured the daily routine of regimental life. At the same time, offensive tactics were being called into question by the lessons of the Boer War. As a final blow, France's Lorraine-oriented war plans were challenged by intelligence indicating that the Germans intended to attack through Belgium, using reserve units in their front lines. Military officers developed three alternative ways of coping with these threats: moderates proposed to meet them by incremental adjustments, a few radical reformers sought to accommodate the threats by means of fundamental organizational and strategic changes, and "neotraditionalists" urged a reassertive reaction against them.

For the first several years after the Dreyfus affair, the military was in disarray organizationally and dispirited individually. Having no other solutions in hand, the military tried to maintain old formulae in organizational policy, tactics, and strategy, making marginal, pragmatic adjustments in the face of changing political, technological, and strategic circumstances. This attitude dominated policy until 1910 and remained an important current in French military life through to the outbreak of war. Its proponents were mainly older officers, often in positions of high authority, who remained true to the relatively moderate doctrines of the 1880s and 1890s. Notable figures in this loose "group" include all of the pre-1910 generalissimos, designated to command the army in wartime, as well as Generals Henri Bonnal, Joseph-Simon Gallieni, and Charles Lanrezac.

After the adoption of the two-year law in 1905, the pressure for more fundamental adjustments to changing conditions increased. One logical direction of change was to accommodate the shorter term of service by turning the standing army into a school for the nation-in-arms. Such a decision would have involved reshaping institutions, beliefs, and operational doctrines to fit the needs of the short-term trainee and the reservist rather than those of the professional soldier. Jean Jaurès's book *La nouvelle armée* was the purest expression of this solution to the contradiction between France's military institutions and the changed political, technological, and strategic circumstances. Within the military, Victor Michel's 1911 scheme for using reservists to bar a German march across Belgium followed a similar logic. Support for this kind of radical accommodation was probably not widespread, even among "republican" officers, but Michel's plan lays out in stark relief the institutional and strategic implications of both the two-year law and the intelligence about German war plans.[50]

Many officers thought that troubling trends should be combated rather than accommodated. Spearheaded by a group of young officers at the war college and in the General Staff, this movement sought to revitalize the army's morale, institutions, and operational doctrines by reemphasizing the tenets of the traditional organizational ideology: the decisive role of morale in warfare, the importance of troop quality rather than quantity, and the crucial significance of the offensive. After Michel's fall in 1911, this tendency came to dominate French military policy. Its key figures included "Young Turks" like Colonel Grandmaison of the General Staff as well as so-called "clerical" and "antirepublican" officers of an older generation such as Generals Foch, Paul-Marie Pau, and Noël Curières de Castelnau.

It is tempting to argue that the views of members of each of these three groups made up a syndrome, linking attitudes on strategy, tactics, military organization, religion, and domestic politics. At the extremes of the reformer-traditionalist spectrum, syndromes can be quite clear. The archetypical traditionalist, for example, was General Pau, the army's chief spokesman during the 1913 debate on the three-year service bill. He believed that the two-year law and the reservists were the ruination of the army; he liked bold offensives and Plan 17 and feared a German *attaque brusquée* using only active units. He was also considered a clerical and an antirepublican.[51] Pau's nemesis, the socialist leader Jaurès, favored a militia system and a defensive strategy; he expected the Germans to use their reserves to go through northern Belgium and thought the fear of a German *attaque brusquée* in Lorraine was groundless.

As one moves in from these extremes, however, other figures

rarely exhibit this absolute consistency of viewpoints. Even among the most reformist officers, an emphasis on the reserves' importance did not necessarily imply a passively defensive orientation on strategic and tactical questions. For example, Michel's 1911 scheme calls for a "vigorous offensive" into Belgium, but it is likely that he envisioned a positional battle along the Anvers-Namur-Verdun fortress line. Tactically, Michel believed in dispersed order, a strong avant garde, and a blend of offense and defense.[52]

Some individuals who wanted to reassert the interests of the professional military also deviate from the expected pattern. Foch was clerical, favored the offense, and was blocked from high posts by republican reformers but nonetheless anticipated a German attack across northern Belgium.[53] Moreover, not all members of this group were clerical traditionalists like Pau. Joseph Joffre had at one point been a Mason. Adolphe Messimy, the civilian war minister who selected Joffre, had had to quit the army because he was ostracized by other officers for believing in Alfred Dreyfus's innocence. These were modern men who wanted to revitalize traditional institutions not out of atavistic habit but as the most effective antidote to Michel's ideas, which they considered disastrous.[54]

Most moderates favored a pragmatic combination of offense and defense and predicted fairly substantial German deployments in Belgium. Almost all supported the three-year law in 1913 but wanted reservists to be better used in the opening battles, and they supported the republican form of government while disapproving of the disruptive reforms of the Louis André ministry. Some, like Colonel Auguste Grouard, leaned toward the reformist end of the spectrum on most issues (favoring the strategic defensive, foreseeing Belgium as the principal theater, and urging a key role for reservists), but most were closer in outlook to Joffre than to Michel. Michel's draft plan won no adherents on the Supreme War Council from any camp. Indeed, those members of the council labeled "reactionaries" and "doubtful republicans" by the leftist press were no more critical of the plan than those labeled "republicans."[55]

Thus Douglas Porch is at least partially right to criticize those historians who portray French military policy as a struggle between aristocratic, offense-minded proponents of an insular, professional army and republican, defense-minded proponents of a nation-in-arms.[56] This caricature ignores the large body of moderate opinion, the scarcity of true antirepublicans by 1911, and the fact that almost all professional officers saw an important role for some type of offensive operations. At the same time, Porch underplays some real cleavages, for example, the distinction between the *offensive à outrance* and more moderate offensive views.[57] What is more important, both Porch and the nation-in-arms historians that he criticizes tend to collapse the distinction between antirepublicanism and institutional protection as motives for denigrating the idea of the nation-in-arms. Although Joffre was an impeccable republican, his policies were still influenced by his *organizational* interest in a longer term of service. Being republican, that is to say, was a necessary but not a sufficient condition for favoring radical military reform.

I consequently differ in the following narrative from both Porch and his opponents in that I discuss French military developments from 1898 to 1911 primarily in terms of organizational interests rather than in terms of political ideology. In response to four different kinds of threats, incremental adjustments failed fully to satisfy the French army; they neither produced an effective military policy nor protected the military's institutional interests. Faced with the choice between a more radical accommodation of these threats and a reassertive reaction against them, the French military gravitated toward the latter, bolstered politically and psychologically by Grandmaison's offensive doctrine.

1. Morale

The humiliation of the army as a result of the Dreyfus affair left the military in a mood of testy despair. In November 1899 Gilbert wrote his publisher that it was probably futile for him to continue writing articles about military policy. In view of "the insolent triumph of the cosmopolitan cabal," he wrote, "what use is there in studying the improvement of our military institutions when the very survival of the army is in doubt?"[58]

The new center-left government decided to take advantage of its victory over the military by thoroughly republicanizing military attitudes and institutions. General Louis André, an avidly republican officer, was chosen as war minister to oversee this reformation. His program included purging the personnel of the central military institutions, politically controlling officers' promotions, discriminating against conspicuously Catholic officers, increasing the number of officers commissioned from the ranks, democratizing access to service academies, changing the authoritarian relationship between officers and conscripts, reforming the military justice system, and instituting a two-year law.[59] By 1905 this program had had a ruinous effect on the morale of professional officers.

[73]

André asserted the authority of the war minister over the General Staff by naming relatively junior officers to head the General Staff and by reserving the right to nominate its various bureau chiefs. Meetings of the Supreme War Council were infrequent, and its vice-presidents (that is, the intended wartime generalissimos) were less prestigious than formerly. Three of them resigned between 1900 and 1907 to protest War Ministry meddling and the deleterious effect of the government's reform program on the fighting capacity of the army.[60]

Even after André's departure in 1905, the decisive criteria for filling top military positions were political reliability and parliamentary connections. The inexperienced General Georges Picquart was chosen as war minister primarily because of his role in exposing the General Staff's falsification of evidence in the Dreyfus case. Similarly, Michel's ascent under André and subsequent ministers was embarrassingly rapid. According to Messimy, Michel's authority among his peers was "nil."[61] But the presence of such antitraditionalists at the top of the hierarchy made it difficult for the army to organize a coherent campaign of resistance to the reform program.

One of the most resented practices was the war minister's control over the promotion of officers. André used Masonic lodges to inform him of officers' political and religious beliefs. Under this system, talented Catholic officers like Foch were often relegated to inconsequential posts in the provinces. Members of Parliament received hundreds of letters from officers asking for political character references. While favoritism in promotion had always been a problem, this particular version had an unusually severe effect on morale. Officers came to feel that their superiors had received their posts only because of political toadyism.[62]

Generally speaking, the life of the typical officer had less and less to recommend it. The promotion rate was slowing, and salaries were low compared to civilian pay. The demise of the three-year law eliminated the pool of spare manpower that had been used for such tasks as maintaining the officers' tennis courts. The officer found that he was expected to lecture his soldiers on civics, hygiene, and agriculture and that "discipline via respect" had replaced the traditional approach he preferred. Applications to St. Cyr, the elite military academy, declined from 3,400 in 1892 to 800 in 1912.[63]

Many of the reforms directly affected the daily pattern of regimental life, including relationships among the officers. General Léon-Frédéric Metzinger, a spokesman for the old guard, was particularly bitter toward the new breed of reform-minded officers that had been promoted from the ranks or graduated from one of the nonelite academies. "Convinced that they have been called to regenerate the army, they pose as intransigent reformers upon their arrival in the corps. Since the parvenus enjoy assured protection from the minister, . . . the veterans must hold themselves in check. The mess table, where one eats without saying a word, one's nose in one's plate, . . . becomes odious and deserted. It is the end of comradery, solidarity, and esprit de corps."[64]

Metzinger saw threats to the social cohesion of the regiment coming from a variety of sources. He bemoaned the change to a territorial system of recruitment, as allowing soldiers social ties outside the regiment, and the elimination of barriers to the marriage of young officers. Similarly, General Charles Kessler remarked on the increasing impact of reservists on regimental life. "When a large number of reservists—that is, men who are strangers to each other, preoccupied with family and business concerns, indifferent to the goal of training the group—are introduced into the unified and compact milieu [of the active regiment], the spirit of the group is changed. It begins to waver and becomes hesitant. Its moral force disintegrates."[65] The view that "the reservists are poisoning the regiments" was shared by many corps commanders, according to a book whose title, *Vers un nouveau Sedan*, captures the pessimistic spirit of the period.[66]

Not all opponents of radical military reform, however, were hidebound reactionaries. Metzinger appealed to a very broad audience when he argued that the French civic ethos was not highly enough developed to replace the traditional bases of military morale and discipline. Even center-left republicans and Dreyfusards, having won their point, began to question the wisdom of further destruction of the old military institutions. These second thoughts were reinforced by the discovery of André's Masonic espionage net, the First Morocco Crisis of 1905, the steady rise of the socialists' share of the vote, and the Midi troop mutiny of 1907.[67]

The military, for its part, generally recognized that its material problems were not great. There was nothing wrong, said the retired Bonnal, that a sympathetic war minister could not set straight in a few months. Similarly, Major Emile Driant, the author of *Vers un nouveau Sedan*, diagnosed the army's disease as moral and organizational rather than material. Sharing this analysis, officers like Grandmaison and Foch set out to provide the spiritual and doctrinal basis for the renaissance of army morale.[68]

2. The Two-Year Service Law of 1905 and the Reserves

In theory, there was a good military argument for the two-year law. By reducing the term of service, France could increase the number of her trained soldiers at no additional cost. This increase would allow her to keep pace with Germany in terms of available manpower, despite the growing disparity between the populations of the two countries. Of course, it would imply an intensive use of French reservists, including some of the older classes, called "territorials." However, neither the civilian politicians nor the military made sufficient efforts to implement the two-year law in a way that would realize its military potential.

Parliament cared more about reducing and equalizing the burden on its constituents than about military results. "To tell the truth, we are infinitely more preoccupied with the question of principle than with the practical consequences of the solution proposed by M. le Ministre," said the bill's reporter.[69] Despite the two-year system's need to rely more heavily on reservists, Parliament tended during this period to reduce the length of the reserves' periodic call-ups.[70] Georges Clemenceau, however, blamed this reduction on the military: "If we have reduced . . . the period of military instruction, it is because we have found that the chiefs of the army did not make good use of the reservists that we sent them."[71] The reservists were commonly used for guard duty or corvée labor and often did not take part in field maneuvers. As a result, in 1907 only about two-thirds of them bothered to show up. Even reserve officers were often absent. This slapdash attitude gave the professional officers further ammunition for the charge that reservists were unreliable.[72] Thus their disdain for the reservists became a self-fulfilling prophecy.

The two-year system posed a peculiarly severe problem for military planners. They had to plan for the use of reserve troops even though the attitudes of the politicians, the officers in the field, and the reservists themselves had hindered the development of their fighting value. As the classes with three-year obligations were discharged, the size of the active French army would decrease by an estimated 110,000 men. In principle, this reduction could mostly be made up by suppressing exemptions, offering reenlistment bonuses, and civilianizing noncombat functions. Even under the best of circumstances, however, reservists would have to take up some of the slack.[73]

Bonnal suggested solving the problem by means of incremental adjustments to existing policies. The strict division of labor between front-line actives and second-line reserves should, he said, be maintained. At the same time, he thought, a high priority should be placed on improving reserve officer cadres and on serious field maneuvers for the reserves. This priority should not, however, extend to the territorials.[74]

This modest accommodation of the two-year system seemed increasingly inadequate to republican officers who held key General Staff positions. In their view, only more intensive use of the reserves could solve the dual problem of a shrinking active army and the need to extend the French left wing to cover the Belgian border. In 1907 General Jean Jules Brun, the chief of the General Staff, told the Supreme War Council that if the infantry regiment was to keep its four-battalion structure, the fourth would have to be constituted exclusively of reservists. Brun proposed as an alternative eliminating the fourth battalion while adding a six-battalion reserve brigade to each active corps. In case of war, this brigade could be put into the front line "after rapid retraining."[75]

Continuing this trend, an order of 1908 required reservists to spend their training period in the field, not in the barracks.[76] Michel reported to the council on these field exercises, calling the reservists "mature," "flexible," "homogeneous," and "disciplined." They were in good physical condition, he believed, and possessed an "excellent spirit." "If each reserve company had 200 men with one captain and one other officer from the active army, it would be the equal of an active company: this is the goal to pursue."[77] Reflecting these assessments and the Belgium threat, Plan 16 of 1909 made use of 463 reserve battalions instead of the previous plan's 320.[78]

The Picardy maneuvers of 1910 brought these matters to the attention of the public and the press. In these exercises, managed by Michel, each corps was supplemented by a fifth brigade of reservists. Charles Repington, the esteemed military critic of the London *Times*, was unimpressed by the French performance and wondered whether the two-year service was to blame. The French press tended to agree.[79] Grandmaison, then a General Staff section chief, used the opportunity to humiliate Michel's collaborator, Alexandre Percin, who served as chief umpire of the maneuvers.[80] Michel was unchastened, however, and shortly produced the even more radical demi-brigade scheme that caused his downfall.

In sum, the two-year law tended to make incremental, "business as usual" solutions to the reservist problem untenable. At the same time, the failure to create truly first-class reserve units made Michel's policy equally vulnerable. This combination of circumstances made it possible for the professional military, spearheaded by a hard core of young ideologues, to reassert its traditional preferences.

3. Lessons about Defensive Firepower

The Boer War of 1899–1902 and the Russo-Japanese War of 1904–1905 provided stark new evidence of the domination of the modern battlefield by defensive firepower and its attendant phenomena, the proliferation of entrenchments and the extension of the front.[81] French reactions to these conflicts suggest that evidence *can* change beliefs even when those beliefs are linked to vested interests. However, they also show that, under ambiguous circumstances, observers will interpret evidence in such a way as to preserve their fundamental views.

French leftist politicians were quick to point to the Boer War as proof of the efficacy of defensive tactics used by nonprofessional soldiers, in this case Boer farmers.[82] However, it was not only proponents of the short term of service who remarked on the new demonstration of the power of entrenched, defensive fire. In 1902 Emile Mayer, a moderate traditionalist on questions of military institutions, used the lessons of the Boer War to predict with astounding accuracy the European stalemate of 1914–1918. Two human walls would face each other, Mayer argued, unable to advance. Each side would try to outflank the other until stopped by mountains, the sea, or a neutral border.[83]

Mayer had been an advocate of the defensive even before the Boer War, but the perceptible rise of a defensive school of thought between 1900 and 1904 shows that the new evidence had an impact beyond merely reconfirming already held views. This school included people of varied political views, ages, and institutional associations. By 1904 this unlikely coalition had succeeded in revising the infantry regulations to increase the emphasis on firepower, dispersed order, and the methodical use of terrain for cover.[84]

Many tacticians, however, denied that the Boer War refuted their earlier views. The incrementalist Bonnal was typical in warning against developing revolutionary tactics suited to improved armaments, arguing that the war had been influenced by unique factors and British errors. "Revolution is a violent remedy capable of killing the patient, and its use is justified only in desperate cases. Present tactics are far from requiring such treatment."[85]

Georges Gilbert also saw the Boer War as confirming his earlier opinions. He claimed that the material lessons of the war were overshadowed by the moral lessons. The Boers had done well against a numerically superior force primarily because of their superior morale. Nonetheless, the Boers had failed, and they had done so primarily because of their passive defensive strategy and the inherent limitations of a nonprofessional force. The British had been unable to press home their attacks because they had mistakenly mixed their veteran troops with raw recruits, becoming a quasi militia: "The more solid

[78]

troops are lost in the mass." The material lessons of the war were worthless, Gilbert added, since the newest weapons, such as rapid-fire artillery, were used inexpertly and in small quantities. He generally reiterated the benefits of the offensive and the dangers of undermining the elite professional army.[86]

Frédéric Culmann, one of the leading military writers of the day, adopted Gilbert's view of the relative importance of material and moral factors in the Boer War. Culmann explained away the Boers' devastating rifle fire in a hundred and one ways, including the assertions that Boers have better eyesight than Europeans and that South African air is exceptionally clear. However, he argued, the real key to the Boers' stubborn defense was the British unwillingness to take casualties. The British suffered only 7.4 percent attrition in major engagements. Anticipating Grandmaison, Culmann argued that the army needed to be instilled with a doctrine of *offensive à outrance* as an antidote to its natural desire to sit safely in the trenches. He specifically denounced Bonnal's concept of the defensive offensive, which in practice "inevitably transforms itself into a pure defensive."[87]

Reactions to the Russo-Japanese War followed a somewhat different pattern. Because the attacking Japanese "won" a series of inconclusive, slow-moving engagements interspersed with long periods of stalemate, most French observers adopted a two-level analysis: on one level, the war showed that the tactical role of defensive firepower could not be ignored, but on a more important level, it had borne out the moral and strategic advantages of the offensive. Consequently, it was generally felt, the more sweeping arguments of the defensive school that had emerged after the Boer War were largely rebutted.

The French official observers in Manchuria, for example, reported quite accurately that the extension of the front was an inevitable result of the strength of defensive firepower. They also pointed out the necessity of entrenchment in offense and defense.[88] While noting the usefulness of machine guns in the offensive, the French observers stressed that their defensive effectiveness had been particularly devastating. "It is above all in the defensive that these machines demonstrated their terrible efficacy, particularly at the moment when the adversaries close to a few hundred meters and the men become nervous and shoot too high. . . . Machines without nerves and without a soul, the machine guns in these circumstances literally mow down the attackers."[89]

Of course, these findings did not daunt the partisans of the tactical offensive. Culmann, for example, noted that the Japanese lost 49,000 men in their human-wave assaults on the entrenchments at Port Arthur, while the Russians lost only 28,200. But the key thing, Culmann argued, was that the attacks eventually succeeded, showing that Japanese morale was the decisive factor and that the material effects of defensive fire, though real enough, were ultimately a secondary factor.[90]

At the strategic level, the French official observers reported the war as "a resounding confirmation of the superiority of the offensive, . . . of the value of maneuver, and of the powerlessness of the defensive and above all of the passive defensive."[91] Even the Russians' numerical superiority and their accumulation of field fortifications had not saved their defensive strategy. But this argument entailed two important biases. First, the Russians fared even worse when they attacked than when they defended. Second, the French, quick to invoke "British ineptitude" to explain failed offensives in the Boer War, resisted invoking "Russian ineptitude" to account for unsuccessful defensive operations in Manchuria, although Russian mediocrity was apparent. More recent analysts have indeed argued that the Russians' adoption of an inert, stalemate strategy alone prevented total disaster.[92]

One other conclusion deserves notice. General Marie Félix Silvestre, the chief French observer, recognized the Russo-Japanese War's lesson that future battles could last days or weeks. However, he argued, such prolonged operations would only happen in the very unlikely eventuality that one side adopted a fortified defense, as the Russians had. In essence, that is, he understood that modern technology made stalemate a theoretical possibility, but he failed to understand the overwhelming incentives for the weaker side (or losing side) to adopt this posture. He believed, therefore, that battles would be decided in one day, not including advance contact.[93]

The Russo-Japanese War reinforced the doctrines that Foch had been disseminating since his term at the war college in the 1890s. The persistent and ultimately successful Japanese seemed to validate Foch's view that "a battle lost is a battle one believes one has lost, for a battle is never lost materially."[94] The bankruptcy of the passive Russian defense similarly seemed, at least superficially, to support Foch's call for an offensive strategy. Finally, the demonstration of the withering effect of defensive firepower did not refute Foch's tactics, since he had always taken it to some degree into account by emphasizing the need for "superiority of fire" at the point of the attack and the use of terrain cover in the final assault.[95] Thus the success of Foch's doctrinal teachings, culminating in their extreme expression by

[80]

Grandmaison in 1911, must be attributed not only to motivated bias but also to the doctrine's credible attempt to deal with the realities of modern war as revealed by the Manchurian campaign. Because the Foch-Grandmaison message was both plausible and more appealing than that of Mayer and the 1904 field manual, defensive doctrines declined in popularity after 1905, even though historians usually see the Russo-Japanese War as a harbinger of the coming stalemate on the western front.[96]

4. *The 1904 Intelligence Coup and Intelligence Estimates, 1905–1911*

In 1904 the French General Staff acquired information indicating that German war planners intended to outflank the French fortresses and field army by violating Belgian neutrality. They learned in addition that the attacking force would be somewhat larger than they had previously been expecting and would use reserve units in the front lines. Instead of 19 active corps and 15 reserve divisions, the new evidence suggested, the French would be facing 20-1/2 active corps and 22 reserve divisions, some grouped into reserve field corps. If anything, this intelligence understated the size of the active forces that Schlieffen expected to deploy against France.[97]

The development of this additional threat to the orthodox French military outlook—and the French response—followed a familiar pattern. After an initial impulse to deny the need to do anything about the intelligence, French military authorities decided to accommodate the threat by incremental adjustments to their previous plan. As the danger grew more credible and less manageable, incremental adjustments eventually gave way to Michel's more radical proposals. At this point, military traditionalists revolted and adopted a view of German strategy that presented less of a challenge to the interests of the French professional military. This pattern of incremental adjustment, radical accommodation, and reassertive reaction parallels the French military's response to the two-year law.[98] Such a similarity is wholly unsurprising, since beliefs about German strategy had important implications for attitudes about the use of French reserves, and vice versa.

In January 1904 the General Staff's intelligence bureau began to evaluate the information it had recently acquired. The bureau showed considerable objectivity and sophistication in accepting the probable validity of the new data while placing it in the context of a nuanced, accurate assessment of the capabilities of different types of German reserve units.[99] With regard to the violation of Belgian neutrality, the intelligence bureau noted that Lorraine would constitute too narrow a field of action for a force as large as the one that Germany could deploy. As early as 1870, the report noted, the elder Helmuth von Moltke had deployed a force half the size of the German force of 1904 on a front of 140 kilometers. Since the distance from Aix-la-Chapelle/ Aachen (near Liège) to Sarrebourg (in Lorraine) is only 250 kilometers, the deployments outlined in the raw intelligence data seemed feasible. According to the bureau's report, they were also corroborated by information about German war games. Yet the intelligence bureau remained perplexed by the continuing construction of rail lines in Lorraine, which seemed superfluous if the front were to be extended.[100] They neglected to consider that the German General Staff might be planning for a large increase in the use of reserve forces, which would explain why more platforms would be needed in both areas. This interpretation of the evidence on railroads and reserves shows that when policy is changing or when there are disagreements about policy, observable indicators may be contradictory and will lag behind policy changes. Consequently, observers can focus on the signals that fit their expectations or interests and ignore the rest. This problem vexed French planning not only in 1904 but also in the critical five years before the war.

The initial reaction of the General Staff's operations bureau, recorded in a 29 January 1904 memorandum, was that the French war plan should not be changed even if the new information were true. If ten German corps were to cross southern Belgium, the march would put them out of action until at least the twenty-first day after mobilization, when they would reach the river Meuse north of Verdun. This delay, the operations bureau believed, would give the French forces in Lorraine time to defeat the inferior German forces left in that sector. In fact, the bureau considered such a situation so disadvantageous to Germany that it suspected that the whole idea of crossing Belgium was a ruse. The Germans might use this deception to induce the French to extend their deployments along the Belgian border and then attack a diminished French force in Lorraine. They could do so either by turning their northern army south instead of west or by sending it directly into Lorraine on the "superfluous" rail lines. In fact, Schlieffen did envision the German right wing wheeling south if the French decided, foolishly as he saw it, to come out from behind their impregnable fortress line and attack.[101]

The operations bureau was quite realistic about the role of the German reserve units. The bureau assumed that the reserve corps in Lorraine would play an active and important part in the decisive

[82]

battle, although they would arrive two or three days behind the actives. The reserve corps and divisions in the right wing would march through Belgium just behind the active corps, covering their flank against the Belgian army, which everyone expected to retreat into northern Belgium. This assessment fitted closely with Schlieffen's actual ideas.[102]

In April and May 1904 the intelligence bureau reported that recent German railway construction near the Belgian border, especially disembarkation platforms that could not be explained by civilian uses, meshed precisely with the new intelligence. "One could rightfully conclude that [the purchased document] is not just a study . . . but that it is a copy of a plan actually envisaged by the German high command, and that it has prompted preparatory measures necessary for its execution."[103]

The chief of the General Staff, deciding that advice should be sought from the members of the Supreme War Council, had the operations bureau prepare a study of the Belgian question for their comments in August 1904. The study cited earlier assessments that "the violation of Belgian neutrality by Germany would be an error from which it would be easy to profit by assuring us superiority in the decisive theater."[104] However, the study noted, several recent developments made this contingency more dangerous. Better railroads now ran through the Ardennes region of southern Belgium. France's northern forts were now less valuable. Unlike those facing Lorraine, they had not been modernized to withstand the new melinite explosives. The increased number of German units would not only allow but actually demand more room for deployment. Improved German fortifications in Alsace, moreover, would permit some of the units designated for that region to be deployed elsewhere. Finally, of course, the study stressed the military importance of the newly built disembarkation platforms around Aix-la-Chapelle/Aachen.

The study noted that the new information implied a German force crossing through Belgium that would not merely threaten one or two points but would cover a front of 100 kilometers. Despite this implication, it suggested that the bulk of the German forces would still be deployed in Lorraine. The French would possess superiority in Lorraine, but their numerical advantage would not be overwhelming. Moreover, the Germans in Lorraine could buy time by falling back to the Saar River. Consequently, a fairly substantial French force would have to be created to parry the German right wing for at least eight days, until a decision had been attained in Lorraine. The operations bureau recommended using eight reserve divisions to cover the Franco-Belgian frontier from Mézières to Stenay, with another eight divisions of even lesser quality backing them up. "This mass of 280,000 second-line troops clearly could not take the offensive against the German First Army, 324,000 strong, of whom 216,000 are active soldiers. . . . It nonetheless would constitute a rather important screen for stopping the invasion by using the water barriers and natural obstacles of this difficult region." More artillery would have to be allocated to these units and the old fortress at Maubeuge would require improvement, the study noted.[105]

The reactions of council members to this report can be divided into three general categories. Some members wanted virtually no change in the French deployment plan. Henri-Joseph Brugère, the generalissimo, claimed that Plan 15, the current plan envisioning the main battle in Lorraine, had not ignored the Belgian hypothesis and that it "provides the means for meeting all eventualities."[106] General Raoul-Marie Donop agreed with Brugère and offered a detailed critique of the operations bureau's concept of a reserve army to screen the border with Belgium. There was no need to counter the German attack across Belgium with any new deployments, he claimed, for the eccentric march of the German First Army would put them far away from the action during the critical fighting in Lorraine. Rather than drawing off major forces to meet this force on the Meuse north of Verdun, Donop urged retreating to Paris to buy still more time. Moreover, he thought the idea of forming a screen from reserve units to be particularly erroneous. It reflected the insidious effects of the "deceptive chimera of large numbers." Without adequate staff, artillery, and cavalry, a motley collection of reserve units could not constitute an independent army. "If we had the good sense to suppress the reserve corps, the theoretical creation of which was the result of a spirit as false as it was alluring, it was not to go ahead now with the formation of reserve armies." Reserve units should only be used in conjunction with active forces, and in no case should the older territorials be used in the field army. While denigrating the value of the reserves, he also took the opportunity to make a passing jibe at the short term of service.[107]

A second group of council members tended to agree with the operations bureau's plan. General Jean-Edouard Dessirier, for example, agreed that the violation of Belgium was a serious possibility and that the reserve army was an appropriate means of hedging against the eventuality. On the other hand, he, like the General Staff, still considered Lorraine the main theater and worried about the possibility of a ruse. Therefore, he believed, the French active forces in Lorraine should not be depleted. His concern also led him to propose that the new reserve army be given an offensive capability, in case the German First Army turned south prematurely, exposing its flank.

A third group agreed that the Belgian invasion route should be covered but argued that reserve units alone could not do so. Expressing a viewpoint that would set the tone for the development of French strategy across the next several years, General Jacques Achille Duchesne argued that the entire French deployment should be shifted slightly toward the northwest. The proposed reserve army would have no solidity; it would have to be reinforced with some of the active forces that the General Staff wanted to use in the Lorraine offensive. This reinforcement implied abandoning that offensive, but Duchesne did not consider this a disadvantage. Even under the best of circumstances, he felt, a decision in Lorraine could not be achieved before the German First Army arrived in the French rear. Thus, while arguing against the reserve army concept, Duchesne was not at all opposed to exploiting the reservists more fully. In view of Germany's overall numerical superiority, he argued, the French would have to use "all the forces at our disposal, particularly our reserve divisions."[108]

In short, the immediate reaction of the French military authorities to the new intelligence was not particularly unreasonable. Only a few of the responses denied the need to make changes at all. Most held the new circumstances to require some kind of an enhanced role for the French reservists.

In this sense, the 1904 response to information about German plans was not unlike that of 1887–1893. In the earlier period, two factors had been conducive to a clear recognition of the problem and a more or less rational response: first, the manageability of the German and internal threats and second, the undeniability of the German army increases. The German threat in 1904, as portrayed in the intelligence data, could be managed by minor adjustments, even if they might touch on the psychologically sensitive issue of the reservists. Besides, the French reserve question was then mostly a potential problem; it was not clear how unmanageable it might later become. But on balance, it seems that the French military authorities were somewhat more inclined to deny the evidence of a problem in 1904 than they had been in the earlier period. Their inclination could be explained either as a result of a perceptual bias or as a reflection of the questionable authenticity of the intelligence data, which were supposedly purchased from a German General Staff officer.

In any case, the main difference between 1887–1893 and 1904 lies in the trend of subsequent developments. In the earlier case, the threat of German numerical superiority eventually subsided. In the latter case, however, the problem grew worse, and incremental adjustments would eventually seem inadequate to handle it. Only then would the strategic and organizational implications of the intelligence provoke a more doctrinaire response.

After 1905 the Germans continued to develop the infrastructure needed to implement the Schlieffen Plan. They expanded the construction of railroads along the Belgian frontier. The fortresses of Metz and Thionville/Diedenhofen were connected to form a huge fortified zone that secured the area between the German right wing in Belgium and the left wing in Lorraine. And, the German war plan continued to use reserve units in an active role. The plans for 1905 through 1907, which adopted Schlieffen's idea of a wide sweep through northern Belgium, designated 20 reserve divisions as integral parts of the attacking field armies. By 1910 this figure had risen to 22.[109]

Between 1905 and 1909 French intelligence became increasingly convinced of the likelihood that Germany intended to violate Belgian territory if war broke out. The deduction was based on German railroad construction along the Belgian border. However, the Germans would use, it was believed, only 14 or 15 reserve divisions in their field army in the west. The intelligence bureau consequently estimated that the German right wing could only extend as far as southern Belgium. In short, the moderate incrementalists who dominated French strategic planning during the period foresaw only the kind of attack that their minor adjustments could manage.

French information about German railroad building across the border from northern Belgium was quite extensive.[110] The construction of disembarkation platforms as far north as Aix-la-Chapelle/Aachen did not, however, necessarily prove that the Germans would cross into northern Belgium. Moreover, the continuation of railroad improvements in Lorraine indicated that the main weight of the German attack might remain on the German left. The French similarly understood that the German doctrine of envelopment made a flank attack through Belgium quite likely, but doctrinal generalities could not reveal whether the flank maneuver would be wide or narrow.[111]

The tendency to underestimate German use of reserves made an extension of the front through northern Belgium seem even less likely. In May 1907 the intelligence bureau of the French General Staff inexplicably estimated that the German field forces in the west would include a maximum of 14 reserve divisions. Although the 1904 information had suggested that the younger Landwehr (territorial reserve) classes would form reserve divisions capable of field operations, the bureau now estimated that Landwehr units would serve only as garrison and siege troops. In no case would they take part in field operations at the beginning of the campaign. Since the intelligence bureau admitted that "we do not possess any exact or precise information on the German plan of operations," it is unclear why the 1904 data were discarded. It is even less clear when one finds that the same report noted that the French had obtained a 1906 war game played by the German General Staff, in which a German right-wing force of 15 active corps attacked the Meuse between Verdun and Namur.[112] (This figure is almost exactly correct for the real German plan of that year, if the reserve divisions echeloned behind the active spearheads are not included.)[113] Despite this accurate and seemingly authoritative information, the French continued to plan for a smaller force of 8 to 10 German corps operating in the sector.[114]

In 1909 the General Staff and the generalissimo, Henri de Lacroix, drew up Plan 16 in order to deal specifically with the threat of a German flank maneuver through southern Belgium, which by then they deemed very likely.[115] The French deployment was moved somewhat further northwest, and the forces adjacent to Belgium were made strong enough to operate offensively. Although this plan was a step in the right direction, it did not go far enough. It completely failed to envision a German march through northern Belgium or the scale of the German attack, foreseeing only 22 active corps and 15 reserve divisions—a total of only 790 battalions. The actual figure in German plans of the time was almost 100 battalions greater. Against this attack, Plan 16 mustered exactly 790 countervailing battalions by incorporating six reserve battalions into each active corps.[116]

Even this organizational adjustment, necessitated by the decline in active strength caused by the two-year law, was a bitter pill for army traditionalists. An accurate estimate of German strength would presumably have led to even more extreme innovations to maintain numerical equality, as the later Michel period suggests. Incremental accommodators like Lacroix were evidently able to see only as much of the threat as their preferred solutions could handle.

By 1910 and 1911 observers who did not share the biases of French military traditionalists were beginning to take quite seriously the German reserve threat and the northern Belgium invasion route. The Russians, the British, General Michel, and General Regnault, an André protégé who had become assistant chief of the General Staff, all provided evidence or analysis that challenged the incrementalist assumptions of Plan 16.[117] For example, in early 1910 the French military attaché in Berlin, Lt. Colonel Pellé, transmitted to Paris an intelligence analysis provided by his Russian counterpart, Colonel Mikhelson. The report presented evidence that each German active regiment had in principle a corresponding reserve regiment and that the Germans were forming some mixed divisions of actives and reservists in order to use more reservists in the field army. The French General Staff responded on two levels. At the level of details, they accurately pointed out that the comprehensive organization of the German reserves in principle was not fully achieved in fact, and they cited a number of examples. At the level of generalities, they continued to maintain that the Germans viewed the increased participation of reservists in the first-line army with "repugnance." At least on this general level, the French response missed the mark. The 1910 table of organization of the German army shows 13-1/2 reserve corps (27 divisions), fewer than the Russians imagined but more than the French foresaw.[118]

During this period one of the standard French arguments against the larger figures for German use of reservists was the German shortage of officers. Since the number of officers was insufficient even for the number of units the French had identified, the provision of cadres for still more units was considered impossible. In April 1910 Pellé transmitted Russian figures showing how the Germans could provide an officer cadre for the reserves by using retired officers, cadets, one-year volunteers, and particularly the 24,000 noncommissioned officers who had left the army with certificates of aptitude for wartime commissions. The French had had these facts all along, but they did not draw the same conclusions from them that the Russians had.[119]

In March 1911 Pellé reported that the British chief of staff, General Henry Wilson, believed that the Germans would attack through northern Belgium, using a large number of reserve divisions in the front line. The German force on the western front could be as great as 70 divisions, Wilson believed, with 40 of them passing through Belgium. Since only three divisions could be marched on the same road, the Germans would have an overwhelming incentive to extend their right flank as far as Brussels and Lille.[120]

In April 1911 the intelligence bureau of the French General Staff obtained a secret aide-mémoire for German staff officers, *Taschenbuch des Generalstabsoffiziers*, dated 1908. Coupled with another German document, dated 1911, this intelligence conclusively established the existence of reserve corps and noted the addition of a machine gun company to the reserve divisions. It showed that Landwehr brigades

[88]

would be entrusted with coastal defense and the protection of lines of communications, presumably freeing divisions and corps formed from younger reserve classes for more active operations.

There was nevertheless room for alternative interpretations. Paraphrasing the *Taschenbuch*, the French analysts noted that "the proportion of reserve formations [in a field army] will depend without doubt on the role given to each army. The armies that have the most arduous task will probably consist only of active corps; reserve corps will, however, enter in a certain number into the composition of armies having a less taxing mission, such as operating around a fortified area or besieging an entrenched camp."[121] In fact, German plans did try to differentiate in this way when possible, but frequently reserve corps had to be used as full-fledged maneuver corps. (The East Prussian campaign of 1914 shows how successful they could be in this role.)[122] However, French intelligence analysts were unwilling to extend their interpretation this far. "Does the introduction of the new word 'reserve corps' indicate a relatively new concept for employing reserve divisions, with the intention, for example, of having them participate more actively than before in the operations of the first line, because a new operations plan might require an extension of the strategic deployment? The document is mute in this regard."[123]

This was enough ambiguity to allow conventional wisdoms to remain unchanged. For example, the war college course on organization and mobilization for 1910–1911 adhered to the traditional outlook. While noting some discussion of reserve corps in the German press, Commandant Stirn told his students that Germany faced the same officer cadre, artillery, and supply service problems as France did in this regard. The Germans, he argued, would no doubt arrive at the same conclusions as the French had.[124]

At the General Staff, however, General Regnault found the evidence of German plans for the intensive use of reserves to be quite convincing. After the war, Regnault claimed that sufficient evidence was collected between March 1910 and July 1911 to give a full and accurate picture of German intentions. Although Regnault did not provide extensive details, his statements make it clear that the intelligence section obtained at least some important materials that are no longer to be found in the French archives. For example, Regnault claimed that in 1911 the French obtained a critique of a map exercise by General Helmuth von Moltke, the younger, in which reserve units were used right alongside the active forces. "Like all interesting documents," it was communicated to the members of the Supreme War

Council. Regnault said that the French knew all about German reserve organization, reserve participation in maneuvers, and the premature retirement of general officers to create a cadre for commanding higher reserve units. Regnault said he had proselytized his views and that they played a major role in the development of Michel's plan.[125]

This connection with Michel made the acceptance of Regnault's intelligence estimates even less likely. Although Regnault produced no smoking gun, the history of French intelligence from 1905 to 1911 suggests that resistance to his views was not based solely on the ambiguity of his information. For no good reason at all, the French gave up their basically correct estimates of 1904 and gravitated to a lower figure. Somehow the claim that there was no information on which to base a judgment was passed off as a valid excuse for discounting the problem. These circumstances suggest that under conditions of ambiguity, the French military authorities rejected Regnault's intelligence estimate because it tended to support Michel's despised organizational scheme.

GRANDMAISON, JOFFRE, AND THE REASSERTIVE REACTION

Grandmaison's doctrine of the *offensive à outrance* helped ideologically to retool the military professionals for their battle against threatening developments. In developing his doctrine, Grandmaison was interested not only in questions of operational doctrine but also in bureaucratic politics and the problem of improving the army's devastated morale. He and other "Young Turks" actively lobbied for a traditional professional army, both in the press and in the General Staff.[126] The extent to which Grandmaison saw himself as reversing the drift toward Michel-type solutions to the dilemmas of military strategy and organization is unclear. What *is* clear, however, is that Joffre used Grandmaison's ideas and his adherents to oppose such solutions.

At the same time Grandmaison's writings are not merely political documents. They resulted from serious study of practical operational problems and manifest considerable awareness of the realities of modern warfare. Indeed, had they been otherwise, they would not have been a credible ideological instrument either for Grandmaison's clique of young officers or for Joffre.

In 1906 Grandmaison wrote a book on infantry training in which, without explicitly taking a position on the two-year law, he repeated most of the arguments originally developed by Ardant du Picq and Gilbert in support of a small, professional army and a long term of service. Fear is the main enemy, Grandmaison explained. The physical effects of firepower influence the outcome of the battle primarily through the impression they make on men's minds. Unfortunately, as modern firepower is becoming more terrifying, the moral qualities of the soldiers in European armies are declining. Consequently, the military esprit militaire must be drummed into them by training. To Grandmaison, training meant repetition of an action to the point of its becoming reflex. Reflexes in combat must be group reflexes, and the tactical group must therefore train together repeatedly in peacetime. Although Grandmaison obviously thought these ideas applicable to the two-year training regime, any reader aware of their historical associations would immediately interpret them as implying a preference for a longer term of service.[127]

Grandmaison rather uncritically associated high morale with the offensive. Military history showed him that victorious armies all shared "an unmitigated offensive spirit, *sans arrière-pensée,* animating both chiefs and soldiers." This spirit, he asserted, was the reason for the recent Japanese victory in the face of "an exceptionally solid enemy." He also advanced, in favor of the offensive, a feeble truism perennially invoked by military writers: "The fact of obliging the enemy to cede territory that he occupies is the only sure sign of success and it is in this sense that one can say: to be victorious is to advance."[128]

When Grandmaison tackled specifics, however, he could hardly be accused of underestimating the power of the defensive. He took pains merely to establish that "the direct offensive is still possible. . . . We have no difficulty in recognizing, however, that the infantry offensive is difficult and costly and that is requires new procedures." In order to cross the killing zone successfully, the infantry must use the lay of the land, avoid attacking in the most open sectors, use fresh troops, use night attacks, and coordinate their advance with suppressive artillery fire. The goal is to achieve fire superiority and approach the enemy in a systematic fashion. A stage nevertheless comes when the methodical, attritional attack bogs down. "In order to go further, . . . one can only advance brutally, without concern for casualties, without economy. . . . The Russo-Japanese War, in showing that the forced frontal attack is necessary and possible, dispenses with the need for further discussion."[129] Grandmaison even admitted that the defender's firepower and concealment exert a profound demoralizing effect on the attacker. He did not, however, conclude that the defender therefore enjoys a moral advantage; rather this advantage shows that the attacker must be morally superior if he is to be successful.[130] In short, only readers who were already convinced of the need for the offensive were likely to be persuaded by Grandmaison's arguments. Others could only infer from Grandmaison's frank realism that his offensive game was not worth the price.

Grandmaison's readership was, however, sympathetic. His traditional concern for building morale—and his traditional approach, which linked morale to the offensive and to group training—struck a responsive chord among professional officers at a time when attacks on tradition had brought the army's military esprit to a low ebb. At the same time, his rejection of some of the old tactics made him seem modern and in tune with changing conditions. As a result, his followers did not have to feel like reactionaries even though his doctrine could help the military to reassert its traditional priorities.

Over the next few years, Grandmaison fought a running battle with those who resisted his views. Called to task during the 1907 maneuvers for decisions that violated the current tactical regulations, Grandmaison responded: "We will change the regulations! We are a group of young officers convinced of the justice of our ideas, of the superiority of our theories and our methods, and are resolved to make them prevail against all opposition."[131] His opposition frequently included the "republican generals" promoted during André's term as war minister for political reasons. At the 1910 maneuvers in Picardy, Grandmaison attempted to humiliate Percin and Picquart and, through them, Generalissimo Michel and his reserve-based innovations.[132] Although the evidence is not conclusive, Grandmaison apparently picked these targets not only on tactical grounds but also because of their political associations.[133]

The yearly maneuvers convinced Grandmaison that the traditional French emphasis on the offensive was a matter more of rhetoric than of action. Both Foch and Bonnal advocated ensuring security with a strong advance guard. But this system led to a preoccupation with the opponent's intentions, Grandmaison believed, rather than seizing the initiative for oneself. Like the defensive offensive, the advance guard system inevitably led to reactiveness and passivity.

To combat this tendency, Grandmaison read two lectures at the Center for Higher Military Education in February 1911. He told his audience that their preoccupation with security and the advance guard had produced a habit of passivity: "To be frank, we no longer attack; after a thousand precautions, we 'counter attack' and that means the 'defensive offensive.'" To correct this habit, the French

army must learn that "in the offensive, imprudence is the best security. An adversary attacked suddenly and everywhere at the same
time is preoccupied with parrying the blows; he no longer maneuvers
and soon becomes incapable of any serious offensive. It is the rapidity
of the engagement that guarantees us surprise and the violence of the
attack that will assure us against the maneuver of the enemy."[134]

Grandmaison's ideas take on special significance when considered
in light of a German attack through Belgium and Michel's proposed
response. As the chief of the General Staff's operations bureau,
Grandmaison knew of Michel's plan, but we do not know to what
extent his lectures were motivated by a desire to refute Michel. Some
sort of implied critique seems obvious. According to Grandmaison,

> We should not be too concerned to know whether our front of deploy-
> ment extends further than that of the enemy. Even if our front should be
> a little shorter than his, insofar as we will have imposed on our adver-
> sary the obligation to defend himself and to parry our blows, it is his
> front that will have to mold itself to ours. There is no other method for
> combating the exaggerated lengthening of the front. This cannot be
> repeated too often.[135]

Perfect intelligence being impossible, the key is to render it unneces-
sary by disrupting the enemy's plan before he can implement it. As
long as the attack is sharp and persistent, minor deployment errors
due to inadequate intelligence will correct themselves.[136]

Michel's plan would have violated every tenet of this view of good
strategy. It was reactive, based on a guess about German intentions.
It featured reserve troops that (we may infer from Grandmaison's
earlier writings) would lack the moral solidity needed for a resolute
offensive. Finally, it succumbed to the temptation to compete in
elongating the front. Michel himself clearly interpreted Grandmaison's lectures as criticism of his plan, since he responded point for
point in a lecture at the Center for Higher Military Education on 24
March 1911.[137]

Michel's plan came under more explicit attack inside the General
Staff. A study by the first bureau (organization and personnel) disin-
genuously claimed that the French had "no information that would
allow making any hypothesis" about the use of German reserve units
in the first-line army. Implying that Michel's fears were purely spec-
ulative, the analysis concentrated instead on the disruptive consequences of Michel's plan for meeting the hypothetical threat. It pointed out that the French had too few officers to enlarge their field army.

Michel's demi-brigade idea would, moreover, entail a dangerous three-day lag in mobilization.[138]

Grandmaison had been transferred to a field command, but his criticisms could not be posted away. The operations bureau portrayed the Germans as a mirror image of the French, believing that reserve forces should only be used for "missions that suit them." Like the French, the Germans would give mobilization priority to the first-line active forces. Because the undemocratic German political system permitted a surprise mobilization, it would be particularly dangerous for the French to delay the deployment of their active corps by waiting to include huge numbers of reservists. Michel's plan, moreover, would leave most of the French forces out of the initial action if the Germans decided not to cross to the left bank of the Meuse. Even disregarding the strategic arguments, the operations bureau was quite frank about the organizational disruption that Michel's plan would cause. "It is necessary only to remark that this mixed force would require very profound changes in our regulations, our habits, our tactical rules, and the organization of our staffs."[139]

Coincident with this revolt inside the General Staff were the untimely deaths of Jean Jules Brun and Maurice Berteaux in early 1911, which deprived Michel of his political backers in the War Ministry.[140] In light of the ongoing Agadir Crisis, the new war minister, Messimy, wanted his generalissimo to enjoy the full confidence of the army. Messimy soon found that Michel was acceptable neither to him nor to the other members of the Supreme War Council. On 19 July 1911 the council met to discuss Michel's strategic plan. During the debate, the vast majority took the view that reserve units were inherently inferior to active forces. They could be usefully employed in secondary functions, but intermixing them with active regiments would only ruin the cohesion and spirit of the first-line forces. The majority also made the unwarranted assertion that "all the information we have obtained indicates that the Germans . . . are counting on their active corps, composed of the youngest and most vigorous elements, to initiate operations rapidly and seek an immediate, decisive battle."[141]

In fact, all the studies by the French General Staff up to 1911 had argued that an *attaque brusquée* would be totally out of character for the methodical Germans, who believed in launching an operation only after they had concentrated their entire force. But the opportunity to capitalize on the mobilization lag that Michel's scheme would entail made the invocation of the *attaque brusquée* threat irresistible.[142] In 1913 this theme would again be invoked, with only slightly greater justification, in the parliamentary battle over the three-year law. The polemical intent behind the use of the argument, it should be noted, changed across the three years. In 1911 the traditionalists (or "neotraditionalists") used the *attaque brusquée* argument to defend themselves against a radical worsening of their position; by 1913 they had discovered that they could invoke similar arguments to regain lost ground.

Michel's successor, Joffre, was given an unprecedented opportunity as both generalissimo and chief of the General Staff to revitalize French military institutions. Like Grandmaison, Joffre placed the highest priority on overcoming the spiritual malaise that had afflicted the army since the André ministry and the introduction of the two-year service. The two-year service still seemed unassailable in 1911, but Joffre's mandate allowed him to reassert the military's organizational autonomy and to boost morale by focusing on the needs and interests of the professional soldiers. Although Joffre considered Grandmaison's views to be extreme, he shared Grandmaison's view that defensive habits were a symptom of the army's malaise.[143] To achieve the military renaissance he was aiming for, Joffre found Grandmaison's rhetoric more useful than the uninspiring views of the moderates. Grandmaison's formulae could rebuild French confidence just as offensive doctrines had done in the 1880s.[144] The *offensive à outrance* also provided a rationale for basing French plans and institutions on French preferences, rather than guesses about German intentions. Thus Joffre, a military engineer with few doctrinal preconceptions, found that the *offensive à outrance* fitted the times and the institutional needs of the organization that he was determined to rebuild. These considerations were far more persuasive than ambiguous intelligence data or the moderates' reservations about the Young Turks' operational doctrines.

Yet these developments were by no means inevitable. In 1911 there were three leading candidates for the newly combined position of chief of the general staff and generalissimo: Joffre, Pau, and Gallieni. All three opposed Michel's ideas, but only Pau seemed certain to push strongly for the reassertion of traditional military interests. Since Joffre was just beginning to get acquainted with broader questions of strategy, tactics, and military organization, he could be more easily captured and controlled by the militant ideologues, but it does not seem that he was chosen for this reason. Rather, Joffre was preferred because he was politically more acceptable than Pau and younger than Gallieni. If Gallieni had been selected, the General Staff would have become centrist in orientation; while a partisan of the offensive, Gallieni considered Grandmaison's ideas to be extreme. He similarly opposed Michel's deployments in the far north of France, but he believed that Joffre's left wing in Plan 17 was too weak. Thus the element of chance (Gallieni's age) played some role in establishing the conditions under which offensive ideologues were able to dominate French strategy. Likewise, the international context was important. Had there been no Agadir Crisis, no subsequent German army increase, and no French "national revival" in response, French military doctrine and institutions might have developed along a different trajectory.[145]

THE JOFFRE REVIVAL

Joffre's emphasis on the internal problems of the military led to bias on questions of operational doctrine, war planning, and intelligence. While he did make some accommodation with strategic reality, he did so only insofar as these adjustments would not jeopardize policies that he preferred for institutional reasons.

Joffre's Plan 17 made only limited use of France's reserve units, but it tried to improve the quality of the smaller number it did use. Plan 17 reduced the number of reserve units that would participate in the opening campaign, removing a reserve regiment from each active corps and dropping 96 brigades from the reserve divisions that would be formed upon mobilization. Yet Joffre did attempt to provide a better officer cadre for that smaller force, and he deployed it closer to the front.[146]

Plan 17 similarly made a greater effort to deal with the danger of a German attack across southern Belgium but rejected the possibility of a major attack further north, which would have implied the use of French reservists to cover the longer front. Henri-Mathias Berthelot, Joffre's more dogmatic operations chief, used Grandmaisonian logic in arguing that a northern attack would be "so much the better" for Plan 17, but Joffre could not convince himself that Berthelot was right. As railroad redeployments in late August 1914 demonstrate, an accurate view of the German offensive would have required not only a shift from right to left but also more reserve units more intensively employed. Over half of the new Sixth Army that Joffre would improvise opposite the Germans' right flank was made up of reserve divisions.[147] In fact, Joffre tried to have both sides of the argument on the need to extend the French left: while denying the need for a major extension, which would have used large numbers of reservists, he simultaneously complained that the two-year term of service did not provide enough active forces for a smaller extension north of Mézières, which he believed *was* necessary.[148] He saw enough of a threat, that is, to help justify the three-year law without seeing too much of a threat, which would have played into the hands of Michel and Jaurès.

In the area of operational doctrine, Joffre also mixed motivated bias and realism. On the one hand, he encouraged offensive thinking, because it "would prevent our maneuver from being dominated from the start by the enemy's decision."[149] That is, the offensive allowed French needs to outweigh guesses about German preferences. On the other hand, Joffre admitted that Grandmaison's views were extreme. Despite the popularity of the *offensive à outrance*, moderation was not completely stifled in the new field regulations, in the war college, and among field commanders.[150]

The glorification of the offensive was a convenient tool for protecting the French army against further encroachments after 1911 and for regaining lost ground. The officer corps still felt beleaguered in this period. The journal *France militaire* declared that the generals remained "terrified" of politicians, while the debate on three-year service provided socialist agitators with an opportunity to provoke mutinies in the regiments.[151] In this political setting, the argument that reservists were incapable of carrying out essential offensive missions continued to protect the institution. Even before the Germans announced a plan in January 1913 to increase their active army, French military publicists had begun agitating for a return to the three-year service.[152] Crucial to their case was, as always, the inextricable connection among offense, morale, and active forces. One writer was even so blunt as to call for the "restoration of a professional army."[153] Members of Parliament parroted these arguments when debating the infantry cadres bill in 1912 and the three-year service bill in 1913.[154] In Ralston's view, "the fact that many of the republican politicians most concerned with military affairs so readily espoused the theories and attitudes currently in vogue with the professional soldiers was decisive for the enactment of the three-year law."[155]

The German army bill of 1913 handed the French military a less esoteric argument for lengthening the term of service: a two-year system could not provide an active covering force sufficient to guard against an *attaque brusquée* by the enlarged German standing army. Although Joffre and most military authorities privately considered such an attack to be a remote possibility, they publicly exploited it as the centerpiece of their case for the three-year law.[156] Planning for the offensive became secondary in the parliamentary debate, although it still played a central role in the military's justification of the three-year law to the government itself. To the war minister, for example, Joffre stressed that the three-year service would give French units "considerable offensive power."[157]

In short, Joffre combined realistic analysis, cynical manipulation, and motivated misperception in his approach to strategic and institutional questions. He aspired to realism, but that was never his highest priority. He was determined above all to reestablish what he saw as healthy military institutions and attitudes. Cognitively, he was more willing than some officers to accommodate himself to inconvenient reality, but only insofar as it did not seriously jeopardize the essence of his program.

The Intelligence Failure of 1914

The French intelligence failure is the most dramatic indication that Joffre based his military policies on motivated misperceptions. Given what he knew by the summer of 1914, his misestimates are difficult to explain solely in terms of the ambiguity of the evidence or the shortcomings of the General Staff's intelligence section. Staff studies, it is true, somewhat underestimated the number of reserve divisions that the Germans would deploy in the west and consequently discounted the possibility of a German march through northern Belgium. But Joffre compounded the error by rejecting staff warnings that a substantial number of German reserve divisions would be formed into field corps and used in the opening battles. This rejection led him to further mistaken deductions: that the Germans could not even extend their right wing as far north as central Belgium, and that France could achieve numerical equality in the opening battles by making only limited use of its own reserve divisions. The worst misestimates were made by Joffre, Castelnau, and Berthelot, who were at the policy-making level rather than in strictly analytical jobs. Their interpretation of intelligence data was colored by its implications for a broader range of policy issues, including the role of French reservists, the length of service, and the status of the *offensive à outrance*. Intelligence and operations specialists, who were less involved with institutional questions, made more accurate assessments of the size and the direction of the German attack. Also more realistic were Gallieni and Lanrezac, the designated commanders of the Fifth Army, which would bear the brunt of a German attack across Belgium.[158]

Joffre's misjudgment of German plans helped to justify the serious misallocation of French forces that allowed the German army to penetrate nearly to Paris in August 1914. Although Britain, France, and Belgium had a potential superiority of about ten divisions on the western front, more than twenty French reserve divisions were absent from the opening battles. By 23 August only four French reserve divisions—as opposed to seventeen on the German side—had seen action in the field.[159] (This statistic is particularly striking, since it does not count the numerous German reserve and Landwehr forces that were used for the secondary tasks of investing fortresses and securing the rear.) As a consequence, the Germans were able to match French forces in Lorraine and the Ardennes while outnumbering the French and the British by 24 divisions to 17-1/2 divisions in the north. On the far left, the British were outflanked and outnumbered by about two to one.[160]

In his memoirs, Joffre is quite candid about his misreading of the role of the German reserve corps and its effect on the campaign: "In view of the fact that the German reserve army corps possessed only a relatively small number of guns at the outbreak of the war, I was inclined to believe that these corps would be placed in the second line and would be employed only for laying siege to fortified places, for guarding communications, defending passive fronts, and occupying conquered territories." As late as 25 August 1914 Joffre and his intelligence staff doubted that German reserve units had even been organized as corps. "It must be acknowledged that this error . . . bore heavily upon the manner in which we organized our concentration, and consequently it gravely affected the opening operations."[161]

Castelnau, in particular, argued that the Germans would not use reserve units in the first line and therefore would be spread too thinly if they deployed into northern Belgium. "If they extend as far as Lille, they will have two men per meter. We would cut them in two. We couldn't wish for anything better."[162] Similarly, Berthelot, one of the principal architects of Plan 17 in the General Staff, apparently believed that the German first-line army in the west would comprise 49 divisions, only nine of them reserve divisions.[163]

These mistakes about the direction and strength of the German attack persisted into the third week of fighting in August 1914. As soon as Joffre learned that Belgium had been attacked, he ordered his left wing to shift slightly to the north and west, an option envisioned in the prewar planning. Joffre and Berthelot, however, continued to believe that the Germans would not cross to the north bank of the Meuse in significant numbers. As late as 18 August the General Staff was considering whether the French Fifth Army should try to outflank the German right wing.[164]

Figure 3. French intelligence estimates, 1913–1914.

	Total German divisions except Landwehr	Active divisions	Reserve divisions	(of which in reserve corps)	Reserves engaged in opening battles	Extension of German left to	German divisions passing thru Belgium	(of which west of Meuse)
Actual German plan[a]	76	44	32	(26)	many	northern Belgium (Mons)	34	(26)
General Staff intelligence bureau[b]	65	42	23	(20?)	surely some, perhaps many	central Belgium (Dinant)	22–24	(0)
General Staff operations bureau[c] hypothesis 1	62–66	40–46	14–20	(all?)	none	defensive screen vs. Belgium	4–6	(0)
hypothesis 2					some/many	southern Belgium (Stenay)	16–20	(0)
hypothesis 3					some/many	middle Belgium (Dinant)	22–26	(0)
Joffre[d] hypotheses 1 and 2 (ditto above)	65	about 44	about 21	(probably none)	few, if any			
hypothesis 3						extreme southern Belgium (north of Verdun)	?	(0)
Galieni and Lanrezac[e]	?	?	?	(some in corps)	some	middle Belgium (Dinant)	22–24	(0)

a. Tyng, pp. 354–60.
b. Etat-major de l'armée, deuxième bureau, "Situation sur le pied de guerre des principales armées européennes," 10 November 1913, 7N1771.
c. Etat-major de l'armée, troisième bureau, "Compte rendu du Plan XVII," June 1914, 7N1771.
d. Joffre, pp. 46–47.
e. See below, chap. 3, notes 178–80.

One of the reasons for this error was the failure to perceive that reserve units were being used in the first line. As of the 18th Joffre believed that the German right wing included only 7 or 8 corps, when in fact it was 16 corps strong. He judged the strength of the German center as 6 or 7 corps, but in fact it contained 10.[165] By 23 August Joffre's intelligence staff had identified German reserve units where they were expected—screening the Belgians around Antwerp. Not knowing of the presence of the reserve corps on the main battlefront, Joffre calculated that the allies enjoyed a considerable superiority. By the 25th Joffre was still underestimating German strength by at least seven corps, most of them reserve corps.[166]

Joffre tried to excuse his persistent misreading of the German reserves' role on the grounds that "our Intelligence Service [had been] disorganized during the preceding years by politics" and "by reason of the changes then going on in the German army."[167] But these complaints about poor intelligence work are difficult to understand, since the French had obtained the German mobilization plan, dated 9 October 1913 and effective as of 1 April 1914.[168] It confirmed previous intelligence indicating the existence of reserve corps and stated explicitly that "the reserve troops are employed in the same way as the active troops." The General Staff, however, thought this statement could only be accepted with some qualification.

> The mobilization plan distinguishes between 'reserve corps' and reserve divisions that are not incorporated into reserve corps. The reserve corps send some personnel into the zone of concentration in the first four days like the active corps, whereas for reserve divisions that are not incorporated into reserve corps, special instructions determine the date on which this personnel should be ready. It does not seem, therefore, that the separate reserve divisions will, at the beginning, play exactly the same role as the reserve corps.

The General Staff noted in conclusion that "the German reserve corps, destined to be used in active operations in the same way as the active corps, has become, according to the new mobilization plan, a more homogeneous and better staffed instrument than previously, even though it is lighter than an active corps."[169]

A June 1914 General Staff memorandum, presumably based in part on the same data, noted that the combat elements of the German active corps were to be completely transported to the front on the tenth day of mobilization, those of the reserve corps on the twelfth day. "From the thirteenth day, therefore, the Germans . . . [will]

have available all their active corps and those reserve divisions (grouped for the most part into reserve corps) that are destined to participate immediately in active operations."[170] This memorandum estimates the number of reserve corps at ten.

Joffre alludes to this document in his memoirs, stressing its caveats about weak artillery and a deficit in the officer cadre rather than its overall message that the reserve corps would be used like the actives.[171] His point about the artillery is certainly valid, but his denigration of the quality of German reserve cadres does not recognize the major efforts undertaken after 1911 to improve the reservists, both officers and soldiers. The Reichstag's generous army appropriations during those years had permitted not only a larger standing army but also improvements in reserve personnel. The larger active force automatically meant a larger number of younger reservists. Furthermore, reservists were called up for retraining more frequently and for longer periods. The number of active officers scheduled to command reserve units was increased.[172] Nonetheless, Joffre allowed himself to be reassured by the reports of the French military attaché in Berlin, who believed that German reserve units, though greatly improved, would still not take part in the opening battles: "We will be facing reserves that are rather well officered and instructed, younger than ours, and their number will grow incessantly. . . . We must gain victory before these reserves intervene."[173] Yet such speculations contradicted direct evidence that the Germans intended to use reserve units in the front line. For example, the Russians had passed along intelligence showing that the Germans intended to deploy a reserve corps in the first-line field army in East Prussia.[174]

There was, nonetheless, enough "noise" mixed in with the "signals" that Joffre could avoid drawing the correct, but disturbing, conclusions. The German war ministers were consistently less enthusiastic about the reserves than were the German General Staff. Partly for reasons of political expediency, they told the Reichstag that mobilizing reserve units was a "delicate" process and promised that there would be "no fathers or husbands" in the front lines.[175] Moreover, in 1913 the French obtained a document allegedly written by Colonel Erich Ludendorff, then Moltke's principal assistant in the General Staff, which told the French exactly what they wanted to hear: the main German attack would be executed in Lorraine by the active army. After the war, Ludendorff denied that he authored the note.[176] We do not know to what extent the French believed this forgery. In any case, Lt. Colonel Buat of the French General Staff wrote his own forgery, during the debate on the three-year law, presenting a similar scenario, which he passed off on the French public as a German war plan found on a railway car.[177]

Such noise swayed Joffre more easily than some of his colleagues. Gallieni, designated to command the French Fifth Army, thought that the five corps allocated to the northern most French army were insufficient to meet the likely strength of the German attack through Belgium.

> Guided by intelligence that we received from the second bureau of the General Staff on the German corps in the Rhenish provinces, on their garrisons, on railroad debarkation platforms of cities bordering Luxembourg and Belgium, and on the military legislation of our neighbors, we formed the hypothesis that the Germans would form a group of three armies that would enter Belgium and take as their respective objectives Longuyon, Sedan, and Hirson.

This force was expected to contain 11 or 12 corps, of which two might be reserve corps.[178] Gallieni resigned his command when Joffre refused to increase the size of the Fifth Army to nine corps.[179] His replacement, Lanrezac, also believed the Germans would send three armies against the zone that the Fifth Army was supposed to cover. In a letter to Joffre of 25 July 1914 Lanrezac objected to the Fifth Army's proposed mission—attacking due east toward Neufchâteau. Basing his argument on a 1911 German war game, he told Joffre that the German right wing would extend as far north as Dinant and thus outflank his position at Neufchâteau.[180]

The estimates of Gallieni and Lanrezac resembled the realistic hypothesis worked out by the operations bureau of the General Staff in that they were more accurate than Joffre's personal views in terms both of the axis of the German attack and of the inclusion of reserves in the front line. Still, Gallieni and Lanrezac were, using the terminology developed earlier, moderate incrementalists. Both were willing to adapt to German plans and to use the defensive when necessary, but neither wanted to adapt in a way that would overturn traditional French military institutions, as Michel had done.[181]

As centrists, they were vulnerable from both sides. Their method for meeting the threat of a German invasion through Belgium was insufficient. Gallieni's Fifth Army, even supported by the British, would still have been outflanked by unexpected German forces operating north and west of the Meuse. And it would still have been outnumbered, assuming the Germans saw their plan through.[182]

Gallieni's plan would at the same time have undermined the myth of a quick French victory in Lorraine. Depleting their offensive forces in Lorraine would have reduced the French to passivity all along the front.[183] As a consequence the argument that only the standing army could carry out the offensive would lose its relevance: there would *be* no offensive. But to abandon the offensive would have given an opening to the socialists, who argued that a reserve-based force could cary out defensive operations as well as an active force. The leftist victory in the parliamentary election of 1914 threatened the reversal of the new three-year law, and the army consequently needed all the arguments it could muster to preserve the three-year term of service.

The General Staff could have proceeded on two tracks—the *offensive à outrance* for public relations purposes, and the "defensive offensive" for its real doctrinal and strategic policy making. In fact, the issue of the *attaque brusquée* does seem to have been handled in this way, although even there the line between public dissembling and self-deception was occasionally blurred. In the long run, ideologies work better when they are sincerely felt, and opportunistic arguments tend to become sincere beliefs. In short, although the Gallieni-Lanrezac view would have been a strategic improvement over Joffre's misestimates, it might still have been strategically inadequate. Above all, however, it would have been ideologically inadequate.

CONCLUSIONS

The development of French military policy between 1870 and 1914 can be explained in terms of three factors: the severity of threats to parochial military interests, the ambiguity of the strategic problem, and the persistence of preconceptions about military doctrine.

Under the Third Republic, the transition from the old professional army to a nation-in-arms threatened the traditional values and interests of the French officer corps. In order to protect these threatened interests, the French military developed an organizational ideology that stressed the necessity for offensive operations carried out by a standing army. The offensive, the military held, was the key to success on the battlefield, and only active-duty soldiers were suitable for offense. The biases resulting from this organizational ideology became more extreme after the Dreyfus affair, which increased the threat to traditional military institutions and practices. These biases were the most important causes of the three major errors of Plan 17: the *offensive à outrance*, the intelligence failure, and the underuse of French reservists.

[104]

Parochial interests were not the only factor shaping strategy, however. One important constraint was the weight of objective evidence on doctrinal and intelligence issues. After the Boer War, for example, a brief doctrinal trend toward the defensive included many military traditionalists. Clear evidence of an upgrading of German reservists between 1887 and 1893 likewise forced the French to adopt similar measures, no matter how distasteful. In most cases, however, the weight of evidence was only a loose constraint on motivated biases. For example, although the Russo-Japanese War demonstrated the tactical advantages of defensive firepower, the broader strategic lessons of the war were less clear-cut. Since the costly offensives of the Japanese did achieve limited success, the French were able to interpret the Manchurian campaign as a vindication of the strategic offensive.

Ambiguity played an important role in the intelligence failure. The information available to the French about German intentions between 1904 and 1914 was less conclusive than the information available between 1887 and 1893. Whereas the clear weight of evidence ruled out any misconceptions that Miribel might have held, Joffre's biases were not similarly constrained. If the motivation to misperceive is strong enough, a little ambiguity will suffice.

The stability of preconceptions constrained motivated bias. Older officers, wedded to the counteroffensive doctrines taught by Bonnal in the 1890s, were unwilling to accept Grandmaison's innovations. Extreme offensive doctrines, though more useful than traditional doctrines for reversing the slide toward a militia system, were unreservedly adopted only by people whose operational views were still unformed—that is, the young officers and uncommitted thinkers like the engineer Joffre. But this constraint should not be overemphasized. Many older officers, like Pau and Castelnau, had quite offensively oriented views and worked easily with the Young Turks on the General Staff in drawing up Plan 17. There was a good deal of continuity from the offensive ideas of Cardot, Gilbert, and Foch to those of Grandmaison. For this reason, preconceptions inherited from the 1880s and 1890s may have facilitated the acceptance of the *offensive à outrance* among officers who had been influenced more by Cardot than by Bonnal.

To sum up these various qualifications, the formation of an organizational ideology does not mean that all beliefs and perceptions are automatically determined by parochial interests. The French case shows a more complex process at work. Specifically, interest-driven perceptions, constrained within a plausibility established by the available evidence and existing beliefs, were most easily accepted by un-committed thinkers (the young officers and Joffre). Allying with those traditionalists who had always thought in such terms (like Pau), this group took advantage of favorable political conditions (the Agadir Crisis and increases in the size of the German army) to reshape French military policy according to their own views.

[4]

Germany: The Elusive Formula
for Decisive Victory

Surrounded by "enemies on all sides, . . . Germany and Austria stand unprotected," Alfred von Schlieffen wrote in 1909. "Around them, behind moat and wall, are the other Powers." France, Britain, and Russia are all "implacable" foes, motivated by the desire for revanche, by commercial rivalry, and by racial antipathy. Despite their numerical superiority in military manpower, these encircling powers do not attack because "Germany and Austria are still too strong. They must first be weakened by internal conflicts" arising from strife among Austria's nationalities and Germany's parties. Then, "at the given moment, the doors are to be opened, the drawbridges let down, and the million-strong armies let loose, ravaging and destroying. . . . The danger seems gigantic."[1]

Four factors shaped Schlieffen's response to this perceived danger. The first was the numerical inferiority of the Austro-German armed forces compared to the forces of the Entente. When fully mobilized, France, Britain, Belgium, Russia, and Serbia would be able to field 199 infantry divisions; Germany and Austria, only 136. This disparity was only partially offset by the qualitative inferiority of Russia's 114 divisions, since Austria's 49 divisions were also below the standards of the German, French, and British forces.[2]

The second factor was the slowness of the Russian mobilization. Whereas France and Germany could mobilize and deploy their whole forces in two weeks, only half of the Russian force could be deployed in that time, giving them between 35 and 40 divisions on the main front. By the twentieth day of mobilization, about three-quarters of Russia's infantry strength would be ready. Only by the fortieth day would the whole force be concentrated.[3]

Third, German forces would have to be divided between the Russian front in the east and the French front in the west. According to traditional Napoleonic and Prussian doctrine, this division constituted an advantage for Germany. Whereas France and Russia had no choice about the apportionment of their forces between east and west, Germany could shift the bulk of her troops in either direction, responding to the dangers and opportunities of the moment.[4]

Finally, Schlieffen's war planning was shaped by his absolute requirement, a rapid, low-cost, decisive victory. In his earlier years, Schlieffen seems to have accepted this requirement as axiomatic. He believed that no self-respecting strategist should reconcile himself to a lengthy, attritional campaign. Only later did Schlieffen advance economic arguments to support his inclination. Drawing on the views of contemporary economists, Schlieffen contended that the capitalist system could not withstand the strain of a long war.

> The [economic] machine with its thousand wheels, through which millions find their living, cannot stand still for long. One cannot move from position to position in battles of twelve days' length for one or two years, until the belligerents are completely exhausted and worn out, both beg for peace, and both accept the status quo. We must attempt to overthrow the enemy quickly, and annihilate him. . . .
>
> [Long] wars are impossible at a time when the existence of a nation is founded upon the uninterrupted progress of commerce and industry. . . . A strategy of attrition will not do if the maintenance of millions of people requires billions.[5]

Schlieffen also echoed the widespread view that Germany would be at a disadvantage in a long war because of her dependence on imported food and raw materials. Russian grain shipments would be cut off in wartime, and a British blockade might prevent imports from most other suppliers.[6] As it turned out, the Russians suffered more and sooner from the disruption of trade than the Germans did—a major contribution to German successes on the eastern front. The Germans did not foresee, however, that Russia's economic vulnerability in a long war would be greater than their own. This predictive failure was in part the result of illusions about the self-sufficiency of Russia's "natural," agrarian economy. In part, it was because no one, least of all Schlieffen, was interested in finding rationales for a long war.[7]

PREMISES AND RISKS OF THE SCHLIEFFEN PLAN

The plans for a two-front war that Schlieffen and the younger Helmuth von Moltke developed were designed to achieve decisive victory in a short time with numerically inferior forces. Although the specifics changed considerably between 1897 and 1914, the general concept remained the same. Over four-fifths of the German army would be directed initially against the French. A large proportion of the German force would cross through Belgium to avoid the French fortress line facing Lorraine and to outflank the French field army. Within a month, the French army would be encircled and destroyed in a battle of annihilation. The German army would then be sent by train to meet the Russian offensive, which would just be beginning.[8]

The German General Staff argued that Germany's numerical inferiority made this strategy necessary and Russia's slow mobilization made it possible. Germany had to use the initial weeks of the war to win a decisive victory that would permanently redress the balance in her favor. Schlieffen thought that this initial victory would have to be won against France, not Russia. Although the Russians were slow in concentrating their forces, Schlieffen believed that they were not vulnerable to a decisive preemptive blow, because fortresses and river barriers protected their concentration. If the Germans attacked with a force large enough to overcome these obstacles, the Russians would simply withdraw into their endless interior spaces, and the French would meanwhile be attacking an inferior German force in the west. Schlieffen consequently felt that he had to find a formula for a rapid, decisive victory against France, leaving only a small screening force in the east while Russia was completing her concentration.

Schlieffen's last war plan before his retirement in 1905 used 23 active corps and 15 reserve divisions in a German offensive on the western front. Although the bulk of these forces were deployed in Alsace and Lorraine on the German left, a strong right wing was to cross the southern tip of Belgium, enveloping the French left north of Verdun. This plan, however, dissatisfied him. He feared that the crucial flank maneuver would be too weak to "shake the cornerstone" of the French position. He consequently prepared a parting memorandum in which he laid out his conception of an ideal strategic deployment.[9]

For the purposes of this exercise Schlieffen did not plan on the basis of the actual size of the German army; rather, he assumed the existence of as large a force as he needed to implement his ideal strategy. Thus he allowed himself 40-1/2 active and reserve corps as well as 6 to 8 Ersatz corps. All but five corps were to deploy north of Metz, crossing the whole of Belgium and the southern appendix of Holland in order to maximize the number of march routes available to the huge right wing. The arc of the envelopment was to extend all the

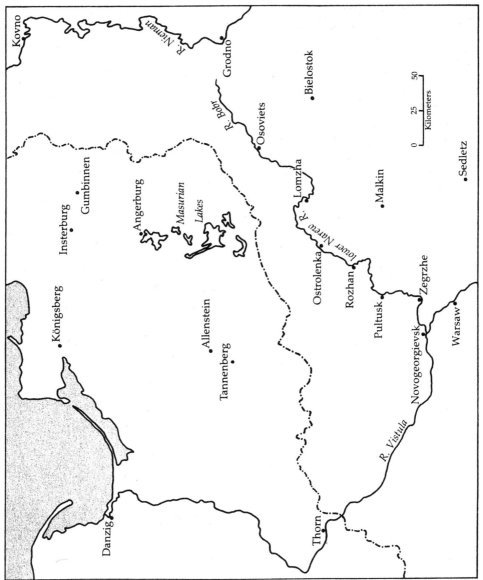

Map 3. East Prussia

way around Paris. Meanwhile, the fortress of Metz would anchor a German holding action in Lorraine.

Schlieffen's successor was the nephew and namesake of the German commander in the Franco-Prussian War. Moltke accepted the general outline of Schlieffen's thinking, but he diminished the ratio of the right wing to the left from 7:1 to 3:1. Three factors account for his alteration.

First, Moltke considered it a mistake to violate Dutch neutrality. Such an attack would add to the number of Germany's enemies and eliminate a neutral "windpipe" through which Germany might be able to import food and raw materials.[10] Foregoing the roads of southern Holland, however, severely limited the number of units that could be marched into northern Belgium.

Second, Moltke, despite increases in the size of the German army, did not have Schlieffen's hypothetical 46-1/2 to 48-1/2 corps at his disposal on the western front. The actual figure for 1914, including Ersatz and Landwehr units, was about 41-1/2.[11] Consequently, Moltke concluded correctly that the right wing would have been too weak to envelop Paris in any event.

Finally, as a result of improvements in the French army and the rise of the doctrine of the *offensive à outrance*, Moltke focused more closely on the risks and opportunities presented by a French offensive in Lorraine. On balance, Moltke thought, a French offensive would play into German hands, for the French could then be enveloped further east than Schlieffen had thought possible. Both to defend against a French attack and to take advantage of it should it occur, Moltke positioned his forces so that they could envelop the French either in front of the French fortress line or behind it.[12]

Reasons for the Plan's Failure

Disciples of Schlieffen have always laid the blame for the German failure of August 1914 at Moltke's door, for his weakening of the right wing. They have argued that the strengthened left wing served only to keep the French safely bottled up behind their fortresses, while the weakened right wing could no longer push home its flank attack. Moltke compounded this error when he transferred two corps from the right wing to East Prussia after the minor Russian victory at Gumbinnen, on 20 August.[13]

Other critics, however, have focused not on details of implementation but on the fundamental flaws of Schlieffen's original conception.[14] All of the operational shortcomings they cite apply even more strongly to Schlieffen's version of the plan than to Moltke's. Germany, they argue, had insufficient forces for the sweep across northern Belgium and France. German forces in the right wing were, moreover, unavoidably debilitated by the long, forced march and by insoluble supply difficulties. Predictably, the French were able to redeploy by rail more quickly than the Germans could advance across Belgium and northern France on foot. And even if the Germans had been able to "envelop" the French army, transfers to the eastern front would have been necessary long before the annihilation of the French could have been completed.

These drawbacks were not only foreseeable—they were all actually foreseen, and by the German General Staff themselves. Schlieffen himself recognized that his plan was "an enterprise for which we are too weak." During the two decades before the war, the forces that the Germans intended to use on the western front were marginally superior in number and fighting capability to those of the French. But the Schlieffen Plan squandered this potential superiority. The violation of Belgian territory meant the addition of six Belgian divisions to the opponents, and it made the participation of four and a half British divisions much more likely.[15]

While the march through Belgium added to the forces facing the Germans, it also depleted the size and vigor of the army that the Germans could marshal for the decisive engagement against France. Several corps were used up besieging or blockading fortresses and guarding lines of communication. The troops that did arrive in France were exhausted from many days of forced marching. Imperfect supply of food, fodder, and ammunition, a problem inherent in operating on enemy territory, further reduced the fighting value of the right wing. The supply trains and occasionally even the artillery could not keep up with the pace of the advance. Had the risky *coup de main* against the Liège fortress not succeeded, these logistical difficulties would have become critical, since Liège blocked German access to the north Belgian rail net. Had even a few simple, planned demolitions been carried out, they would have devastated German logistics. The German attack, moreover, made it easier for the French to get the most out of their forces. The low-quality troops garrisoning secondary French fortresses tied down elements of the active German field army. Reserve units deployed around Paris, and elsewhere in the French rear, were almost automatically added to the fighting strength of the French field army because of the depth of the German penetration. As Schlieffen himself realized, the attacker's "strength dwindles constantly as the defender's increases . . . particularly in a country which bristles with fortresses."[16]

Schlieffen had hoped to compensate for these disadvantages by forming six to eight Ersatz reserve corps, which would march behind the right wing. This force would protect the flank and rear of the German right wing from a French attack out of the superfortress of Paris, while the envelopment of the French field army was being completed. By 1914, however, only six and one-half Ersatz *divisions* had been formed, and they were deployed on the German left, not behind the right wing. Consequently, the envelopment maneuver was attempted without a significant flank guard.[17]

Although the Germans realized that they would not have superiority on the front as a whole, they nonetheless hoped to overpower the French at the decisive point. According to Schlieffen, "if one is too weak to attack the whole, one should attack a section."[18] If the Schlieffen plan worked, the German right wing would be able to outflank and outnumber the French left wing, ultimately forcing the whole French army to fight a disorganized battle with an inverted front. If the French were to reinforce their left wing to meet the attack, however, a mere frontal engagement of equal forces would result. Even if this frontal engagement resulted in the French being "pushed toward the Alps," as one of Schlieffen's scenarios envisaged, such an outcome could hardly be desirable for the Germans.[19] The large Paris garrison would then be threatening their flank and rear, while the long time required for a frontal victory would allow the Russians to collect all their forces and carry out an offensive in the east. Schlieffen's writings are usually disdainful of this kind of "ordinary, frontal victory."

In the first draft of his 1905 memorandum, Schlieffen expressed the "hope that [the enemy] will not succeed in so extending his left wing that, in the face of all the fortresses, its envelopment becomes impossible." In his next draft, he exhibited more confidence: "The French will not hesitate to shift troops from the main front to the endangered subsidiary front, or to move up reserves, for example the corps from the Alpine frontier. . . . This will hardly succeed so far as to block the area and to provide their left wing with desired extension and strength."[20] It is difficult to determine on what he based his confidence. In part, Schlieffen hoped to pin down superior French forces in Lorraine by attacking exposed positions like the city of Nancy. He also appears to have counted on delay and disorganization as the French implemented a decision to redeploy. Nonetheless, he clearly did not overestimate the degree of surprise that the march through Belgium would achieve. "The breadth of Belgium is considerable; it will take so long to cross it that the French will have time for all kinds of countermeasures. There can be no question of surprise."[21] Nor did he count on the French doing the Germans the favor of choosing to attack in Lorraine instead of defending in the north.

In 1914 the French did the Germans more favors than Schlieffen had expected, attacking in Lorraine and the Ardennes and generally failing to perceive the threat posed by the German right wing until the very last minute. But the French were nevertheless able to redeploy their forces in time to achieve a numerical superiority opposite the German right by the battle of the Marne. While the German right was advancing at the speed of the footsoldier, the French left was quickly reinforced by rail between 25 August and 4 September.[22] The defensive strength of the fortress line facing Lorraine allowed the French to deplete their forces in the sector without risking a sudden German breakthrough.

Nothing about this railway maneuver was unforeseeable. In fact, Schlieffen had proposed that the "French" commander use exactly this strategy in a 1905 staff exercise. Schlieffen, according to his son-in-law, pointed out the opportunity of "improving the apparently desperate situation by quickly transporting all troops which could be spared from less busy sectors of the front, and all the forces behind the front, to behind the French left wing; there they could be formed into a new army group to counter-envelop the German right wing."[23] The Germans, moreover, would use the same technique of railway redeployment in August 1914, to defeat the Russian invasion of East Prussia. In short, although German planners seem to have understood the theoretical opportunity for French countermeasures, they failed to draw the proper conclusions.

The General Staff's analysis of the problem of shifting German forces from the French to the Russian front followed a similar pattern. In several staff exercises between 1897 and 1903, Schlieffen envisioned transporting 2-1/2 to 11 corps from France to the east at times ranging between the twenty-third and twenty-ninth days of mobilization. In 1909 Moltke told the Austrian chief of staff, Franz Conrad von Hötzendorff, that a decision would be reached against France in three weeks if the French attacked and in four weeks if they remained on the defensive. Nine to ten days later, the German units deployed against France would start to arrive on the Russian front.[24] At other times, German estimates were more pessimistic. In the event of a frontal engagement with a fairly strong French left, Schlieffen estimated on one occasion, the German victory would be delayed until M+56.[25] In discussing a 1905 war game, Schlieffen remarked:

> The theory of decisive battle . . . is roughly this: we go with all our forces into France, fight a decisive battle which, of course, ends in our favor, and on the next morning at the latest, the trains are ready and the victors roll eastwards to fight a new decisive battle on the Vistula, the Niemen or the Narew. That is not the way of wars today. After the battle comes the pursuit . . . and this takes a long time. You can take Sedan as a decisive battle. If the German armies had been transported to the Vistula on September 2d, 1870, what would have become of the campaign in France? If we want to make war in France for several months, we can't ignore the Russians entirely.[26]

When Conrad asked what Germany would do in the east if there were no decisive victory against France, Moltke responded in an even more pessimistic vein: "I will do what I can. We are not superior to the French."[27]

Perhaps the most common criticism of the Schlieffen Plan is that it made the fear of a two-front, general war in Europe a self-fulfilling prophecy. Because of the time pressures in the plan, any Russian mobilization would require an immediate German attack on France. Thus there could be no chance to localize a Balkan conflict—no chance for either side to posture militarily, negotiate, and demobilize. The Schlieffen Plan prepared for the worst case in a way that ensured that the worst case would occur.

The Schlieffen Plan similarly helped to bring about the British blockade that it was in part designed to avoid. The fear of blockade helped the Germans to rationalize the need for the quick victory that could only be obtained by violating Belgian neutrality. But that violation helped to bring Britain into the war, and the feared blockade became a reality. Had Germany respected Belgian neutrality and generally remained on the defensive in the west, British neutrality would have been reasonably likely. Indeed, as late as 1 August 1914 Foreign Minister Edward Grey was suggesting that Britain could remain neutral on precisely those terms.[28] Two recent historians of Anglo-German relations argue that Britain's only substantial motive for war was to prevent German hegemony on the continent. They speculate that hegemony would not have been at issue had Germany fought the war defensively, and Britain would probably have stayed neutral.[29]

Schlieffen and especially Moltke were quite sensitive to the Schlieffen Plan's shortcomings. In a 1913 memorandum, probably in response to a request from Foreign Secretary Gottlieb von Jagow to reconsider the planned invasion of neutral Belgium, Moltke expressed serious doubts about the political advisability and operational feasibility of the Schlieffen plan.[30] But all the alternatives at the time seemed worse.

Alternatives to the Schlieffen Plan

Yet despite the conclusions of the General Staff, strategically sound alternatives to the Schlieffen Plan were available. Drawing on the war plans of the elder Helmuth von Moltke in the 1880s and the 1915 campaign on the eastern front, several German observers have argued that the best strategy available to Germany in 1914 was to defend in the west and to wage a limited offensive in the east. While such a strategy would have had a better chance than the Schlieffen Plan of achieving Germany's political and security aims, it could not have promised rapid, low-cost, and decisive victory. Since Schlieffen and the General Staff placed an absolute value on these latter criteria, schemes for a more likely, but also more costly and more limited victory were not even considered.

The elder Moltke planned for a two-front war in the 1880s that differed markedly from the Schlieffen formula. In the west, Moltke planned to remain on the defensive, taking advantage of the shortness of the Franco-German border, the fortresses of Metz and Strasbourg, and the strong line of defense offered by the Saar River and Vosges Mountains. He expected that even an inferior German force could, if necessary, hold this line for months.[31] In the event of a French advance through Belgium, the lower Rhine would offer a virtually impregnable barrier against exploiting the maneuver. In the east, Moltke sought to use Germany's advantage in mobilization speed to destroy Russia's exposed forces around Warsaw. After this victory, Moltke would have established a defensive line along the Vistula River, a line that would have been shorter and less vulnerable than the convex, 750-kilometer Russo-German frontier. Moltke expected his limited victory in Poland would enable him to transport a large force to the French front. Having suffered terrible attrition from the Saar defenses, the outnumbered French invaders would be counterattacked near the German railheads on the Saar. On the basis of these limited victories, the diplomats were expected to negotiate an end to the war, probably based on the status quo ante.[32]

By the 1890s, however, the chances of a quick victory in Poland seemed less likely. The Russians had improved the fortresses protecting their concentration, while their peacetime deployments in Poland were both larger and less exposed. Even in later years, when Russian strength was at its nadir, the Russians were careful to concentrate their forces safely out of reach of a sudden German attack. As a result, German schemes for an immediate offensive in the east came to involve deeper penetrations, more troops, and longer periods of time. For example, in 1912 the German General Staff played a war game at the Austrians' request in which the main offensive was directed against Russia. The "Russians" retreated in front of an invading German force of 18 army corps, which reached the Kiev-Vilna line on M+35 without having achieved a decisive victory. By M+45 the "French" had turned the flank of the Metz fortress, and the German force in the east decided to retreat.[33] Yet despite the conclusions of the German General Staff, at least one eminent German military authority, General Sigismund von Schlichting, continued to believe in the feasibility of the elder Moltke's formula. He urged an "offensive with limited goals," culminating in a victory around Warsaw and a shift back to the west for a battle on the defensive line between the fortresses of Metz and Strasbourg.[34]

The actual course of the war in 1915 seems to confirm the viability of a strategy based on defense in the west and offense in the east. On the western front, German forces successfully defended against a larger allied force, despite the fact that their defensive line was more than twice as long as it would have been had Belgian neutrality been preserved. On the eastern front, the Germans and Austrians deployed 109 divisions against 100 Russian divisions for their May offensive. After a breakthrough in the open plains south of Cracow, the joint offensive pushed the Russians out of Poland by the end of the summer. The intention of Erich von Falkenhayn, the new German chief of staff, was to dig in before reaching Russia proper; he focused instead on solidifying the Austrians' hold on the Balkans and the lines of communication to Turkey.[35]

Together with the elder Moltke's plans, this operation has served as a model for such critics of the Schlieffen Plan as Ludwig Beck, chief of the Army General Staff from 1935 to 1938, and Hermann von Staabs, chief of the General Staff's railway section under Schlieffen. Their alternative schemes would have used the forces of Schlieffen's right wing for a limited offensive in the east, while defending the short Franco-German frontier with comparatively few forces.[36] Several factors favored the eastern operation.

For both sides, positional defense would have been more difficult in the broad, open spaces of Poland and Galicia than in the cramped,

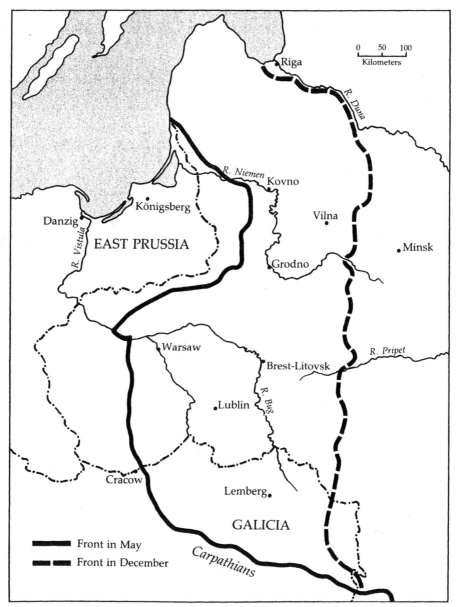

Map 4. The Eastern Front in 1915. Adapted from James E. Edmonds, *A Short History of World War I* (London: Oxford University Press, 1951).

fortified theater in the west. Moreover a defensive strategy in the west would have subtracted the Belgian and probably the British armies from the forces facing Germany. Even if France had built up a considerable numerical superiority, it could not have used it effectively on the narrow Franco-German frontier. Germany, meanwhile, would not have been at a disadvantage if the war had dragged on, since she could have obtained food and raw materials from eastern Europe and probably by sea. Furthermore German strength would not have been sapped by repeated attempts to attack Verdun or by other counterproductive efforts in the west. A limited offensive in the east would have answered Austria's security needs more directly than a risky grab for total victory in the west, and due to the slowness of the Russian mobilization, the Germans could have occupied the western half of Poland virtually without opposition. Finally, there would have been at least some chance that the French, in view of the strong socialist showing in the 1914 election, would have hesitated to aid the Russian "aggressor."[37] Hence, if the Germans and Austrians could have scored a reasonably quick, limited victory in Poland and Galicia, followed by a nonpunitive peace, they might have managed to keep the war localized.

Despite these advantages of a defensive or limited offensive strategy, one might nonetheless defend the General Staff's quest for a decisive victory as reasonable on several grounds. First, a limited offensive strategy would have required a negotiated settlement to end the war. The superheated nationalistic atmosphere of 1914 makes it difficult to imagine the Germans scoring a few battlefield victories and then calmly negotiating a restrained Balkan settlement with the chastened Russians. In rebuttal, it might be argued, the atmosphere would have been less heated if the Germans had anchored their security on a fortified frontier in the west. Hysteria about "encirclement," the Russian army increase, and Austria's relative decline would have been less acute, since German forces could still have carried out the easier defensive strategy despite an adverse fluctuation in the balance of power. Unburdened of the Schlieffen Plan, Germany's Balkan policy would have lost its "now or never" character. With a more secure Germany, the "Third Balkan War" would have been harder to start, easier to limit, and more feasible to terminate.

Second, it might be argued that the Schlieffen Plan was not only reasonable but, considering how close it came to succeeding, brilliant. If Moltke had only been more resolute in planning and execution, Germany might have solved all her problems with one throw of the dice. The problem with this argument is that the Schlieffen Plan did *not* come particularly close to succeeding. Despite French errors that facilitated the Germans' task, the Allied left wing outnumbered the German right by the battle of the Marne, 35 divisions to 20-1/2.[38] This imbalance was the result not of some error in Moltke's fine-tuning of the plan but of an unalterable fact: the Allies had more forces in the theater as a whole and greater ease in maneuvering them. Moreover, as a recent study of the logistics of the Schlieffen Plan concludes, even if the Germans had somehow won on the Marne, "there is every reason to believe that the advance would have petered out. The prime factors would have been the inability of the railheads to keep up with the advance, the lack of fodder, and sheer exhaustion."[39]

Third, as L. L. Farrar argues, Germany's foreign policy required military planners to prepare for a short, offensive, decisive war that would create the conditions for Germany's political expansion at an acceptable cost. If expansion were valued highly enough, the adoption of the Schlieffen Plan would have been rational, despite its serious operational difficulties. Farrar links Moltke's limited war plans to Otto von Bismarck's status-quo diplomacy, and Schlieffen's plan for decisive victory to the aggressive "New Course" adopted by Kaiser Wilhelm after 1890. Observing that "Schlieffen could have stood on the defensive against both France and Russia with greater prospect of success than Moltke because Germany was stronger," Farrar deduces that the Schlieffen plan was necessary only if Germany wanted to overturn the status quo. But he presents no direct evidence that the Schlieffen Plan was designed to suit the needs of an expansionist foreign policy; rather, he carefully states that Schlieffen merely "reflected the prevailing mood."[40]

Indeed, there is no evidence that Germany's foreign-policy makers played a direct role in shaping the Schlieffen Plan. Kaiser Wilhelm is reported to have expressed a preference for attacking first in the west, but there is no evidence that this was more than a passing whim or that it influenced the war planning of the General Staff.[41] It is certainly not the reason that Schlieffen was selected to replace Alfred von Waldersee, who had been Moltke's immediate successor as the chief of staff. Waldersee's dismissal had more to do with personalities and politics than with military issues, and Schlieffen, as Waldersee's deputy, was his logical successor. The kaiser must also have found Schlieffen, an apolitical technocrat, a welcome contrast to Waldersee.[42] Although civilian authorities knew the general outlines of Schlieffen's plan to violate Belgian neutrality, they rarely expressed any opinion about it. Baron Friedrich von Holstein of the Foreign

Ministry said that "if the Chief of Staff, especially a strategic authority such as Schlieffen, believes such a measure to be necessary, then it is the obligation of diplomacy to adjust to it and prepare for it in every possible way." In 1912 Foreign Secretary Jagow urged that the need to violate Belgian territory be reevaluated, but a memo from Moltke ended the matter.[43] Civilians had, in short, little if any impact on the shape of German war plans.

If the congruence between Germany's offensive military strategy and its revisionist foreign policy is more than a coincidence, therefore, the explanation must lie in Farrar's more subtle point—that both were independently caused by Germany's increasingly assertive mood after 1890.[44] But this argument, too, has weaknesses. Although Schlieffen favored a decisive, offensive strategy, he was less assertive and bellicose than were Moltke and Waldersee, who favored a strategy to achieve limited aims.[45] Thus the change in operational strategy after 1890 has less to do with the mood of the "New Course" than with Schlieffen's style of strategic analysis and with changing Russian deployments in Poland, which made the old strategy more difficult to implement.

In Schlieffen's case, security and expansion are difficult to disentangle as motives for his strategy of decisive victory. In "Krieg in der Gegenwart" and other memoranda, he wrote as if there were no conflict between Germany's interest in security and her aim of decisive victory in the political-economic rivalry with the Entente.[46] Schlieffen saw the Entente as implacable, seeking the opportune moment for an unrestrained war of annihilation; it is not surprising, then, that he favored a decisive, offensive strategy, which relied neither on the prudent forebearance of the enemy to keep the war limited nor on negotiations to end it. Thinking of the war in this way allowed Schlieffen to avoid a choice between security and expansion, since both seemed to require his preferred strategy.

In conclusion, there are several grounds for arguing that the Schlieffen Plan was a rational strategy, despite its operational drawbacks. Probably the strongest of these arguments is that Schlieffen and the General Staff viewed Germany as a dissatisfied power and for that reason could not have accepted a defensive posture. The main problem with this justification is that Schlieffen sought security as well as expansion. Schlieffen and his colleagues ignored the possible conflict between security and expansion, assuming that their plan for a decisive victory was the best way to satisfy both requirements. In fact, a more defensive strategy would probably have served Germany's security interests better. Instead of recognizing the trade-off between the two values and rationally choosing between them, Schlieffen unfairly denigrated the defensive alternatives to his preferred offensive plan, making defense look undesirable on both counts. After about 1894 no serious consideration was given to defensive, limited, or eastward-oriented schemes. When such alternatives were evaluated, they were designed to fail, and they were held to a tougher standard than was the Schlieffen Plan. Even if the General Staff's preference for high-risk, high-gain strategies was rationally tenable, it was also bolstered by a biased assessment of the alternatives.

EXPLAINING THE GENERAL STAFF'S BIAS

The elder Moltke and his successors at the General Staff viewed war as inevitable, given the grasping and pugnacious nature of men and states. They also believed that war was, on balance, beneficial: it allowed young, dynamic cultures (like Germany's) to sweep aside the decadent cultures that were holding back the advance of civilization.

This outlook implied the need for an offensive doctrine. If war is inevitable, there is a premium on undertaking it as the moment of superiority, and only an offensive strategy is useful for a preventive or preemptive strike. If wars are to be seen as beneficial, they must be fought in a way that achieves great profit at minimum cost and above all resolves the issues that caused the fighting. Only a rapid, decisive victory can meet these criteria.

The German military's view of the nature of war reflected a "tooth and claw" outlook that to some extent prevailed in civilian as well as military circles throughout Europe. But even in Germany the military consistently took a more Hobbesian approach than civilian authorities did to problems of peace and war. Bismarck continually had to turn away the military's requests for preventive wars. In July 1914 Theobald Bethmann-Hollweg likewise made last-minute attempts to urge moderation on the Austrians, which were undermined by Moltke's efforts in favor of an immediate Austrain decision to mobilize.[47]

These differences in degree can largely be explained by differences in the focus of attention and areas of responsibility of civilian and military officials. The soldier's duties require him to focus on the potential for conflict among states, threats to his country's security, and military means to counter them. Nonmilitary solutions may not occur to him, or they may seem unrealistic or pointless, since he presumes that war is in any case inevitable. In terms of the explanatory models introduced in chapter one, the soldier simplifies his analytical task by focusing on the military aspects of international politics—a simplification that biases his strategic choices.

The views of the German military may also be explained as a motivated bias, rooted in the military's professional interest in preserving the function of war as a beneficial social institution. The extraordinary rise in the social prestige of the German military after the nation-building wars of 1866 and 1870 suggests that this consideration was hardly trivial. If, on the other hand, wars are expected to be long, costly, and indecisive, they are likely to be seen as aberrations that need to be stamped out—hardly a climate of opinion conducive to the prestige and health of military institutions. Although civilian authorities may benefit from successful wars, they do not have the same stake in the perpetuation of war as a beneficial institution. Though any military organization has an incentive to argue that war can be a productive endeavor, the spectacular successes of the Wars of Unification permitted Moltke and his successors to argue the case for short, victorious wars with a special degree of credibility. The historical backdrop also gave them a set of expectations and a reputation to live up to.

A second point worth noting about the German General Staff's bias is the dogmatization of doctrine. Under the elder Moltke the doctrine of the rapid, decisive victory by means of encirclement constituted a flexible guide for strategic planning. When circumstances favored other solutions, Moltke bowed to them. Schlieffen reduced Moltke's strategic precepts to a dogmatic formula that was applied regardless of circumstances. This simplification can be explained in part by individual differences between Moltke and Schlieffen. Whereas Moltke was a pragmatist whose outlook derived from his broad personal experience, Schlieffen was a theoretician who worked out his concepts over a wargaming table in the offices of the General Staff. Moreover, his dogmatization of strategic thinking served the institutional need for a standardized doctrine, to simplify the work of the General Staff and to facilitate the training of young officers.

Finally, the operational analyses of Schlieffen and his General Staff manifested a systematic bias in favor of the prevailing doctrine and the preferred war plan. In some instances, this bias was simply the result of a lack of imagination and open-mindedness. The General Staff had been thinking about a single solution so exclusively and for so long that they lost the ability to appreciate alternative perspectives. Thus the only plan that they could imagine for an offensive in the east was a mirror image of the Schlieffen Plan for the west. In other instances, however, their analysis violated basic standards of fair, logical argumentation as they denigrated alternatives to the preferred strategy. Although the General Staff never succumbed to an excessively optimistic view of the Schlieffen Plan's chance for success, they made its risks seem necessary by arbitrarily disparaging defensive options.

[5]

Germany: The "Necessary" Is Possible

Between 1870 and 1914 German war planning was dominated by three figures—the elder Helmuth von Moltke until 1890, Alfred von Schlieffen between 1890 and 1905, and the younger Helmuth von Moltke from 1906 until the outbreak of war. All three hoped to solve the problem of a two-front war by means of a rapid, decisive battle of encirclement on one of the fronts. They favored this formula, despite its operational difficulties, largely because it suited the institutional interests and professional outlook of the German military. The elder Moltke eventually bowed to operational realities and abandoned the quest for a rapid, decisive victory. Schlieffen, however, dogmatized and institutionalized Moltke's doctrine of encirclement, rigidly applying it to the practical tasks of war planning and unfairly denigrating alternative solutions to strategic problems. The younger Moltke was grimly aware of the shortcomings of the war plan that he inherited from Schlieffen. He was nevertheless caught up in the ideology of the rapid, decisive victory and so could conceive of no acceptable alternative.

MOLTKE'S ENCIRCLEMENT DOCTRINE

The elder Moltke, while recognizing that railroads and increased firepower tended to favor the defender, nonetheless saw no profit in strictly defensive strategies. Prussia needed the capability to win short, decisive wars in order to complete the unification of the German nation and to carry out preventive attacks on her warlike neighbors. To serve those ends, Moltke devised his doctrine of encirclement, which made railroads and firepower compatible with the requirement for a short, decisive war. Frontal attacks, the doctrine held, could not lead to decisive victories because of the defensive advantages of modern firepower. Decisive results could only be achieved by using all available rail lines to deploy the army on a broad front, thereby outflanking the enemy, threatening his lines of communication, and encircling and annihilating him.

Under modern conditions, Moltke realized, wars would have to be short and decisive if they were to contribute in a positive way to the achievement of national goals.

> The character of modern warfare is revealed in the striving for greater and faster decisions. The strength of armies, the difficulty of feeding them, the costliness of keeping them in a mobilized state, the disruption of trade and transport, business and agriculture, as well as the army's high degree of readiness and the ease with which it is deployed—all these militate for the speedy ending of wars.[1]

But if modern conditions demanded short wars, modern military technology was making decisive, offensive operations more difficult. As early as 1865 Moltke had expressed the opinion that improvements in firepower were making tactical defense easier than tactical offense.[2] After the Franco-Prussian War, this view became even more pronounced. "My conviction has been won over to the tactical defensive by the improvements in firepower. In the campaign of 1870 we continually took the offensive and took the enemy's strongest positions, but with what sacrifices! It seems to me to be more favorable to go over to the offensive after first parrying the enemy's attacks."[3]

Moltke also contended that railroads favored the defender, who would have the full use of the rail net in his own territory.[4] While Moltke's 1866 and 1870 campaigns have been interpreted as a vindication of the doctrine of short, decisive, offensive wars of maneuver, they only served to heighten Moltke's awareness of the logistical limitations on offensive envelopment.[5]

Despite his understanding of the defender's advantages, Moltke resisted strictly defensive strategies. The brevity and decisiveness of the campaign were his principal concerns. Within the limits of these concerns he sought to avoid the attacker's most serious disadvantages in devising his encirclement doctrine. In order to use the full capacity of the rail net to deploy the army in the theater of war, Moltke typically detrained his forces along an extended front (which also facilitated the supply of the large force). Instead of concentrating his forces before the battle, as Napoleon had done with his smaller armies, Moltke concentrated them during the battle itself, using his extended wings to envelop and attack the enemy's exposed flanks. The comparatively weak center of Moltke's formation would ideally use the tactical advantages of defense to avoid being overwhelmed before the envelopment maneuver could be completed. In the most desirable circumstances, the battle would take place fairly near the railheads, so that marching distances and supply problems would be minimized. In 1870, however, the French attack was slow in developing, so Moltke had to supplant his initial plan for a battle of envelopment near the border by a series of offensive improvisations that led deeper into French territory.[6]

Moltke's Views on War and Politics

Moltke strove to mesh his operational doctrine with technological realities, but his encirclement doctrine was not dictated by the proliferation of railroads and improvements in firepower. Defensive doctrines would have been more fully compatible with those developments. Moltke's doctrine was, rather, shaped by his views on the nature of war and international politics. Wars would be frequent, he believed, and they should be employed as a normal, productive tool of statecraft. These conditions demanded that they should be short and decisive.

On the most general philosophical level, Moltke expressed the zero-sum outlook typical of European professional officers of the time: "Man's life, indeed the whole of nature is no more than a struggle of the new against the old, and the life of national entities is no different." In the conflict-ridden world he perceived, "It is only the sword that keeps the sword within its sheath."[7]

Many civilians in Moltke's Germany shared the view that "war between states is the natural state of affairs" and that war is an engine of cultural development.[8] This militant nationalism, exemplified by Otto von Bismarck as the chancellor of "blood and iron," made it easier for the military to gain acceptance for its view of the pervasive role of force in international relations. The great military victories of 1866 and 1870, which created the unified German Reich, did much to promote this outlook among civilians. Nonetheless, the military remained at least until 1890 more wedded than the civilian authorities to the conflictual view of international politics. The military was more inclined to urge preventive war and less willing to recognize the possibility of diplomatic solutions to political disputes.

Moltke was all too quick to perceive international disputes as proclaiming the inevitability, sooner or later, of war between the parties.

As early as 1860 he was foreseeing the inevitability of a clash with the Napoleonic ideas of "plebiscite, nationality, and natural frontiers, . . . expedients suitable for any purpose."[9] Similarly, in 1871, at a time of relatively good relations between Germany and Russia, a Moltke war-planning memorandum noted that one day Russia would have to turn against Germany, because of contradiction between the material interests and customs of the two states. As Alfred Vagts remarks, "Estrangement between Russia and Germany began first with the soldiers . . . rather than the diplomats; it never extended to the bankers."[10]

Since wars were inevitable, Moltke felt that their timing should be largely a matter of military expediency. In 1867 Moltke saw in the dispute over the sovereignty of Luxembourg an ideal pretext for provoking a war against France before Louis Napoleon could reform his army along the lines suggested by the lessons of the Austro-Prussian War of 1866. In order to sway Bismarck's decision, Moltke advanced some unlikely opinions about the great military value of the Luxembourg fortress. Moltke ultimately accepted Bismarck's judgment that the timing was inopportune because of the attitude of neutrals and German public opinion, but he continued to believe that "in time his stand will cost us many lives."[11]

In this case, Bismarck was no less interested than Moltke in the question of the expedient time to launch a war against France, but Moltke's professionally limited perspective led him to overemphasize the purely military aspects of the matter of timing. The fact that Moltke was highly attuned to political issues compared to most military professionals makes this conclusion even more striking.[12]

In 1887 Moltke again urged preventive war, this time against Russia, on the grounds that waiting would decrease Germany's chance of success. Although every important military figure in Germany shared this view, Bismarck again argued that German aggression would put "the full weight of the imponderables . . . on the side of the enemies we have attacked." Bismarck at one point admitted in principle that it is "the government's duty, . . . when a war becomes truly unavoidable, to choose a time for waging it at which it will exact the least sacrifice and hold the smallest danger for country and people."[13] But Bismarck consistently disagreed with Moltke and the military on two issues: when the point of inevitability had been reached, and what constituted a favorable moment.

Moltke's ethnic sensibilities made it more difficult for him to perceive states like Austria and Denmark as implacably hostile. He was nonetheless willing to prescribe war as the best and ultimately unavoidable means for settling disputes, even within the Germanic family of nations. In 1860 he wrote that a short, offensive war against Austria "would put an end to the internal dissentions in Germany, would place the smaller states under the hegemony of the victor, and would create in Central Europe a powerful state, equal, indeed superior, both in power and influence to any of its neighbors."[14]

This vision of a passage at arms as the ultimate solution to political problems was reinforced by the victory of 1870–71. After that campaign and the concomitant founding of the German Reich, novelist Gustav Freytag wrote that "never perhaps did any army have . . . such a deep poetic sense of the fact that the dreadful work of the battlefields served a higher ethical purpose," in expressing the "poetry of the historical process."[15] Not only were the barriers to Germany's political and historical development overturned, they were overturned in a way that immensely enhanced the army's prestige. As a consequence, it is not surprising that the German military was eager to learn the lessons of 1870 regarding the creative historical role of armed conflict.

For all his erudition, Moltke was not exempt from the military view that armed force was the only reliable means for resolving international difficulties. "Our diplomats have always hurled us into misfortune," he told his brother; "Our generals have always saved us."[16] His emphasis on military solutions to political problems helps to explain his disagreement with Bismarck over the treatment of defeated France in 1871. Moltke urged the imposition of harsh peace terms in order to cripple France's postwar economic recovery, limit its armed forces, and give Germany an impregnable line of defense. Bismarck considered the option of a less punitive peace that would leave the door open for Franco-German reconciliation, but Moltke thought such hopes illusory. He believed that only by keeping France weak could peace be assured.[17]

After the Franco-Prussian War, Moltke recognized that technological and social trends were making his formula for short, decisive victories more difficult to implement. By April 1871 he was already writing that, in the event of a two-front war, "we cannot hope to rid ourselves of one enemy through a quick, successful offensive in the West, and then turn against the other foe. We have just learned how hard it is to bring even the victorious struggle against France to an end."[18] It was nonetheless difficult for him to imagine diplomatic solutions to Germany's security problems. In the last analysis, he preferred to rely on preventive war rather than on Bismarck's diplomatic balancing act.

These differences between Moltke and Bismrck have been explained in two ways. The first explanation stresses the parochial interests of the military; the second, the narrow focusing of attention on one's own specialty. Bismarck himself subscribed to the former view. Explaining his disagreements with Moltke on preventive war and the conduct of military operations, Bismarck stated: "It is natural that not only the younger, ambitious officers, but also the experienced strategists of army General Staffs find it necessary to use their own ability and the strength of the troops they lead to play a part in the course of history."[19] In other words, the professional soldier develops an outlook that justifies—even glorifies—his function.

Gerhard Ritter, however, argues that the cause was not primarily parochial interests but rather a parochial focus of attention.

> In his capacity as chief of the General Staff Moltke had no particular occasion to concern himself with questions of history and politics other than those that created tensions among the great powers and might thereby lead to war. His jurisdiction did not extend to the evaluation of possible peaceful solutions. The limited historical perspective in his military writings thus derived from the contingencies of his work and goals, and as such it is quite understandable. To create the kind of fighting morale that must inspire an army requires an appropriate view of history.[20]

Even if one accepts both Bismarck's and Ritter's hypotheses, it is debatable whether Moltke's outlook was particularly biased. His predictions of imminent attack by Germany's neighbors, although often wrong, were not totally implausible. His zero-sum interpretation of nineteenth-century international politics, moreover, differed only in degree from Bismarck's own. If Moltke's outlook was realistic, the priority he gave to rapid, decisive, preventive offensives does not constitute bias. Perhaps the criterion of bias in this case should be whether Moltke recognized the operational risks of a short-war strategy, whether he was willing to abandon that strategy when the risks became too great. As Moltke's war planning after 1870 shows, by this criterion he qualifies as unbiased.

Moltke's Plans for a Two-front War

After 1870 Moltke sought to apply his envelopment formula for short, decisive campaigns to the problem of a two-front war against France and Russia. The bulk of the German forces would seek rapid victory on one front and then shift to the other. Especially in his later years, however, Moltke seems to have expected only limited victories and counted heavily on the staying power of a positional defense in the west, to buy time for a possibly lengthy campaign against Russia.

In the 1870s Moltke intended to attack France and defend against Russia. He chose this plan primarily because a rapid decision would be more difficult in the vast spaces of the eastern theater of war.[21] Beginning in 1879, however, Moltke decided to attack Russia first, seeking a rapid, limited victory around Warsaw while defending against France with only 4½ army corps. Two main factors contributed to this change, the more important being the completion of the formidable French fortress line. This line made any rapid decision against France impossible unless the French foolishly decided to fight in front of their brand new fortresses. Moltke believed that they would attack only if they were faced by a small German force. In this way, he planned to lure the French out of their fortresses and near to his railheads just as the bulk of the German army was being shifted from east to west. The second factor leading Moltke to reverse his strategy was the strengthening of Russian deployments in Poland. This new Russian strength not only increased the danger of an early Russian offensive should Germany attack France, it also created a more profitable target for a German preventive attack.[22]

Toward the end of the 1880s, however, the likelihood that a concentric attack on Warsaw would bring a quick, significant victory decreased. Continuing major increases in Russian peacetime deployments turned the forces around Warsaw from a tempting target into a serious obstacle. An *attaque brusquée* against this position could only result in an inconclusive frontal engagement. Consequently, Moltke and his deputy Alfred von Waldersee planned a deeper envelopment, crossing the Narew River to the east of Warsaw.[23] Moltke realized that this plan would prolong the campaign in the east, requiring extended defense in the west. But he did not worry about the strength of the Saar defensive line. He believed that the French would be wary of attacking in such a narrow corridor, flanked by two fortresses and filled with geographical obstacles. The German defenders would be well supplied by rail and would enjoy the advantage of defensive firepower. Any attempt to outflank the position through Belgium would be stopped by the Rhine, forcing the French to do battle with Holland at their backs and the German army threatening their communications. The French would be unlikely to abandon the security of their fortresses for such a dubious enterprise. As a result, a "seldom seen event may occur; two armies prepared for battle will stand opposite each other, neither wishing to begin battle."[24]

In sum, Moltke developed a remarkably successful doctrine for short, victorious wars, but he never reduced it to a dogma, a universal recipe for success. Strategy remained for him "a system of *ad hoc* expedients, . . . the development of an original idea in accordance with continually changing circumstances."[25] When circumstances seemed to require positional defense and the risk of drawn-out engagements, he drew the necessary, if distasteful, conclusions. The same cannot be said of his successors.

Schlieffen's Strategic Doctrine

Schlieffen borrowed Moltke's doctrine, but he did not apply it in Moltke's skeptical, pragmatic fashion. His use of encirclement, for example, was much more dogmatic than Moltke's, judging by several criteria. The first involves insensitivity to circumstances. Whereas Moltke had recognized that circumstances might preclude a rapid decision, Schlieffen dogmatically insisted on a rapid, decisive campaign by means of an encirclement battle regardless of the circumstances. The second concerns insensitivity to discrepant information. Whereas Moltke became more favorable to defensive strategies as a result of the Franco-Prussian War, Schlieffen resisted the defensive implications of the Boer and Russo-Japanese wars, except on the lowest tactical level. The third criterion is reliance on deduction. Whereas Moltke had viewed strategy as "a system of *ad hoc* expedients," Schlieffen relied much more on deductions from a set of abstract principles. The final criterion is narrowness of approach. Although Moltke's views on war and strategy were marked to some degree by a narrow, professional focus, his experience and outlook were broader than those of most professional officers. As a result, he was not totally insensitive to the possibility that diplomacy might play a constructive role in strategy. Schlieffen, in contrast, relied solely on military tools.

The need for cognitive and organizational simplicity favored the trend under Schlieffen's tenure toward a narrow, stable, deductive, standardized doctrine. Other factors intensified the dogmatic trend: the comparative centralization of German military institutions, the relatively high degree of doctrinal consensus in support of encirclement, and the lack of major disturbances from the environment, such as a major European war or a domestic political upheaval.

Schlieffen's Views on War and Politics

Schlieffen held to the same conflictual philosophy of international relations as Moltke did. Judged by his comments on the Franco-Prussian War and his reviews of the strategic situation in 1909 and 1912, Schlieffen saw implacable hostility as the normal relationship among European states. Only Germany's military capabilities prevented an attack by her competitors. Ultimately, war alone could resolve the impasse of political competition. "It is to be hoped that England's will may not for ever be decisive, and that Germany will one day regain the position of power necessary to her economic prosperity. Without a war this will scarcely be possible. How it will come about remains to be seen."[26] He praised Bismarck but failed entirely to appreciate the subtlety of his policies, seeing him simply as "the diplomat of blood and iron, who used his sword to cut the tangles of politics on the battlefield. The herald in battle, the mighty warrior, whose powerful voice roused Germany's sons to fight the enemies of the freedom and greatness of the Fatherland, was a soldier in all but name."[27]

Schlieffen's insensitivity to political nuance led him to take the two-dimensional, militaristic, zero-sum view of international politics more literally than Moltke did. Moltke had understood, at least to some extent, that diplomacy could help strategy by creating favorable conditions for starting, fighting, and ending a war. Schlieffen's strategy tended to assume that the diplomatically worst case was inevitable, even though, especially before 1911, the Franco-Russian alliance was not so tight as to rule out scenarios more favorable to Germany.[28] Limited war on one front might have seemed appropriate under some diplomatic circumstances—had Schlieffen been more politically imaginative. He ignored such possibilities entirely.[29]

Schlieffen's war planning reflected the view that political goals were best served by total military victories and that military operations should consequently be guided solely by the best means to achieve a decisive outcome.[30] As a result, many commentators have portrayed Schlieffen as nothing more than a narrow technician. Walter Görlitz, for example, remarks:

Schlieffen's complete imperviousness to anything that lay outside the sphere of his professional interest could at times be astonishing. Once on a Staff journey . . . the adjutant who was accompanying him drew his attention to the magic of the Pregel Valley that lay before them in the morning sun. Schlieffen looked at the scene, remarked, 'An unimportant obstacle,' and relapsed into silence. In human relationships he was equally insensible. One of his closest colleagues, General von Kuhl, relates how on every Christmas Eve he received a military problem the solution of which had to be returned by Christmas Day.[31]

He implies that Schlieffen focused narrowly on operational effectiveness rather than on the broader questions of political aims and "grand strategy." But on the contrary, the Schlieffen Plan entailed tremendous disadvantages from a strictly operational standpoint. Its logic stemmed entirely from the assumption that a formula for a short, decisive campaign had to be found. As noted above in the discussion of Moltke's strategy, this assumption is based not so much on operational advantages as on the need to reconcile the practice of war with the belief that war is normal, inevitable, and beneficial. In this sense, Schlieffen was not only a narrow technician but also a biased one.[32]

Dogmatization

Even one of Schlieffen's strongest critics admits that his strategy was based on "simple and impressive ideas."[33] Once the necessity of a rapid, decisive victory is accepted, the rest of Schlieffen's doctrine follows with inexorable logic. The division of the opposing forces in a two-front war gives the advantage to the force located between them. It allows that force, even if inferior to the combined strength of its opponents, to defeat them piecemeal—first on the one side, then on the other. The first battle, of course, must be waged with all available forces and must produce a truly decisive outcome: "We could not use a Solferino; it must be a Sedan or at least a Königgrätz [Sadowa]."[34] As Schlieffen's chosen examples indicate, only a flank attack, which threatens the opponent with envelopment and the loss of his communications, can produce a decisive outcome in a short time. Especially in light of the defensive strength of modern firepower, frontal attacks will at best produce partial, "ordinary" victories. Indeed, the attacker himself can make use of the holding power of the defense in a frontal engagement for "about the only way to find the means for a strong flank attack is by weakening the forces facing the enemy front."[35]

These strategic notions are obviously derived from the elder Moltke's style of operations. Schlieffen's doctrinal system simplified and systematized them, occasionally to the point of caricature, and ap-

[134]

plied them to all kinds of operational problems in all kinds of settings, virtually without discrimination.

For example, Schlieffen applied his formulae of envelopment and "hit-and-shift" in every conceivable circumstance: at the tactical level, at the corps level, at the level of the front, and at the level of the war as a whole; when the opponent is stronger and when he is weaker; when the underlying aim is defensive and when it is offensive. Under no circumstances is positional defense encouraged, except as part of an encircling maneuver.[36] (This idea that the same two principles should be applied universally and exclusively would never have occurred to Moltke, even though he inspired the principles.) The Schlieffen plan itself is the clearest example of mechanically applying a formula for success to inappropriate circumstances. The "encirclement" of the French army by means of Belgium may have looked like Sedan or Sadowa on Schlieffen's gaming table, but the differences in scale, logistics, and the balance of forces meant that it played out like Solferino: an ordinary frontal engagement of the kind Schlieffen abhorred.[37]

Schlieffen's dogmatic rigidity is also to be found in his attempt to plan in advance the entire course of the campaign. This practice was a sharp departure from Moltke's, which was to devise flexible deployments that could be used offensively or defensively in response to changing circumstances. According to Moltke, "No strategic plan goes with any certainty beyond the first encounter with the enemy's main forces. Only the layman believes he can see in the course of a campaign the carrying through of an initial idea, thought out in advance, considered in every detail, and adhered to right to the end."[38]

Schlieffen's dogmatism reaches its zenith in his approach to military history. He wrote his study *Cannae* to prove that "flank attack is the essence of the whole history of war." It is generally agreed that his idealized treatment of Sadowa in that volume renders Moltke's victory over the Austrians barely recognizable.[39] General Sigismund von Schlichting likewise criticized Schlieffen's attempt to use the campaign of 1805–1806 to confirm the validity of the Moltkean doctrine of envelopment, pointing out the fundamental differences in operational scale and logistical technology.[40] Even Schlieffen's apologist, General Wilhelm Groener, admits that Schlieffen's goal was not to be a scientific historian but rather to "teach the art of leadership by impressive examples and to show the German leaders of future wars the 'coloured splendours' of the actual secret of victory of all times."[41]

Schlieffen approached the military classics in the same way he approached military history. In Clausewitz, he sought not a philosophical statement about the essence of war and its relation to politics but rather a recipe for victory. "The enduring value of the work *On War* lies in its emphasis on the theory of annihilation. . . . This doctrine led us to Königgrätz [Sadowa] and Sedan."[42]

Schlieffen's tendency to dogmatize Moltke's doctrine can be explained largely in terms of cognitive and organizational incentives to simplify and systematize. A standard doctrine, based on "simple but impressive concepts," made the unity of effort of the General Staff easier in working out solutions to strategic problems. It also facilitated the education of new staff officers and the uniform training of the troops. In the event of war, commanders could be confident that their subordinates would understand and carry out their orders in a predictable manner, and that colleagues to their left and right would not be operating on the basis of conceptions radically different from their own. Although Schlieffen did not achieve full standardization of thought, especially among older officers who still believed in the efficacy of frontal attacks, he did succeed in indoctrinating a generation of young, true-believing staff officers, like Groener and Hermann von Kuhl, who oversaw the implementation of the Schlieffen Plan.[43]

The difference between someone who has worked out beliefs through hard-won personal experience and someone who has simply systematized the ideas of another is likely to be very great. Thus it is not surprising that Moltke himself did not succumb to these incentives to dogmatize his principles. Schlieffen was a theoretician, so his beliefs were largely shaped by the criteria of "good theory": parsimony, simplicity, logical coherence, and breadth of applicability. Moltke was a pragmatist. His judgments were largely shaped by the myriad special circumstances that he had faced in his long and varied career as a commander and a strategist.

A French comparison sheds light on the German experience. The French counterpart to the dogmatization of doctrine under Schlieffen is Henri Bonnal's neo-Napoleonic doctrine, which in the 1890s distilled and standardized many of the ideas developed in the previous decade. Yet Bonnal's reduction of ideas to a single, standardized dogma was far less complete than Schlieffen's. Motivational factors eventually worked against Bonnal's middle-of-the-road doctrine, whereas they reinforced Schlieffen's formula of the short, victorious war. Moreover, the Boer War was more of a problem for Bonnal's doctrine, which emphasized frontal engagements, than it was for Schlieffen's, which had always reckoned to some extent with the benefits to the defender of advances in firepower. Finally, Schlieffen, as the long-term chief of the powerful General Staff, enjoyed institutional advantages in advancing his views that no Frenchman ever did.

Bolstering the Dogma

Even Schlieffen's admirers admit the presence of a willful, biased element in his doctrinal thinking. Eberhard Kessel, the editor of his letters, notes that Schlieffen adopted a "voluntaristic" approach to strategy reflected in his favorite motto: *"das Denkbar ist erreicht,"* roughly "mind over matter." Kessel argues that the *Einseitigkeit* (one-sidedness or prejudiced, doctrinaire character) of the Schlieffen Plan was its strength, not a weakness. In this case, one-sidedness should not be considered a synonym for delusion. Rather, it was a prerequisite for maximizing the chances of success of a bold conception. In Kessel's view, the Schlieffen Plan could work only if it were implemented by a firm, purposeful, confident will, strictly focused on a fixed goal and the necessary means to achieve it. This argument implies that the younger Moltke ruined the plan by hedging against possible failure.[44]

Such thinking was popular within the military of Schlieffen's era. Colmar von der Goltz, for example, remarks that, "As in all great decisions in war, so in the formulation of the project of operations, a certain amount of bias is of paramount necessity. Whoever cannot descend to that will never, in the presence of a large number of equally plausible views, succeed in grasping one single great purpose; he may, perchance, prove himself to be a subtle reasoner, but never a great general."[45]

Sometimes Schlieffen's operational biases seem to go beyond overconfidence and into manipulated inconsistency. For example, Schlieffen assumed that the Germans could carry out rapid changes of front to execute his plan, but he denied that the French could do the same to foil it. In a staff ride in 1901, presumably with the western front in mind, Schlieffen remarked that "the heavy armies of millions of men can make changes of front only slowly and with great difficulty. They are therefore extremely vulnerable on their flanks and in their rears."[46] However, the basic idea of the Schlieffen Plan, which expected rapidly to shift the front of the whole German army, makes the shift of a few French divisions from Lorraine to the Belgian border seem trivial by comparison.

There is a similarly serious inconsistency between Schlieffen's assertion that the offense could extend its wings by weakening its center and his reluctance to admit that the defender could and would do the same. "If the defender deploys a long front, the enemy has every opportunity to break the weak line at the point he chooses to attack. . . . This is the disadvantage of the defense." General Friedrich von Bernhardi, in his critique of Schlieffen's "Krieg in der Gegenwart," pointed out that the defender could extend his front by thinning his center more easily than the attacker could. "The defender being superior to the assailant in a frontal attack on account of the effect of modern arms, he can spare more forces in front than the latter, and consequently meet the envelopment in superior force."[47]

These inconsistencies bolstered Schlieffen's preferred doctrine and war plan, and helped to preserve the hope for a short, victorious war.

Rationality and Rationalization

Naturally, there were limits to Schlieffen's tendency to dogmatize. Even dogmatic beliefs must maintain some plausible connection with reality. Schlieffen was certainly no more remote from reality than many other European commentators on strategy and tactics.

Like Ferdinand Foch, Schlieffen was more dogmatic in his pronouncements on questions of grand strategy and abstract doctrine than in his treatment of operational specifics. With regard to the logistical frictions that disproportionately hamper offensive operations, for example, Schlieffen understood the problem quite well but did not draw the logical conclusions for doctrine or war planning. In an 1896 critique of a staff problem, Schlieffen pays considerable attention to the marching limitations of an army corps.[48] However, in the 1905 Schlieffen Plan, he remarks only that the long forced march across Belgium will require "very great exertions." He evidently agreed with his collaborator on the General Staff, Freytag-Loringhoven, who believed that "a leader's strong will" was sufficient to override logistical frictions if the leader had good officers and troops.[49]

A similar pattern prevails in the area of tactical doctrine. Schlieffen was quite willing to admit that the Russo-Japanese War demonstrated the tactical strength of the defensive and that "the manifestations which came to light in the Far East will also be repeated in a European war."[50] In fact, Schlieffen was willing to recognize an even more unsettling lesson of the Russo-Japanese experience: whenever the defender was threatened with envelopment, he fell back quickly and effectively, turning the engagement into an ordinary frontal battle.[51] Schlieffen's conclusion, however, was not that the defensive had become a desirable option in certain circumstances, nor even that

[138]

rapid, decisive victories were becoming extremely difficult to achieve. Rather, he exhorted the attackers to redouble their efforts, advancing "from position to position, day and night, advancing, digging in, advancing. . . . The attack must never come to a standstill as happened in the war in the Far East."[52] In essence, Schlieffen had not changed his opinion of 1893: "The armament of the army has changed, to be sure, but the fundamental laws of combat remain the same, and one of these laws is that one cannot defeat the enemy without attacking. . . . One must attack when one has the means in hand to do so, and one must attack so as to annihilate [the enemy] to the greatest possible extent."[53] In this way, Schlieffen defended his central beliefs with an a priori reasoning that was virtually impervious to evidence. At the same time, he freely adjusted peripheral views (should the shovel be used in an attack?) according to the latest data.

In issues of grand strategy Schlieffen's apparent rationality concealed a significant measure of rationalization. Schlieffen's views on the economic consequences of a long war, for example, constitute an ex post rationalization rather than an ex ante rationale. The first indication of his concern with this question appears in 1901, long after his basic doctrinal orientation was established and four years after he had decided that the invasion of Belgium would be unavoidable.[54] Schlieffen moreover made no attempt to have the General Staff examine the specific economic consequences of a long war and even discouraged nonmilitary analysis of this type. In comparison with both the elder and the younger Moltke, Schlieffen had little interest in such economic questions as how to feed the army and the civilian population during wartime.[55] Indeed, he seems mainly to have interested himself in economic matters as a source of rationalizations for a strategy that he preferred for other reasons.

SCHLIEFFEN'S PLANNING FOR A TWO-FRONT WAR

The general shape of the Schlieffen Plan resulted from the doctrinaire application of strategic principles, especially the requirement of a rapid, decisive victory. Although Schlieffen examined several alternatives to the violation of Belgian neutrality between 1891 and 1897, he found none that met his crucial criterion. He did not delude himself about the difficulties of the Belgian operation: drawbacks, afterall, had to be considered in order to devise the best possible plan for a rapid victory. Agonizing over how far to extend his right wing and how to divide his forces between right and left, Schlieffen evaluated alternatives rationally and without prejudice as long as they did not challenge the essence of his preferred strategy.[56] In contrast, he often violated normal standards of rational consistency when he evaluated defensive options or plans for only limited victories. In addition to attacking these plans on the grounds of abstract principle, he would also criticize them on specific operational grounds, applying a double standard for favored and unfavored plans.

Offense in the East

Improvements in Russian railroads, fortresses, and troop deployments had by 1890 greatly diminished the feasibility of the German plan for a rapid encirclement of Warsaw.[57] Schlieffen, at the time Waldersee's deputy, analyzed the alternatives in a February 1890 memorandum, which urged avoiding the heavily fortified Lower Narew by extending the envelopment further to the east. Characteristically, he argued that "the goal of our operations must be a great, decisive battle as soon as possible." This battle could not be achieved by attacking the left bank, where few forces could be encircled, or the Lower Narew, where the Germans would face prepared positions. He proposed to attack further east, toward the less formidable fortifications of Osoviets and Grodno, in order to avoid the strong points on the Narew and to achieve a more complete envelopment of the Russian field army. Yet Schlieffen also had his doubts about this plan. "Times come in every year when operations must stand still. If the war should break out in the rainy season [when rivers would overflow], we will have to consider if it were not better to leave weak forces in the East and attack in the West."[58] These doubts notwithstanding, Waldersee and the retired elder Moltke agreed in April 1890 to adopt Schlieffen's more easterly offensive.

Soon after succeeding Waldersee as chief of staff, Schlieffen concluded that the offensive in East Prussia would have to be abandoned, thereby freeing forces for use against France and alongside the Austrians in Silesia. Only a small, defensive contingent was to be left in East Prussia. His principal objection to an attack from East Prussia was that it could not achieve rapid, decisive victory. Even in the event of a successful crossing of the fortress and river barriers, "we would not achieve a decisive battle or the destruction of the Russian army, but a series of frontal battles." He argued that "even if the fortifications at Lomzha [on the Narew] do not have a very great defensive capacity, they would require the use of heavy artillery, a bombardment, an assault, and, consequently, a loss of time that would always allow the enemy to reinforce the threatened point." At best, the Russians would retreat into "the interior of their enormous empire."[59]

Schlieffen's own analysis implied that great gains might be made by an offensive in the east, but he considered these gains inadequate because they fell short of a decisive victory over the Russian army. His unwillingness to accept anything less than a truly decisive victory in the east rested in large part on his belief that a protracted defense in the west would be untenable.

Defense versus Offense in the West

Schlieffen's planning for military operations in the west shows a considerable bias against defensive strategy that cannot be fully explained in rational terms. The arguments that were central to his case against a positional defense contain various inconsistencies and double standards. His opposition to a defensive campaign was based almost completely on his theoretical doctrines, and he manipulated the evaluation of specific operational scenarios to support his theoretical insistence on decisive, offensive operations.

In his first operational memorandum after becoming chief of staff, Schlieffen grudgingly admitted that the French army could not be attacked behind the impenetrable French fortress line, so "we shall have to let them run up against us."[60] However, Schlieffen believed, the French would not attack at the outset of the campaign, and therefore, the first decision would have to be achieved against Russia. For protection against France during the eastern offensive, Schlieffen urged the construction of fortresses at Molsheim and Sarrebourg. "However much it goes against our traditions to build fortifications, we cannot, as the weaker side, reject the means used by our opponent to paralyze our military plans."[61]

Within a year and a half, Schlieffen had decided that rapid victory was impossible in the east. He immediately abandoned the idea of a positional defense in the west. He argued that the passive defender was vulnerable to outflanking if he were too concentrated and vulnerable to frontal penetration if he were deployed too thinly.[62]

With regard to the threat of frontal breakthrough, Schlieffen argued that the German positions around Sarrebourg were too weak to withstand an attack by superior French forces.

> Even if the defense were carried out in depth, it would be too weak not to succumb eventually to a superior force. . . . The attacker will only

attack a part of the prepared position, but there he will be able to develop a considerable numerical superiority. . . . In order to avoid this result, one could try to counterattack along the whole front [in order to relieve the pressure on Sarrebourg], but this would involve attacking a numerically superior force, which is precisely what we want to avoid.[63]

Schlieffen concluded that the Germans had to collect sufficient forces in the west to launch their own attack. "To win, we must endeavor to be the stronger of the two at the point of impact. Our only hope of this lies in making our own choice of operations, not in waiting passively for whatever the enemy chooses for us."[64]

The elder Moltke had drawn diametrically opposed conclusions about the prospects for a defense along the Saar, seeing advantages in the very circumstances that Schlieffen saw as fatally disadvantageous. Schlieffen worried that the center would give way and that the rest of the front would have to counterattack to save the threatened positions. But this is exactly the kind of battle that Moltke hoped for: drawing the French into an enveloping sack between two strong wings near the German railheads.

With regard to the danger that the Saar position might be outflanked, Schlieffen argued that the French had to attempt a flank maneuver on a broad front if they were to bring all of their forces into the field of battle. Because of the absence of sufficient roads between Metz and the Belgian border, Schlieffen calculated, such a flank maneuver would be impossible without violating Belgian territory. Thus German war games based on the premise of German defense in the west normally assumed that the French would attack across Belgium.[65] The elder Moltke had welcomed the prospect of such a move by the French, on operational as well as political grounds, but Schlieffen saw it as a grave danger to the Saar position.

One explanation for Schlieffen's relative pessimism is that his hypothetical defenses in the west generally employed fewer German forces than had Moltke's actual war plans. For example, Moltke's 1888 plan for offense in the east and defense in the west used only seven active corps against Russia, leaving about eleven active corps against France.[66] In contrast, Schlieffen's winter war game for 1901–1902 left only seven active corps against France. The "French" attacked this force from both north and south of Metz, evidently violating Belgian territory. The "Germans" decided not to retreat behind the Rhine, a decision that Schlieffen approved for reasons of military and civilian morale. Defending the Moselle north of Thionville/Diedenhofen, the German force was encircled and annihilated.[67] The best interpretation that can be put on the choice of this defense in the west is that Schlieffen's doctrinal emphasis on decisive victories led him to deploy an extremely large force in the east, where in this war game he sought to achieve the initial decision. A more skeptical interpretation is that he sought to prove the impossibility of defense in the west and therefore chose a hopeless scenario. This latter hypothesis may seem extreme, but a 1905 war game seems to demand such an interpretation. Although Schlieffen allocated a few more divisions in the latter case to the defending force in the west, he arbitrarily assumed that the British, Dutch, and Belgians had all joined in the French offensive.[68]

Despite this apparent bias against defense, General Kuhl, a supporter of the Schlieffen Plan, reports that in war games conducted by the German General Staff the hypothetical French offensives often miscarried. French attacks in Lorraine, for example, faced a myriad of difficulties.

> Each time, the French attack against Germany turned out to be difficult. An offensive between Metz and Strasbourg, with the mass of the army pressed into a narrow space and deployed in depth, almost regularly miscarried. The narrow space was bordered by Strasbourg, the Kaiser Wilhelm fortress [Metz-Thionville/Diedenhofen], and the Vosges mountains. The French could have been attacked from Metz, Strasbourg, or the Saar. They could have tried to attack our left or right with part of their forces. If they were to turn the Metz-Diedenhofen fortified area from the north, they would have had to enter the territory of Luxembourg and probably also that of Belgium. German forces, held ready around Trèves or further north, could have attacked their left flank. If the French right wing had penetrated into Alsace, its progress would have been stopped by Strasbourg and La Bruche.
>
> Every time, there resulted a separation of the French army into several defiles, a separation that would have been still more accentuated if the French right had tried to cross the Upper Rhine. In all the operational scenarios, the Metz-Diedenhofen fortified region gave the Germans a great advantage in facilitating troop movements and lateral redeployments, at the same time as it provoked a disjunction of the French line.[69]

A French attack through Belgium, the mirror image of the Schlieffen Plan, also looked unpromising.

> Another possibility that was offered to the French was to use only limited forces for the frontal engagement, sending the majority of their force through Belgium and Luxembourg. In order to insure the security

of their right wing, they thus would have had to invest Metz-Di-
edenhofen. The attack could have become a vast wheel, pivoting on
Verdun and facing the lower Mosselle. The French left would have lost
any point of support and could have been attacked by us from the
Rhine. If, to avoid that, the French had wanted to leave a flank guard on
their right, facing the Moselle while continuing to march to the Rhine,
we could have threatened its right flank. . . .

To exonerate Schlieffen, Kuhl argues not that a defense in the west
was impossible but that it would have required too many forces and
that it would not have produced decisive victory.

The most varied measures for countering a French offensive were discussed. Taking a position on the Nied and on the Saar to confront a
principal attack from Lorraine did not seem like a good idea. All positions can be turned and enveloped and thus become untenable. Taking
refuge in a position is the beginning of the end if one does not have
forces elsewhere to come to its relief. Moreover, the defensive is merely
frontal resistance and cannot annihilate the adversary. Annihilation can
only be achieved by movement, not immobility. Consequently, if the
adversary penetrates between Metz and Strasbourg, he should be enveloped by two wings, maneuvering from Metz and the Vosges. . . .
   In any case, it was evident that, despite the difficulties that a French
offensive would have encountered, in order to counter it effectively the
Germans would have had need of significant forces; with a few army
corps, success would have been impossible.

"Significant forces" would not, of course, be available if defense in
the west necessarily implied an ambitious offensive by huge German
forces in the east. However, if the Germans adopted a more limited
offensive in the east, sufficient forces would be available for defense
in the west. Kuhl's own analysis implies that the forces required for a
successful defense in the west would have been considerably smaller
than those demanded by the Schlieffen Plan. It seems likely that a
defensive posture in the west would have freed enough forces to
achieve a successful, but limited, offensive in the east. This solution
did not, however, fit Schlieffen's doctrinal formulae and was not
considered.
   Another indication of the biased nature of Schlieffen's approach to
the question of defense in the west is his double standard for evaluating the feasibility of defense along the Saar. In 1894 he believed that
the position there was indefensible, but in the 1905 drafts of the
Schlieffen Plan he counted on the very weakly occupied Saar position
to hold until the German right wing could bring its forces to bear.[70]

Another double standard is to be found in his assessment of the value of fortresses. He repeatedly stated that the modern French fortress line was unassailable and "need only remain weakly occupied." However, he resisted the conclusion that the Germans could use a fortress line to reduce forces needed in a defense in the west, asserting that "a modern fort is a place where the engineers and artillerymen carry on veritable orgies of expenditure but are still never ready."[71] The fortresses that Germany did build were due to the influence of the ideas of Goltz; Schlieffen probably opposed them.[72]

In sum, Schlieffen's bias against the defensive is the main indication that his war planning for the western front was dominated by nonrational processes. Further evidence is provided by his double standard, discussed earlier, regarding the ability of the French defenders to extend or shift their front to meet the German right wing. Two final factors, Schlieffen's estimates of French intentions and his assessment of the logistical feasibility of his plan, also support to some extent nonrational interpretations.

French Intentions and Logistical Dilemmas

In order to help rationalize the violation of Belgian neutrality, Schlieffen believed that the French would march through Belgium even if the Germans did not. As we have seen, Schlieffen's fear that the French would outflank Metz from the north, through Belgium, was a major factor in his argument against defense in the west. A French march through Belgium would also pose a danger if the Germans attacked only in Lorraine. In this regard, Schlieffen believed the French were "practical and unscrupulous."[73] He regularly assumed French violations of Belgian territory in war games, even before German incursions had taken place—a complete contrast with the elder Moltke's assumptions about likely French moves.[74] Schlieffen's supposition also seems inconsistent both with the intelligence that the German General Staff had on French war plans and with Schlieffen's views on the impossibility of a rapid shift in the French front.[75] Indeed, the French military did not even seek permission to violate Belgian neutrality at the outbreak of war until 1912, and even then the impetus was a dilemma caused by the threat of a German attack through Belgium. The French needed to deploy troops on the Belgian frontier to hedge against this threat, but they feared that this force would be left out of the action if Belgium was not invaded. To solve this problem, they sought permission to advance through Belgium regardless of German actions. The civilian authorities, however, rejected the request because of Belgian and British objections.[76]

Ritter implies that changes in Schlieffen's estimates of French offensive intentions were determined by his need to rationalize changes in his war plans. In 1891, when Schlieffen intended to attack Russia first, he believed the French would only attack after a delay. In 1892, however, Schlieffen sought the initial decision against France but was perplexed by the problem of attacking the French behind their fortresses. To resolve his perplexity, he conveniently assumed that the French would come out from behind their fortifications in order to attack.[77] This precipitous change in judgment is doubly suspicious because the German decision to shift its offensive from east to west took away the principal incentive for the French to attack.

Despite this apparently motivated misperception, Schlieffen's long-term judgment of the likelihood of a French offensive was fairly realistic. In general, he believed that the French would probably remain behind their fortresses unless a large German force were deployed against Russia.[78] He devised a 1901 war game based on this notion, in which seven German active corps attacked the Russians during their concentration period, primarily in order to induce the French to attack. Some of these corps were shifted back to the Saar for the decisive battle against the French attackers, in the manner of the elder Moltke. According to Kuhl, this idea was given up because Schlieffen feared that the forces needed on the Saar would not be able to disengage in the east.[79] Another idea for getting the French to fight in front of their fortresses was to bombard the exposed city of Nancy. Schlieffen accurately concluded that French public opinion would not allow Nancy to be abandoned.[80] Ultimately, however, he felt that an engagement only one day's march from the Toul fortress could not yield decisive results, since the French could easily fall back to safety in the event of a partial German victory.[81] As a consequence, he devised the march through Belgium, which he believed would work whether the French attacked or not. If the French took to the offensive, the German right wing would wheel directly south instead of extending its arc of maneuver all the way through Brussels to Paris.[82] In short, Schlieffen resorted to a self-serving estimate of French intentions only in 1892 and, to some extent, in 1894, when it helped him to rationalize the shift from east to west. Thereafter, the plan to advance through Belgium eliminated the need to believe that the French would do Germany the favor of attacking. Moreover, it is noteworthy that, despite his temporary assessment that the French would attack, Schlieffen kept looking for a means to avoid the French fortresses.

The implication is that even during the 1892–1894 period, Schlieffen may have entertained strong doubts about his self-serving estimate.

Finally, it might be contended that Schlieffen's relative lack of concern with the logistical problems of the right wing constitutes a bias that cannot be explained in rational terms. In a cavalier manner, Schlieffen depended on forced marches, the extensive requisitioning of provisions from "the rich lands of Belgium and northern France," undestroyed Belgian railways, and motor transport that scarcely existed in 1905.[83] However, the General Staff neither ignored nor denied the logistical difficulties of the Schlieffen Plan. They rather accepted them as unavoidable, since no alternative to the march through Belgium fulfilled the General Staff's strategic requirements. As a result, the emphasis of logistical analysis was on how to succeed despite these difficulties, not on whether they made success unattainable.

In fact, Schlieffen's 1905 concept probably entailed less risk of logistical disaster than did the younger Moltke's subsequent plans. In order to insure a steady flow of supplies to the German right wing, Schlieffen planned to connect with the Belgian rail net by means of the undefended Dutch region of Maastricht, whereas Moltke's only rail link to northern Belgium ran through the Liège fortress. Even if this fortress were captured, the Liège rail line could be quickly and thoroughly destroyed. Invading Holland might have been too high a price to avoid this danger, but at least the plan shows that Schlieffen was appropriately pessimistic about some of the logistical barriers to his march across Belgium.[84]

WAR PLANNING UNDER THE YOUNGER MOLTKE

The younger Moltke, chief of the General Staff from 1906 to 1914, had a quite realistic view of the political and operational drawbacks of the Schlieffen plan. Moltke, however, remained captive of the doctrine of the rapid, decisive victory and, therefore, could imagine no acceptable alternative to Schlieffen's strategic formula. In the words of the biographer of General Groener, the head of the General Staff's railroad section, "German strategists understood their problem and sailed right into it."[85]

Guiding Assumptions

Following the militant, nationalist traditions of his profession and his state, Moltke believed that "Germany is the only possibility for the further spiritual development of man" and that Germany should not shrink from war as a means to achieve its historic destiny.[86] During the 1911 Moroccan Crisis, he wrote his wife that "If we again slip away from this affair with our tail between our legs and if we cannot bring ourselves to put forward a determined claim which we are prepared to force through with the sword, I shall despair of the future of the German Empire. I shall then resign. But before handing in my resignation I shall move to abolish the Army and to place ourselves under Japanese protectorate; we shall then be in a position to make money without interference and to develop into ninnies."[87]

Still, Moltke's belligerence was not primarily caused by his will to conquer but rather by his fears for Germany's security. Foreign Minister Gottlieb von Jagow reports this March 1914 conversation with Moltke: "The prospects of the future seriously worried him. Russia will have completed her armaments in 2 to 3 years. The military superiority of our enemies would be so great then that he did not know how he might cope with them. In his view there was no alternative to waging a preventive war in order to defeat the enemy as long as we could still more or less pass the test. The Chief of the General Staff left it at my discretion to gear our policy to an early unleashing of a war."[88]

The younger Moltke believed no less than Schlieffen and the elder Moltke in war as an engine of historical progress and as the ultimate solver of political and strategic problems. This outlook placed a premium on finding a formula for short, victorious wars, whose cost would not negate their political-historical benefits. Given this perspective, it is not surprising that Moltke found the idea of a positional defensive strategy to be incomprehensible. With regard to Russian strategy in the Manchurian War, he wrote that "there was never such a crazy way of making war as long as the world has stood."[89] It is of course difficult to determine whether Moltke's abhorrence of positional defense resulted primarily from his political and philosophical outlook or from his socialization in the prevailing strategic doctrines of Schlieffen and the General Staff.

The career of Groener, however, suggests that socialization in the prevailing political and philosophical outlook and in the prevailing strategic doctrine were simply two sides of the same coin. At the General Staff academy, which Groener entered in 1893, the campaigns of the elder Moltke were used to demonstrate not only the approved operational doctrines but also "the speedy military resolution of complicated political problems. . . . Struggle was an integral part of human nature and international wars could be most mercifully controlled by rapid, conclusive engagement. . . . Problems were solved and life rejuvenated." On the operational level, Groener learned that flank attacks could produce rapid, decisive victories and that frontal attacks and positional defense were to be shunned at all costs.[90] On the philosophical level, Groener was soon contributing to the indoctrination of other officers, writing articles on the beauty and virtue of war and its role in promoting culture.[91]

The link between Groener's philosophical militarism and his operational views is particularly clear in his August 1914 war journal and letters. "In order to achieve great things in war," he wrote, "one should always aim for completeness, never be content with half measures; the golden mean is not suited for war." Groener was pleased that the General Staff was now in charge of Germany's destiny and could correct the errors of the diplomats. The army would do a "thorough job" and give Germany a hegemonic peace that would last a hundred years. However, he feared that Theobald Bethmann-Hollweg and other "weaklings" would seek a compromise peace.[92]

The thinking of the younger Moltke about the specifics of planning for a two-front war was dominated by the General Staff's traditional goal of a rapid decision against one of the opponents. In 1909 Moltke told the chief of the Austrian General Staff, Franz Conrad von Hötzendorff, that he believed a "relatively equal division of the German forces between France and Russia to be a serious mistake."

> In order to be successful against one of our foes we must defend ourselves against the other with the minimum of forces. Our primary effort must be to achieve a quick decision. This is hardly possible against Russia. The defense against France would absorb so much strength that the forces available for the offensive against Russia would not suffice to force a decision. The broad maneuvering space and the unfavorable terrain would waste too much time.[93]

The initial victory had to be sought in the west.

Despite this view, Moltke was quite realistic in assessing the disadvantages of the German strategy for a rapid victory against France. His February 1913 memorandum, responding to Jagow's request for a reevaluation of the need to cross Belgian territory, reflects a considerable understanding of the political costs of this move. In particular, he realized that it would bring Britain into the war, but he saw no acceptable alternative. He rejected the idea of asking for a guarantee of British neutrality in exchange for a German pledge to respect Belgian neutrality. Even if Britain kept her word, such an agreement would mean abandoning Germany's only hope of ending the war quickly.[94]

Under the younger Moltke, the General Staff's analysis of logistical problems and the probable length of the war shows a similar pattern of willful realism. Difficulties were not denied, they were accepted as unavoidable. The emphasis was on how to overcome barriers to the implementation of the preferred strategy, not on whether these barriers were so great as to make the preferred strategy untenable.

Logistics

In August 1914 the long march through Belgium significantly drained the fighting capabilities of the German right wing. Infantry strength was depleted by exhaustion and illness. Although food for the soldiers was supplied fairly satisfactorily by requisitioning, fodder for the horses was more of a problem. Forced to subsist on unripe grain, animals were weakened and some even died, reducing the effectiveness of cavalry and artillery units. Siege operations were occasionally held up because of disruptions in the supply of ammunition.[95] These difficulties, which would have been much worse had the Belgians destroyed the rail link through Liège, were probably not the main reason for the German defeat at the Marne. They nonetheless constituted an important and foreseeable disadvantage of the Schlieffen plan. Moltke and his collaborators on the General Staff understood these difficulties but refused to see them as grounds for abandoning the march across Belgium.

In theory, German logistical doctrine recognized that "an assured system of supply is one of the first conditions of success for an Army at war. Want of food may stop an army in its victorious career, and even in certain circumstances bring it to ruin." In offensive operations, it was believed, supplies should be gathered primarily from local sources and secondarily by bringing them up from the rear.[96] Occasional supply difficulties might warrant a change in operational plans: "When the conditions of supply are very unfavorable it may be necessary to advance more slowly, or to stop the advance altogether, in order to allow the depots being brought nearer." The emphasis, however, was on overcoming such problems, not on bowing to them.

Military history teaches us that good troops can and must endure hardships for a time without losing their efficiency.

A certain recklessness commensurate with the stakes that are being played for may consequently, under certain circumstances, really be based on sound judgment. But such a theory must never, on any account, be used as an excuse for crass ignorance or carelessness. On the contrary, we must scrupulously endeavour to secure for the troops the very best supplies available, and allow this consideration to carry due weight in drawing up our plans of operations.[97]

Groener, as the official most directly responsible for the logistical implementation of the Schlieffen Plan, embodied precisely this spirit: although a careless or cavalier attitude about supply arrangements was unthinkable, high stakes demanded great risks. His October 1906 memorandum on supplying the Schlieffen Plan's right wing shows an awareness of almost every possible pitfall. He agreed with Schlieffen that the rich lands of northern Belgium and northern France would contain abundant food supplies, but he feared that requisitioning would slow the march of the right wing.[98] Nor was supply from the rear a satisfactory solution. Horse-drawn supply trains would inevitably fall behind the advancing columns, especially in the rather likely event of significant railroad demolitions in Belgium. "If the railroads are thoroughly destroyed, . . . the moment would come when the armies would have to stop and let the supply columns catch up." Motorized trucks could solve this problem, "but it will be a long time before we are in a position to equip our supply columns with an adequate number of such transport means."[99]

None of this indicated to Groener that the Schlieffen plan might be a mistake. Just as Schlieffen had demanded "great exertions" by the marching infantrymen of the right wing, so Groener demanded the same of their supply services. "All the authorities must be ruled by a strong will to strive with all their powers, so that the operations will not be crippled by supply difficulties. The feeling of responsibility must be so great that in difficult circumstances people free themselves from procedural hindrances and take the responsibility for acting in accordance with common sense."[100]

In fact, the supply of the right wing operated more or less as Groener expected. All of the difficulties he had anticipated did occur, but none of them crippled the advance in a decisive way. Requisitioning of foodstuffs was generally effective, and some supplementary supplies for the First Army were brought up by rail. The superficial demolitions of the northern Belgian rail net were quickly repaired, so that at least low-speed, low-volume traffic could be put through. The gap between the First Army and its railhead, as great as 80 miles on 26 August, was reduced to 40 miles by 30 August. This distance, within the General Staff's prewar calculation of 75 miles as the maximum sustainable radius, was acceptable. Trucks also proved to be an important link in the supply line, especially for high-priority cargo such as ammunition.[101]

Supplies kept flowing not because of Germanic clockwork precision but, as Groener had anticipated, because of creative muddling through. General Müller, chief of staff of the communications zone of the First Army, recalls:

> The hurry and stress of the first few months of the war were so great that I was unable to find time to issue written administrative orders. The whole doctrine of supply had been somewhat upset by the rapid advance and the service of supply could not, therefore, adhere closely to previously accepted principles. For this reason, it did no special harm when we were issued at Stettin, during the period of organization of the communications zone, all the various regulations dealing with the service of supply, etc., but without the changes and corrections to bring them up to date. These regulations were carried along, nailed up in a packing box; but, as far as I know, the box was never opened until the army withdrew behind the Aisne.[102]

Perhaps the most serious logistical threat to the German right wing lay in the potential destruction of the rail lines running through Liège, which constituted the only connection to the north Belgian rail net. A U.S. Army study later calculated that the destruction on that line of the Meuse River bridge, two tunnels, and a steep grade would have prevented the Germans from sending any trains across northern Belgium before 7 September. The battle of Mons would thus have taken place more than one hundred miles from the railhead. The Marne was about twice as far.[103] The demolition of the Liège line was prepared in advance and actually ordered by the Belgian commander, but the order was not carried out. Groener calls it mere "luck" that the "extremely important" tunnel east of Liège remained intact.[104]

Can the General Staff's attitude toward the logistics of the Schlieffen plan still be characterized as unbiased? Moltke's 1913 memorandum, as reconstructed by Ritter, seems unwarranted in its optimism. "The capture of a modern fortress by a coup de main would be something unprecedented in military history. But it can succeed and must be attempted, for the possession of Liège is the sine qua non of our advance. . . . Once our troops have entered the town I believe that the forts will not bombard it but will probably capitulate."[105] In fact, the German brigade that captured the town found itself completely cut off from the rest of the German force by the guns of the Belgian forts.[106]

The critical issue is in any case not so much the Germans' excessive optimism about an easy and early seizure of the fortress as their optimism about capturing the railroad intact. There is little evidence on how they aimed to do this, but they were probably counting on a combination of speed, surprise, Belgian irresolution, and poorly designed demolitions.[107] While it is difficult to second-guess a successful operation, it is also difficult to describe the Germans' acceptance of so great a risk as unbiased, since the lesser risks of alternative strategies were deemed prohibitive. As in Schlieffen's day, Moltke's General Staff confronted operational difficulties in a forthright manner only insofar as such problems did not directly challenge the essential features of the preferred strategy.

Planning for a Short War

Under the younger Moltke, the General Staff became increasingly concerned that a European war might last as long as two years. Neither military nor civilian officials, however, wanted to spend scarce resources to hedge against the chance of a long war. This decision does not necessarily indicate a failure to recognize that the war might drag on. Rather, it probably represents a conscious choice to spend resources on programs that would help Germany to win the war quickly. As in the case of logistics, Germany's strategists "understood their problem and sailed right into it."

Under the elder Moltke, the General Staff and the War Ministry had interested themselves in the implications of a naval blockade for the sufficiency of Germany's food supply in an extended conflict. The Trade and Agriculture ministries argued, however, that a full blockade was impossible and therefore that no special preparations were needed.[108] Economic analysis lapsed under Schlieffen, but the tenure of the younger Moltke brought a renewed emphasis on planning for a long war.

Like his uncle, Moltke was concerned that an initial victory might not suffice to end a war in which national passions were engaged. In 1905 he told the kaiser that the next war would be "a war between peoples which is not to be concluded with a single battle, but which will be a long, weary struggle with a country that will not acknowledge defeat until the whole strength of its people is broken; a war that even if we should be the victors will push our people, too, to the limits of exhaustion."[109] Moltke was concerned that German morale might not hold up under such conditions.

[153]

The army command has the greatest interest in the avoidance of an economic crisis on the home front so that the soldiers may be heartened that the well-being of their families at home is secured. Economic collapse and hunger during a war would greatly heighten mass nervousness and invite the most unreliable elements of the people to forcefully push their revolutionary aims. The morale of the troops, which is the most important and sensitive instrument of victory, would suffer heavy damage if unsteadiness would spread about at home.[110]

Reflecting these concerns, Moltke instigated studies and conferences on wartime food and raw materials requirements. Although they realistically anticipated an effective British blockade, Moltke still hoped that the Netherlands might constitute Germany's "windpipe" in a long war, and he reversed Schlieffen's decision to invade the Maastricht area in part for that very reason.[111]

Moltke's concerns about the possibility of a long war did not, however, result in significant material preparations.[112] Although the need for such preparations was understood, programs that would help Germany to win a short war rated higher priority. Even these high-priority projects were underfunded, in the view of the General Staff. Despite huge increases in the size of the army in the three years before the war, Erich Ludendorff, the chief architect of this expansion, was removed from the General Staff because he kept demanding further increases.[113] Similarly, Groener's logistical shopping list included five new Rhine bridges, seven new trunk lines in the west, and faster locomotives in order to cut the mobilization against France by three days. He was given one bridge and none of the rest. It is no surprise that attempts to hedge against the chance of a long war remained unfunded.[114]

This preference should not be blamed solely or even primarily on the military outlook. In discussions with the Interior Department on wartime food supplies, for example, Groener argued in favor of stockpiling enough grain to hedge against a two-year blockade; the civilians rejected the proposal on grounds of cost.[115] German economists, although they extensively discussed the possibility of a long war, likewise urged an offensive strategy that would shorten the war and wage it outside German territory.[116]

The German military's failure to prepare for an extended conflict of economic attrition has traditionally been explained as the result of a "short-war" illusion."[117] But there is an alternative explanation that better fits the clear evidence that the General Staff did consider the possibility of a long war. Given the financial limitations of Germany's central government under the Wilhelmine system and the preferences of nonmilitary elites, the General Staff consciously decided to give priority to those army increases needed to carry out a short-war strategy. Although the correctness of this decision can be challenged, it was at least in part grounded on rational calculation and not simply on illusions about the length of the coming war.

CONCLUSIONS

The German war plan implemented in August 1914 invited failure in several ways. It had the effect of increasing the forces arrayed against Germany in the west and of helping to provoke a British blockade. It also defied the realities of time and space, marching the ill-supplied troops of the German right wing to exhaustion while the French shifted to meet the threat by rail.

The German General Staff understood the risks of their plan but could imagine no acceptable alternative. Yet as the 1915 campaign showed, the Germans could have successfully defended their western frontier with a numerically inferior force, thereby freeing sufficient forces for a limited offensive in the east. Had this strategy been followed from the start, Britain might not have entered the war. Germany would have been in a good position to continue the war successfully or to negotiate its end on reasonable terms.

After about 1890 the General Staff abandoned consideration of such strategies of limited aims. A limited offensive could not produce a rapid, successful outcome by military means alone. Ending the conflict after a limited victory required diplomatic means as well. Schlieffen, the chief of the General Staff between 1891 and 1905, refused to rely on diplomatic efforts to end war, seeing diplomats as causing Germany's problems and only soldiers as capable of resolving them.

A quick end to the war was an absolute requirement in the eyes of Schlieffen and the General Staff. Because of their belief that war should be a frequent, beneficial, and normal tool of statecraft, they were loath to plan for the possibility of a long war, which would inevitably bring into question the role of war as a normal method for solving international political problems. Schlieffen and the General Staff consequently relied solely on military means to achieve the rapid, decisive victory that they considered indispensable.

In order to justify his choice of a highly risky strategy for total victory, Schlieffen unfairly denigrated the more limited alternatives, which were militarily and politically sounder than his own plan. This denigration, which involved logical inconsistencies and a double standard for evaluating strategic options, reflected a pervasive, systematic bias in the thinking of the General Staff, for which three factors account.

Operational thinking was skewed by the professional narrowness and the professional interests of the military planners. Narrowness led the General Staff to overrate the inevitability of war and underrate the role of diplomacy in solving international disputes. Interests gave them a special stake in the continuation of the Moltkean tradition of short, victorious, spectacularly beneficial wars, which resulted in the glorification of the military by German society.

Doctrinal tendencies based on these traditions were dogmatized as a result of the need for cognitive simplification and organizational standardization. This trend was facilitated by the difference in individual style between Schlieffen, a theoretician of narrow personal experience, and the elder Moltke, a pragmatist with a broader background.

Finally, the General Staff became intellectually and organizationally committed to Schlieffen's doctrine for a short, decisive war and to the war plan based on that doctrine. This commitment led to their bolstering the preferred strategy by unfairly denigrating the alternatives. However, the General Staff rarely bolstered the preferred strategy by playing down its own risks, doing so only when a possible setback would have ruined the whole plan (as in the risk that the Liège bridges would be destroyed). At least to this extent, "these men saw what they had to see if what they felt they had to do stood any chance to work."[118]

[6]

Russia: Bureaucratic Politics and Strategic Priorities

Russian war planners had incentives to attempt offensives on both the German and the Austrian fronts. Attacking German East Prussia would relieve German pressure on France in the opening weeks of the conflict, while attacking Austrian Galicia would be geographically easier and politically more appealing in light of Russia's imperialist aims in the Balkans. At the same time, offensives against both enemies entailed serious risks. A campaign in East Prussia would have to contend with geographical barriers and a dense German rail net, which would facilitate the defenders' maneuvers. A major campaign in Galicia, though operationally simpler, would draw forces away from the effort against Germany, on which the survival of France might depend.

By 1912 the Russian General Staff had become convinced that the Germans would initially deploy the vast majority of their forces against France, leaving only 16 to 25 divisions in East Prussia. (Actually, the Germans would leave only 13 active and reserve divisions there.) This conviction doubled the Russian incentive for an early offensive against Germany. First, the Russians worried that France might be defeated if she had to face the whole weight of the German army alone. Their fear was heightened by disrespect for the "undisciplined" army of the French Republic, compared to awe at Prussian military efficiency. With France prostrate, the Germans could then dispatch the Russians at their leisure. The Russians therefore had an incentive to attack Germany at the outset to draw forces away from the French front. Second, even if the French army fared well or if the struggle in the west dragged on inconclusively, Russia had an incentive to strike at Germany's vulnerable rear as a way of ending the war quickly and favorably.

Russian planners also saw incentives for attacking Austria. In strict-

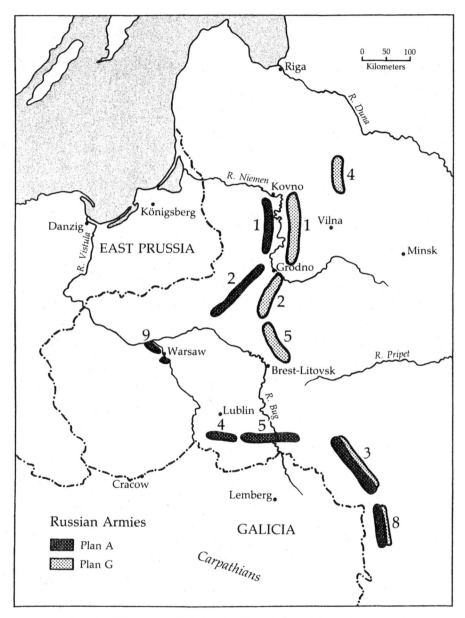

Map 5. Russian Plans A and G for the Prussian and Austrian campaigns.

ly operational terms the wide, flat plains of the Austro-Russian frontier area constituted ideal terrain for a Russian offensive and offered no natural barriers that the Russians could use to set up a strong defensive line. Thus the Russians, even if they were to defend against Austria and attack Germany, would have to leave a very large force facing Austria in order to protect the lines of communication of the offensive against Germany. The offensive against Austria also offered political advantages. Its proponents argued that the Austro-Hungarian Empire would disintegrate if its army suffered a major defeat in Galicia. Slav regions would spontaneously defect to the Russian victors, they argued, and a separate peace with Vienna might be possible. An early success against Austria would encourage Rumania and Italy to side with the Entente at the same time as it would protect Serbia from an Austrian invasion. Finally, it would contribute in the most direct manner possible to the achievement of Russia's imperial aims in the Balkans and the adjacent Turkish Straits.[1]

Yet the prudence of offensives of this kind was called into question. Limited numbers of Russian forces were available for an early offensive. Almost all military writers in France and Germany believed that a decisive battle on the western front would take place in the third or fourth week after mobilization. The French General Staff, particularly after 1911, pressed their Russian allies for an offensive by the fifteenth day of mobilization of sufficient size to attract two or more additional German corps to the eastern front. By this date, however, the Russians would have been able to concentrate only half of their forces on the German and Austrian fronts. Moreover, the supply echelons of these units would not have been ready for an advance by that date. Even by M+21 Russian superiority over the Germans and Austrians would have been slim. Only in the second month could a more comfortable superiority have been achieved.[2]

The geography of East Prussia, where the Russians correctly anticipated that Germany's forces would be deployed, posed further problems for Russian planners. In particular, the impassable Masurian Lakes region complicated the Russians' offensive task. If the Russians attacked only from the northeastern side of the lakes, they could at best push the Germans slowly westward, with no threat to the Germans' flanks or rear. A decisive outcome would be unlikely. However, if the Russians attacked around both sides of the lakes in order to cut off the Germans' escape route westward, they would be dividing their own forces into two vulnerable parts. The Germans might then capitalize on their rail mobility to defeat the Russians piecemeal. Even if they avoided this fate, Russian planners worried that an offensive into East Prussia would tie down a disproportionately large Russian force for several weeks. They feared that such an attack would do too little to help the French during the critical early period of the struggle in the west. As a result, they became interested in putting more direct pressure on Germany by an attack from the left bank of the Vistula toward Poznan, Thorn, and ultimately Berlin. The prerequisite for this attack, however, was that its flanks and rear be protected from attacks by either the Germans in East Prussia or the Austrians in western Galicia. In theory, they could be protected either offensively or defensively. The problem was that this protection would use up most of Russia's forces, especially those that could be deployed in the first few weeks of mobilization. This situation gave an incentive to clean out East Prussia offensively and then add the forces used in that operation to the subsequent invasion west of the Vistula.

In sum, the Russians' strategic aims and situation gave them incentives for offensives against both Germany and Austria. At the same time, the operational risks of an early offensive, particularly against Germany, were considerable.

THE OVERCOMMITTED OFFENSIVES OF 1914

The first operational directives of the Russian high command in August 1914 called for a three-pronged offensive against Germany and Austria-Hungary. The first prong was an invasion of East Prussia around both sides of the Masurian Lakes. This advance, pitting about 17 Russian divisions against 13 German divisions, was to begin during the third week of mobilization, that is, before the supply services of the attacking forces had been adequately organized. The second prong was a semicircular advance into Austrian Galicia from the north and east. By M+18 the Russians had collected 35 divisions for this operation against about 30 Austrian divisions.[3]

The final element of the plan was the buildup of an improvised army around Warsaw, which would carry the offensive into the heart of Germany after the other two offensives had secured its flanks and communications. This third axis of attack was added at the very last minute, because the actual circumstances of August 1914 were more favorable than Russian planners had anticipated. The German deployment in East Prussia was smaller than expected; considerable Austrian forces were tied down in the Balkans; and Italy, Rumania, and Sweden all stayed neutral. The Russians hoped to build up a force of ten or more divisions around Warsaw during the third and fourth weeks of mobilization. In part, this concentration entailed depleting the forces that had been planned for the invasion of East Prussia.

As it turned out, this three-pronged advance was a serious overcommitment of the limited forces that Russia could bring to bear during the early weeks of the campaign. The early offensives particularly overtaxed the Russians' limited logistical capabilities.

The German defenders in East Prussia concentrated first against that portion of the Russian force advancing from the northeast of the Masurian Lakes. Although the Germans enjoyed a numerical superiority in the engagement at Gumbinnen, they suffered heavy losses in an ill-advised frontal attack. The Russians, however, failed to pursue the retreating Germans, in part because they had outrun their supply lines. German forces were meanwhile shifted rapidly by rail to face the other Russian army, which was advancing from the southwest of the lakes. The smaller, less mobile, ill-supplied Russian force was encircled and annihilated at the battle of Tannenberg. This outcome should not have surprised the Russians, since the whole course of the campaign had been closely prefigured by German war games, about which Russian intelligence was well informed.[4]

The Russian offensive in Austrian Galicia also encountered serious difficulties. Because of last-minute changes in the Austrian deployment, the Austrians were concentrated much further west than the Russians had anticipated on the basis of purloined war plans. Consequently, the full brunt of the Austrian attack fell on the two Russian armies advancing southward from Poland. The two Russian armies advancing westward from the Ukraine were left temporarily out of the action, the lack of roads and chaotic supply arrangements hindering their advance. As a result, the forces intended for the Warsaw army had to be diverted to southern Poland to shore up weak spots in the Russian line. This diversion gave the Russians a considerable superiority on the Austrian front as a whole, and the Austrians were eventually driven back to a defensive line in the Carpathian Mountains. No knockout blow was delivered, however, in part because exhaustion and logistical limitations prevented rapid pursuit of the retreating Austrians.[5]

The Russian offensives, all in all, fell short of their planners' expectations. The Galicia operation was successful in gaining territory, but it failed to destroy the Austrian army or to cause the breakup of the Austro-Hungarian Empire. It also used up the forces allocated to the Warsaw army group for the third prong of the Russian offensive. The gravest costs were incurred in the East Prussia operation, however,

where the Germans captured 100,000 soldiers and 400 pieces of artillery.[6] The only offsetting benefit was that the Germans had transferred two corps to East Prussia from their forces in Belgium after the
minor Russian victory at Gumbinnen. These units were still in transit
when the major engagements were being fought both in the east and
in the west.

There is no indication that this trade-off of costs and benefits in East
Prussia represented a calculated risk on the part of the Russian high
command. Although proponents of a single attack on Galicia had
accurately identified the dangers of invading East Prussia, the General Staff acted as if those dangers were slight. The Russians were
hardly expecting to sacrifice 100,000 men as the price for putting
pressure on Germany on the eve of the battle of the Marne. Rather,
the Russians expected to pressure Germany with a series of rapid,
cumulative victories, not with defeats.

Had the Russians understood their problem better and recognized
the constraints imposed by their situation, they presumably would
have designed an offensive plan with fewer risks. Under the relatively favorable conditions of August 1914, the Russians could have
devised a more prudent plan that would have sacrificed only those
aims that were unachievable, not the real benefits of their offensive
plans. They could have abandoned the idea of a Warsaw army and
apportioned its forces to both the East Prussian and the Galician
fronts. They could have attacked East Prussia with a large force from
the northeastern side of the lakes and defended with a small force
along the Narew, southwest of the lakes. The chances of catching the
rail-mobile Germans in a foot-mobile Russian pincer were in any
event negligible. It would have been wiser to give up the illusory
hope of a brilliant victory in order to eliminate the risk of being beaten
piecemeal. Finally, they could have delayed the advance by two days
so that the Russian supply echelons could have been better organized. This minor change would have allowed for a more systematic
exploitation of results on both fronts, a prospect that would have put
greater real pressure on the Germans while increasing the chance of a
decisive outcome in Galicia.

It is worth noting that the Russians' inclination to do too much with
too little did not suddenly appear in August 1914, when the decision
was made to create a third axis of attack from Warsaw. Given the
Russians' anticipation of as many as 25 German divisions in East
Prussia, their two-pronged prewar plans were just as overcommitted.

Three factors are especially important in explaining the dangerously overcommitted Russian offensives of 1914. The first is the intramilitary struggle between those who wanted to give top priority to the German front and those who sought first priority for the Austrian front.

General Iurii N. Danilov, the quartermaster general and the principal operations planner within the General Staff, produced a plan in 1910 that would have deployed more than twice as many forces on the German front as on the Austrian front. He believed this deployment was necessary both to hedge against the possibility of a major German attack and to press the Germans if they left only a weak force in East Prussia. In order to achieve these aims, he was willing to conserve forces on the Austrian front.

Opposing Danilov was General Mikhail V. Alekseev, the influential chief of staff of the Warsaw military district and ex officio chief of staff of the Austrian front in the event of war. Alekseev argued that Danilov was overrating the danger of a German attack and that there was no good way to overcome the difficulties of invading East Prussia. Alekseev therefore urged a defensive campaign with few forces against Germany and a major offensive against Austria. In the absence of an overarching authority to establish a clear priority between the two fronts, the dispute was settled by a de facto compromise that allowed both offensives to take place, but with fewer forces for each. The compromise solution was thus more offensive and more overcommitted than the original preferences of either side.

Considering Danilov's high estimate of the number of German forces likely to be deployed in East Prussia, it is somewhat surprising that he viewed this compromise as feasible. Its terms allowed his offensive in East Prussia a numerical superiority of fewer than five divisions, leaving both arms of the Russian pincer vulnerable to piecemeal destruction. Why, then, did he accept an apparently risky compromise rather than simply capitulate to Alekseev's plan, which had attracted strong support among military district staffs? Alternatively, why did he not adopt a less risky maneuver in East Prussia, abandoning the division of the Russian force into two converging armies? Likewise, why did Danilov adopt a further overcommitment in August 1914, when the surprisingly favorable situation led him to improvise a third axis of attack?

Two factors help to explain Danilov's choices. The first involves biases introduced by the simplification of strategic analysis. For example, Danilov and the Russians generally tended to omit logistical considerations from their war games, maneuvers, and strategic planning. The practice was encouraged by the need to avoid embarrassing senior commanders whose staff skills were questionable. By underemphasizing logistical frictions, the Russians failed to appreciate one of the major barriers to successful offensive operations.

The second factor explaining Danilov's plans was his tendency to see the "necessary" as possible. Danilov's optimism about his East Prussia operation was driven by his larger pessimism about Russia's inability to stand alone against the bulk of Germany's strength. A skeptic about Russia's ability to withstand the rigors of competition with her more advanced neighbors, Danilov believed that Russia had to take maximum advantage of Germany's temporary weakness in the east at the beginning of the war. Russia's prospects would only get worse as the war continued, especially if the French suffered serious reverses. Working with this gloomy prognosis, Danilov had to count on quick, decisive victories in the initial stage of the war. Again to borrow Richard Neustadt's phrase, what Danilov saw as necessary, he also saw as possible.

[7]

Russia: The Politics and Psychology of Overcommitment

The story of Russian war planning from 1910 to 1914 can be told in terms of the intellectual and political battle between Generals Iurii N. Danilov and Mikhail V. Alekseev and the changing circumstances that determined which of the two enjoyed the upper hand. Danilov's defensive plan of 1910 reflected Russia's weakness after the Russo-Japanese War, uncertainty about German and French behavior in the event of war, as well as Danilov's personal pessimism about Russia's ability to compete with the awesomely efficient Germans. By 1912, however, the rationale for caution was mitigated by increasing Russian strength, the tightening of the Russo-French alliance, and the accumulation of intelligence indicating that Germany intended to strike France first should war occur. Alekseev, the chief of staff in the Warsaw Military District, used this opportunity to press forward his scheme for a major offensive against Austria. He won considerable support from key figures on many of Russia's military district staffs, who were attracted both by the operational soundness of the plan and by the imperial expansion that would follow upon its success.

Although the appealing offensive against Austria remained politically sacrosanct, the responsibility for implementing the new strategy had by 1913 passed back into the hands of Danilov and the General Staff. Danilov's pessimism now expressed itself in the form of tightened strategic cooperation with the French, who, he feared, might succumb to the initial onslaught and leave Russia without an ally in the unequal struggle against the Germans. As a result, Danilov concluded, a hasty attack into East Prussia was necessary to relieve the perhaps fatal pressure on France in the early weeks of the war. Russia had insufficient forces to mount offensives against both Austria and Germany, but Danilov was politically unable to forego the former and believed the latter to be a strategic necessity. Seeing the necessary as possible, he embarked upon the overcommitted offensives of August 1914. Russian war planning, then, is the story of two contrasting views of Russia's strategic goals and potential, played out against the backdrop of a shifting military balance, tightening alliances, and the decentralized anarchy of Russian intramilitary politics.

DANILOV'S DEFENSIVE PLAN OF 1910

The Russian war plan of 1910 was more defensive and more oriented toward Germany than any other Russian plan made between 1880 and 1914. General Danilov, the principal draftsman of the plan, allocated 53 divisions to the German front and 19 to the Austrian front. His deployments abandoned Warsaw, the forward fortresses, the Narew River barrier, and indeed most of Poland. Forces deployed against Germany and Austria were to advance after completing their concentration, if circumstances permitted. Rail and road improvements were, however, planned with strictly defensive operations in mind. The abandoned forward zones were to be stripped of all supplies.[1]

Danilov gave two reasons for concentrating forces far from the frontier and primarily against Germany. One was Russian military weakness after the Russo-Japanese War, including the continuing lag in the speed of Russian deployments, and the other, the possibility of a large-scale German attack against Russia and the uncertainty of adequate French support.

The Russo-Japanese War and its attendant political and economic difficulties had a ruinous effect on the Russian army. Matériel stocks were drawn down and not replaced because of Russia's financial crisis, which lasted almost until 1910. Official targets for the stockpiling of equipment and supplies would not even be approached until 1913 or 1914.[2] Between 1906 and 1908 as many as one-third of Russia's soldiers were used for internal security duties, which sapped morale and interfered with training.[3] Moreover, Russia's defeats in Manchuria had called into question the fitness of existing military doctrines, organizational forms, and commanders. The first few years after the war were spent debating the doctrinal and institutional implications of the defeat. Significant reform and reorganization were delayed until 1908 and 1910, when funding was increased and policy-making powers were concentrated in the hands of the war minister.[4]

Russian military figures warned at several times during this period that the army's devastated condition made the use of force dangerous against even Turkey, not to mention Austria or Germany.[5] Such was the state of disorganization even as late as 1909 and 1910 that it would have been "utterly impossible to make war," according to General A. A. Brusilov, who commanded the Russian Eighth Army. In Brusilov's high-priority corps in the Warsaw military district, supplies were barely sufficient even for peacetime requirements, and the transport service was in chaos.[6]

It was clear from these conditions that the plan for war against Germany and Austria would have to be changed. At the most elemental level, the railroads were no longer in a condition good enough to transport the troops on the schedule that had been devised before the Russo-Japanese War. The General Staff's first inclination was to salvage as much of the existing plan as possible. They produced a variety of schemes for pulling back most of the zones of concentration toward the interior of the country, but leaving an exposed deployment around Warsaw. This stop-gap measure won little support. A chief objection was that the Germans could attack Russian forward units before they had completed their concentration.[7] The General Staff began to consider alternatives almost immediately. Danilov's idea of abandoning the forward positions entirely, presented in general form in early 1908, won sufficiently broad acceptance to survive several personnel changes among Danilov's superiors and a major institutional change subordinating the General Staff to the War Ministry.[8]

Uncertainty about the choices of other powers was the second factor shaping Danilov's war plan. Especially important were the General Staff's pessimistic assumptions about the size of the force that the Germans would allocate to the Russian front. Although Danilov admitted that Germany would probably direct its main effort against France in the event of a two-front war, he nonetheless believed that Germany would leave a formidable force of 25 divisions in East Prussia. He expected this force to attack on the tenth day of mobilization in an attempt to disrupt the slower Russian concentration. As a result, he argued, the Russian zones of concentration should be withdrawn out of reach of a disruptive attack.[9]

This estimate of German strength, although more accurate than Danilov's earlier views, was still higher than what Germany actually planned for the eastern front, and it was adopted despite hard evidence of Germany's actual intentions. Danilov's 1910 memo explicitly states that the Russian General Staff had obtained information about a German war game in which a German army built around three or four active corps remained on the defensive in East Prussia. Using an advantageous combination of terrain, railroads, and fortifications, this army destroyed a superior Russian force. This game reflected not only Germany's prewar intentions but also the actual course of the 1914 campaign. Danilov nonetheless rejected it in favor of his own scenario. (It is unclear whether Danilov considered his hypothesis to be an estimate of the most likely German action or a worst case that no prudent planner could ignore.)

Danilov's case for withdrawing the zones of concentration toward the interior did not rely on the *attaque brusquée* hypothesis alone. Perhaps even more important was his desire to hedge against the possibility that Germany might deploy the majority of its forces against Russia, which he considered likely if the occasion for war were a Russo-Austrian dispute that did not directly affect French interests. Danilov's 1910 intelligence estimate portrayed the French as overly concerned with the peaceful pursuit of material well-being, influenced by antimilitarist concepts, and no longer interested in revanche. Judging by the lack of French support for Russia in the recent Bosnia Crisis, Danilov concluded that the possibility of French neutrality could not be ruled out.[10] The war minister, V. A. Sukhomlinov, expressed similar views in a December 1909 document outlining the rationale for his program of military reforms. Painting a bleak picture of the diplomatic situation, Sukhomlinov there contended that Russia had to depend primarily on its own forces.[11]

The third factor favoring a defensive war plan was Danilov's tendency to work from the worst-case assumption that Sweden, Rumania, Turkey, Japan, and China would all participate in a war against Russia.[12] Danilov's critics have argued that this long list of potential enemies was wildly unrealistic: "He left out only the Martians."[13] The Russian military attaché in Stockholm at the time would later claim that his opinion that Sweden would stay neutral in any European war won him enemies in St. Petersburg.[14] However, Danilov may have recognized that these were worst-case assumptions. Understood in this sense, none of his fears were particularly implausible. For example, the French ambassador to Stockholm believed in May 1909 that the Swedes had signed a military pact with Germany.[15]

Not all of Russia's strategists shared Danilov's worst-case pessimism. Alekseev offered a formula that purported to guarantee a safe concentration of the Russian army without automatically abandoning the area between Brest-Litovsk and Warsaw. Alekseev's December 1908 memorandum argued that, if Germany's main force went west, the Russians could safely deploy as far west as Malkin and Sedletz. Warsaw and the important crossings of the Vistula River would still remain in front of this zone of concentration, but they could be temporarily defended by their fortress garrisons. To make the Malkin-Sedletz deployments strong enough to resist a German *attaque brusquée*, Alekseev reassigned forces that other plans typically allocated to the Rumanian frontier or St. Petersburg. In making these adjustments, Alekseev explicitly rejected worst-case diplomatic assumptions: "The wish to secure all our borders spreads our forces too thinly and, moreover, completely disregards the work of diplomacy." The idea of fighting all conceivable enemies at the same time he rejected as simply "impossible."[16]

Alekseev considered it "doubtful" that Germany would send most of its forces to the east, but he admitted that the Russian plan had to hedge against this possibility. The force destined for the Malkin-Sedletz zone would simply detrain further to the rear, between Brest-Litovsk and Bielostok—that is, precisely where Danilov's westernmost army would deploy.[17]

Alekseev saw several reasons for defending the Polish salient. The Russian army, in Danilov's plan largely crowded into the region north of the Pripiat swamp and east of the Nieman River, would find it difficult to switch over to the offensive should Germany leave fairly weak forces in the east. The logical direction of a Russian attack from such a deployment was into East Prussia, but Alekseev believed that an invasion of East Prussia, with its myriad possibilities for stubborn defense, would be "fruitless."[18] In contrast, a force deployed in the Polish salient could turn south, toward the inviting plains of Galicia. Moreover, the more westerly deployment would help to protect Russian bridgeheads on the left bank of the Vistula, the only path that would offer "decisive results in the struggle against Germany." In addition, Alekseev argued, his planned deployment in Poland would answer the contingency in which Russia would be fighting "not with a coalition, but with Germany or Austria separately."[19]

Both Alekseev and Danilov considered a massive German attack unlikely, but both tried to hedge against the possibility. Neither seems to have relied much on French efforts, and at this stage neither cared much about relieving France's strategic burden. Although Alekseev's December 1908 memorandum warned against pessimistic diplomatic assumptions, a memorandum he wrote earlier in the year matched Danilov's bleakness. Alekseev despaired not only about opposition from Sweden, Rumania, Japan, and Turkey but also about the likelihood of wartime uprisings in the Russian provinces of Finland, the Caucasus, and Central Asia.[20] Thus at this point, the difference between Danilov and Alekseev lay not so much in their operational assumptions as in their propensities to take risks. Danilov was content to plan for the worst case, whereas Alekseev sought to plan simultaneously for the best and the worst.

This difference in attitude reflects a small, but consistent, difference between Danilov's and Alekseev's views on other issues: offense and defense in general, Russian imperialism, and Russia's ability to compete with the first-class powers. In each case, one finds Danilov to be the more pessimistic, primarily concerned with avoiding disaster until Russia could be modernized and strengthened.

Danilov's personality provides the key to this difference. All sources agree that he was exceedingly dour, having little taste for the dash and heroics normally associated with the officer's profession. He had dreamed as a youth of becoming a mining engineer, but his father forced him into the army. Indeed, his painstakingly technical approach to military duties recalls the engineer's style.[21]

On the general question of offense versus defense, Danilov appears to have been more defensively minded than Alekseev in both tactics and strategy. In 1913, for example, Danilov scathingly criticized the suicidal tactics of the *offensive à outrance,* which be said would lead to the French being slaughtered like "the Prussian Guards at St. Privat."[22] Alekseev, on the contrary, criticized Russian officers for their defensive habits, glorified offensive operations in his analyses of the Russo-Turkish War, and urged an ambitious envelopment strategy for the campaign in Galicia.[23] During the 1915 campaign, Danilov would advocate a somewhat more defensive strategy than Alekseev would.[24]

Perhaps more important was Danilov's sense of the limits of Russian power and the need to tailor Russian goals to those limits. He believed that Russia's reactionary political and social system fettered the development of the nation's potential. Danilov urged caution until the needed reforms could release Russia's latent power. "The very organization of the Russian army, hindered in part by the inertia of tradition, in part by financial considerations, and in part by the industrial weakness of Russia, was appropriate only for a passive defense within the borders of the state."[25] Danilov consistently opposed adventurous policies, both in areas where he thought Russia had no real interests, like the Far East, and in areas where he thought real interests were at stake, like Turkey. Russia's limited resources had to be husbanded for the main front.[26]

Alekseev, in contrast, heavily emphasized "the historical tasks of the Russian people" and laid somewhat lighter emphasis on Russian backwardness.[27] Despite his protestations about the need to conserve forces for the principal front, in 1907 he joined the chief of the General Staff, F. F. Palitsyn, in urging a forward deployment in Manchuria. This idea was opposed by both the War Ministry and the Foreign Ministry.[28] Similarly, in a 1908 memorandum, Alekseev suggested the construction of strategic rail lines not only on the Austro-German front but also in the Caucasus, Central Asia, and the Amur region in the Far East.[29]

Yet it was Danilov's cautious approach that gained official sanction as the basis for the actual war plan of 1910. The speculation about the reason that Danilov's view prevailed points to the confluence of several factors. During Palitsyn's tenure as chief of the General Staff, Russian war plans reflected a desire to avoid the choice between abandoning the Polish provinces and possibly disrupting the Russian army's concentration. Palitsyn was too much of an imperial nationalist to choose the former and too much of a pessimist to choose the latter. According to A. M. Zaionchkovskii, Palitsyn at different times tentatively approved the draft plans of both Danilov and Alekseev. In terms of the actual war plan, however, Palitsyn still clung to the idea of a weak force in the Polish salient, a concept that both Danilov and Alekseev had criticized as the worst of both worlds.[30]

Palitsyn was dismissed at the end of 1908 as part of a general reorganization of Russian military institutions. War planning was not an issue in this alteration, but the planning process was nonetheless greatly affected. The war minister, Sukhomlinov, sought to insure the subordination of the chief of the General Staff by choosing nonentities to fill the post and keeping the turnover rate high. Since Alekseev had left for a post at Kiev, Danilov remained the most senior and intellectually most able figure at the General Staff. Sukhomlinov himself played little if any part in operational planning.[31] Thus Danilov had if not a free hand, then at least an opportunity to push his ideas to the fore.

Danilov's defensive plan for a rearward concentration found favor from other sources. A large number of Russian units had traditionally been stationed in Poland during peacetime in order to compensate for the limitations of Russia's rail system. Upon mobilization, only the reservists needed to fill out these units required transportation from the interior; they would join their units at the zone of concentration. In this way was the transportation burden minimized. In 1910 this system was changed in favor of a territorial basing scheme. Henceforth, like the other European powers, Russia would station each active unit in the region from which it drew its reservists. This scheme was supposed to simplify mobilization and make it immune to enemy disruption.[32] Of course, the territorial system also meant that a large fraction of the active army had to be stationed in the interior and a smaller fraction in Poland. This "side-effect" was in fact a major incentive for adopting the new scheme. It permanently stationed the troops near the locus of civil disorders, a shift that had occurred anyway after 1905. Finally, it ensured that day-to-day expenditures on the troops would benefit all parts of the empire instead of accruing disproportionately to the Poles.[33]

Against these myriad benefits, the territorial system had one major disadvantage. Many more troops, with their horses and equipment, would have to be transported long distances to the front in the case of war on the empire's western border. Despite planned railroad improvements, this need could only retard the already slow process of transporting and concentrating the army. In fact, it took longer to complete the Russian concentration in 1912 than it had in 1900.[34] This fact worked in favor of Danilov's plan in two ways: first, concentrating closer to the interior would reduce transportation distances and time, and second, concentrating close to the frontier would entail increased vulnerability to enemy disruption. Ironically, one of the original architects of the army reform, of which the territorial basing system played a major part, was Alekseev. Sukhomlinov and Danilov simply carried out those ideas when the money became available.[35]

A final factor that probably facilitated the acceptance of Danilov's plan was the Bosnia Crisis of 1908–1909. The German ultimatum that ended this diplomatic debacle came as a cold slap of reality to those who had resisted the implications of Russian military weakness. The ambitious policies of the foreign minister, A. P. Izvolskii, yielded to P. A. Stolypin's demand for a breathing spell until Russia regathered her strength. While there is no evidence that this policy change directly affected strategic planning, it seems likely that the circumstances and trends of opinion that gave rise to the former may also have influenced the latter.[36]

ALEKSEEV'S OFFENSIVE PLAN OF 1912

Danilov's war plan attracted heavy criticism, especially from the commanders and staffs of the military districts. They were the people who had to fill in the operational details of the war plan for their respective zones of concentration. In wartime, they would become the commanders and staffs of the various armies.

Some critics questioned the need for the field armies to deploy so far to the rear. The staff of the Vilna district, for example, suggested changes in the deployment of the First and Fourth Armies that would allow an easier transition to offensive operations.[37]

The most violent objections related, however, to the Danilov-Sukhomlinov plan to abandon the fortresses in the forward part of the western theater, for example, around Warsaw. Danilov and Sukhomlinov had argued that resources devoted to modernizing and garrisoning these fortresses would be better spent on the field army. Their opponents included not only military district staffs but also Palitsyn, the Grand Duke Nikolai Nikolaevich (the commander-in-chief in 1914), and two briefly tenured chiefs of the central General Staff.[38] They generally wanted the forts to be modernized and garrisoned to protect areas of high political value, like Warsaw, and to facilitate a rapid transition to the offensive. Danilov argued, however, that such a demand would divert a prohibitively large amount of scarce resources from the field army. A political compromise, which apparently involved the tsar and Stolypin, devoted a whole field corps to the garrisoning of the Novogeorgievsk fortress at the confluence of the Vistula and the Narew near Warsaw. Novogeorgievsk should be defended "to the last bullet and the last crust of bread," but the other exposed fortresses were to be abandoned.[39] Thus even at the height of Russia's strategic retrenchment in 1909–1910, there remained considerable reluctance to admit the full implications of Russia's strategic weakness. The debate does not seem to have hinged on different estimates of the value of the clearly obsolete fortresses, the costs of improving and garrisoning them, or likely German plans. Danilov's factual analysis was based on the strong precedents provided by General Staff and War Ministry studies dating back to 1905.[40] Rather than a question of facts, the debate seems to have been a question of values and of propensity to take risks. Defenders of the forward fortresses were apparently willing to run significant risks to maintain those vulnerable positions. For example, General Skalon, the commander of the Warsaw military district, admitted that a defense of the Polish "triangle" had become virtually impossible, but at the same time he considered the abandonment of Warsaw to be politically unthinkable.[41]

An improvement in Russia's strategic circumstances made it possible by 1912 for the military district staffs to challenge Danilov's strategic pessimism in a more credible way. After a year of growing dissatisfaction with the 1910 plan, Sukhomlinov, Ia. G. Zhilinskii (the new chief of the General Staff), Danilov, and the chiefs of staff of the

[173]

military districts met in Moscow in February 1912 to discuss alternatives.[42]

Taking the initiative in these discussions was General Alekseev, still the Kiev chief of staff and the chief-of-staff-designate of the Austrian front. Alekseev argued that the prevailing political and strategic circumstances virtually ensured Germany's deploying most of her forces against France. But the Russian war plan of 1910 was poorly designed to capitalize on Germany's eastern weakness. It could only lead to an unproductive offensive into East Prussia, where a minor German detachment could immobilize a numerically superior Russian force. Instead, Alekseev urged a defensive screen of six corps facing East Prussia and an attack on Austria with the rest of Russia's forces. "Austria is undoubtedly our greatest enemy. In the quantity of deployed forces *she* will be the most dangerous enemy. Successes gained against Austria promise us the most valuable results." A committee of the military district quartermasters was given the task of working out a draft plan based on Alekseev's conceptions. Their plan shifted the Second Army into the Polish salient facing East Prussia and the Fourth and Fifth armies into the Polish salient facing Austria.[43]

Alekseev explicitly argued that the Russian army had improved sufficiently to carry out offensive operations.[44] This belief that great improvements had been achieved was widespread among the military. In April 1912 the deputy war minister, A. A. Polivanov, told the Duma that "the nightmare of unpreparedness" of the postwar period had been "left behind."[45] Even the cautious General Staff became less fearful that the Germans would use captured Russian rail lines to invade. In 1912 they began to relax their opposition to the construction of new lines in the frontier area.[46] The Russian military press adopted a tone of guarded optimism: though there were still many shortcomings, much had been accomplished.[47]

Nonetheless, it is far from universally agreed that the Russian army was ready for offensive operations or even for war of any kind. Russia gave France tepid support during the Agadir Crisis of 1911, because of the army's unpreparedness and the risk of provoking a revolutionary uprising. Both political and military officials repeatedly told the French and one another that Russia would not be ready for another two or three years.[48] Facing a real possibility of war during the Balkan Crisis of autumn 1912, the Russian military demanded and received an emergency appropriation to start redressing still critical shortages of matériel.[49]

The development of offensive plans was not necessarily precluded by these indications of temporary unpreparedness. Although the offensive war plan of 1912 went into effect almost immediately, it was probably influenced by the desire for a strategy that would correspond to the anticipated improvements of future years.[50] A General Staff directive of 1913, for example, said that district mobilization plans should be drawn up so as to remain valid for three or four years.[51]

Another factor encouraging Alekseev's bolder war plan was the Russian perception that France was becoming a stronger and more reliable ally. After the Agadir Crisis and the revival of French nationalism that it catalyzed, the fear that France might sit out a Russo-German war lost much of its credibility. At the same time, the Russians believed that the obvious boost in the morale of the French army would make it a more formidable opponent for Germany.[52] Based on information forwarded by the French in late 1911, the Russians also began to see active British participation on land and sea as more likely.[53]

These circumstances made it more difficult for the Germans to deplete their western frontier for a primary attack on Russia. They also implied that a German attack in the west would face considerable resistance. Even if the Russians did not have absolute confidence in their potential allies,[54] they could at least fall back on the idea that even a French defeat would leave the "victorious" German army crippled.

> Victorious or defeated, [the French army] will have inflicted on the German army such losses that the latter will no longer be capable of a second major effort on a distant front. Thus, the mass of Russian armies will find the path open before it. Even in defeat, the French army will have delivered Europe from German hegemony. The other peoples [of Europe] will be quick to size up the bad position in which the Austro-Germans will find themselves after their Pyrrhic victory.[55]

This idea was not new in 1912, but the greater reliability and strength of the French army began to make a German Pyrrhic victory look to the Russians like a worst rather than a best case. Under these circumstances, the need for a strictly defensive strategy became more difficult to argue.

As a consequence of these developments, Russian estimates of probable German deployments in East Prussia, not only by the military district staffs but by the central General Staff as well, became more optimistic. Everyone agreed that it was very improbable that

Germany would deploy most of her forces in the east. Moreover, serious consideration was for the first time given to the possibility that Germany might leave only three active corps and ten reserve divisions in East Prussia.[56] These somewhat more optimistic (and, as it proved, more accurate) estimates were not based on dramatic new intelligence about German war plans. Zaionchkovskii is probably wrong when he suggests that the greater optimism stemmed from the influence of French estimates. In fact, the Russians realized that the French had no firm documentary basis for their views.[57] The Russians based their optimism on inferences drawn from the changed strategic situation, not from clandestine intelligence.

Yet this Russian optimism was at best guarded. The General Staff, the staff of the Warsaw military district, and the ad hoc quarter-masters' committee formed at the February strategy meeting were all concerned about the possibility that Germany would launch an *attaque brusquée* with five to seven active corps (25 divisions, including reserve units). Starting as early as M+7, such an attack could seriously disrupt the Russian concentration if the Russians, anticipating an early offensive of their own, tried to detrain too near the frontier. Even after 1912 Russian plans always hedged against this danger. The quartermasters' committee also worried that the Austrians, who could mobilize faster than the Russians, might disrupt the concentration of the Russian forces deployed in southern Poland. The committee held that because of this danger, the Russian armies would have to start out on the defensive.[58] (French intelligence analysts argued that Russian calculations typically overrated this danger by overestimating the throughput capacity of the Austrian rail lines.)[59] In general, then, the constituency supporting Alekseev's call for a more offensive plan can hardly be charged with rampant overoptimism.

Finally, the political and operational advantages of attacking Austria rather than Germany favored Alekseev's plan. The quartermasters' committee accurately assessed the operational difficulties of a Russian invasion of East Prussia. It was particularly concerned that even a force of three active German corps would be able to tie down a much larger Russian force. If the German contingent were threatened with decisive defeat, it could simply evacuate East Prussia and retreat behind the fortress barrier along the Lower Vistula. From this position, it could effectively delay the use of the large Russian force bottled up in East Prussia for the later stages of the Russian offensive. Meanwhile, the Germans and Austrians could capitalize in other theaters on this waste of Russian assets. The quartermasters consequently urged a defensive posture with regard to East Prussia, even if the Germans deployed only three active corps in the province. They suggested stripping the Second Army of some of its forces and using them in the main offensive in Galicia.[60]

These concrete operational arguments were particularly persuasive for the district chiefs of staff and quartermasters who held the initiative in strategic planning at the time. Zaionchkovskii calls the 1912 "Austria" plan a "commanders' plan," because it gave the field commanders full scope in using their forces to achieve a decisive victory. Alekseev had complained that district staffs found earlier plans frustrating, because they did not give much guidance for planning the eventual transition to offensive operations. At the same time, the "Austria" plan took account of the practical limitations on what strategy could demand of the troops. No advance was to start before the armies and their rear services were fully concentrated.[61] Moreover, dangerous and fruitless offensives in disadvantageous terrain were avoided. The central General Staff should also have recognized these operational considerations, but it is perhaps natural that the future commanders and staffs of the field armies and corps should have placed greater weight on them.

Several political factors worked in favor of Alekseev's plan. The anticipated effect of a Russian victory in Galicia on the attitudes of Italy, Rumania, and the Slavic populations of Austria-Hungary has already been mentioned. More fundamentally, Russia's ambitions had always been directed primarily toward the Turkish Straits and the Balkans, and her hatreds toward Austria, which blocked her path. Although there were bilateral disagreements with Germany, the main source of Russo-German conflict was Germany's support of Austria. By 1914 this situation had changed somewhat. German penetration of Turkey, as revealed in the Liman von Sanders affair, became a threat to Russian objectives in its own right. But in 1912 such a trend was not widely foreseen. The military defeat of Austria was seen as the surest route to achieving Russia's traditional geopolitical aims.[62]

Grassroots opinion in the Russian officer corps particularly favored a militant policy toward Austria-Hungary. A Russian military newspaper was quite frank about at least one reason for this attitude: "The failures of the last war caused the army to embark on a program of intense, productive labor. The fruits of this labor provide the opportunity to show firmness and decisivensss in international relations. Every [diplomatic] offensive ought to delight the army, since this is the best indicator of its value, the best proof of our military might and the productiveness of the labors of these past years."[63] For most officers, such feelings were primarily aimed at Austria. As late as 1913 a French exchange officer could report that his Russian colleagues did "not seem to have developed any hatred with regard to Germany."[64]

These differential feelings were not limited to military officers. For the conservative bourgeoisie, Germany was not only feared but also respected and admired as a model of efficient, technologically progressive authoritarianism.[65] Both perceived economic interests and pan-Slav ideology led the bourgeoisie to focus its ambitions and hatreds primarily on Austria, the Balkans, and the Straits. When war finally broke out, the bourgeois press was virtually unanimous in demanding that the main effort be directed against Austria.[66] Rightist reactionaries frequently went even further in their pro-German sympathies, seeing Russian dependency on Germany as preferable to the thoroughgoing modernization of Russian society that an effective strategy of competition with Germany would require.[67]

As a consequence of these notions, Russian strategists had occasionally flirted with the idea that the Austrian theater could somehow be decoupled from the general European conflict. In the 1880s and 1890s political traditionalists had wanted a diplomatic deal that would give Russia a free hand in the Balkans and Germany a free hand against France.[68] The theme of localizing conflict in southeast Europe also appears in several of Sukhomlinov's remarks from 1909 to 1913. Sukhomlinov hoped that the combination of Austrian weakness and growing Russo-French power would force Germany to abandon her ally. In a burst of optimism after the First Balkan War, he told the French attaché that he anticipated "the disorganization of Austria-Hungary when [Emperor] Franz Joseph dies, not just in the limited sense of a separation of Austria and Hungary but a complete dismemberment, with the German territories going to Germany and the Slav peoples uniting with already existing states of the same ethnicity."[69] Alekseev and his protégé V. E. Borisov had similar inclinations. At least between 1908 and 1910 they were arguing that the Russian war plan should allow for a single-front war against Austria alone.[70] Perhaps more realistic was Alekseev's later idea that Austria might quickly accept a separate peace after a Russian victory in Galicia. Considered alongside the theory of a German Pyrrhic victory in France, this idea amounts to a formula for a localized Austro-Russian conflict. It is noteworthy that Alekseev continued to advocate tailoring Russian strategy to fit the goal of a separate peace even when it became operationally disadvantageous. In the first winter of the war, Alekseev used the separate peace argument to get fresh troops for futile attacks on Austrian positions in the snow-covered Carpathian Mountains.[71] The incident suggests that political conceptions (and

misconceptions) may have been even more important than operational incentives in leading the Russian military in 1912 to choose the
Austrian front for its principal offensive.

THE RESPONSE TO ALEKSEEV'S PLAN

Between March and May 1912 the General Staff and the military
districts transformed the draft proposals into an actual war plan,
officially sanctioned by the tsar. As the district quartermasters had
recommended,[72] the plan contained two versions: Plan A, which directed the principal offensive against Austria, and Plan G, which was
based roughly on Danilov's 1910 plan for a defensive against Germany. Plan A would go into effect automatically, unless the Russian
commander-in-chief decided that the German force deployed against
Russia was so large that Plan A could not succeed.[73] The number of
German units that would trigger Plan G was not specified in advance.
One Warsaw military district document, probably authored by General N. A. Kliuev, indicated that six or seven German active corps in
East Prussia might be a sufficient threat.[74] It is more likely, however,
that Plan A was intended to apply only if the Germans had significantly more than 25 active and reserve divisions in the east, a contingency that everyone considered quite remote.[75] Even Plan A,
therefore, had to provide a hedge against a German attack of moderate size.

Plan A, as officially adopted in May 1912 and refined during the
remainder of the year, differed in important respects from Alekseev's
original conception. Alekseev had hoped to leave only twelve divisions in a defensive stance on the front facing East Prussia; the plan
actually adopted in May allocated over 29 divisions to this front.[76] On
the Austrian front, Plan A's later versions transferred three divisions
from the Fourth Army, facing the Austrians' left from the Polish
salient, to the Third Army, facing the Austrians' right from the
Ukraine. Accompanying this change was a change in operational
strategy that deemphasized Alekseev's aim of enveloping the Austrians' left flank.[77]

These revisions primarily resulted from opposition to Alekseev's
views by Danilov and Kliuev, the chief of staff of the Warsaw district.
Kliuev, chief-of-staff-designate of the East Prussian front, was more
concerned than Alekseev about the danger of a disruptive German
attack. He was willing to transfer some of his forces to Alekseev's
Austrian front only if the Germans left just three active corps in East

Prussia. In his view, the decision to make this transfer would have to await positive confirmation of the Germans' actual deployment. Any other plan that weakened the Russian forces facing East Prussia would entail too great a risk.[78]

The General Staff, under the guidance of Danilov, also continued to be concerned about a disruptive German attack. Danilov was, of course, not completely insensitive to improvements in Russia's strategic position. Even before the February meeting with the district staffs, he had instigated a change in the 1910 plan that would have detrained the First and Fourth armies closer to the German frontier in order to facilitate an eventual offensive.[79] Still, his alteration was cautious in comparison to Alekseev's scheme. Colonel Stogov, one of Danilov's deputies, warned Alekseev that the Austrians would be able to disrupt the concentration of the Fifth Army if it were deployed as far forward as Lublin. If this Austrian attack were coordinated with a German thrust into the Polish salient, Russian forces in Poland might be cut off and encircled. Stogov consequently urged deploying around Brest-Litovsk—that is, precisely where the Fifth Army was to concentrate according to the 1910 plan.[80]

Similarly, Stogov believed that Alekseev's plan to envelop the Austrians' left flank was still too risky, even in its attenuated form. The forces carrying out this flank attack would have to be concentrated quite far to the west, around Ivangorod. Even if the Russian concentration there were not disrupted by an *attaque brusquée,* there was still the danger that German reinforcements from France might arrive while the Russian flank maneuver was still in progress. "Once there is no hope of the French holding the Germans for 3 or 4 months, then we must, thinking only of ourselves, act cautiously and collect against Austria in the Kiev district 3 armies on 3 railroad lines, strengthen the Odessa army and Brest-Litovsk and attack the Austrians only from the Kiev military district by the left flank along the Carpathians."[81] The transfer of three divisions from the Fourth to the Third Army was probably influenced by this outlook.[82] Thus Danilov and the General Staff were only slightly less cautious in 1912 than in 1909–1910, when their caution had greater justification.

One additional factor working against Alekseev's plan was Russia's commitment to her French ally. In meetings between the chiefs of the French and Russian general staffs, the French repeatedly pressed for an early Russian offensive against Germany. They thought the Russians should attack with forces sufficient to require the Germans to deploy at least five or six active corps in the east. For this attack to affect the outcome on the western front, the French argued, the Russians should begin it at the end of the second week of mobilization. Successes against Austria would have little effect on the outcome on the western front.

The cautious Danilov had always resisted French pressure for a guarantee that the Russian attack would begin before sufficient forces, including their supply services, were completely concentrated. In April 1911, for example, he informed the French that an attack against 25 German divisions could begin only on M+23.[83] Danilov's February 1912 changes in the deployment of the First and Fourth armies may have been designed to help achieve this relatively modest aim.

However, Danilov did not attend the annual meetings between the chiefs of staff, perhaps because of his inadequate knowledge of French. Thus the Russian side of the talks was managed entirely by the chief of the General Staff. During the critical period between 1911 and 1914, this post was occupied by General Zhilinskii. More a politician than a soldier, Zhilinskii had served as a military attaché and as a staff aide to the admiral who was the figurehead commander in the Russo-Japanese War.[84] As chief of the General Staff, Zhilinskii involved himself very little in the details of war planning, leaving them to Danilov.[85] Thus Zhilinskii was disposed neither by his background nor by his everyday duties to pay attention to the dire operational implications of the French demands.

Whereas Danilov's inclination (at this time, at least) was to accommodate the French only insofar as he could reconcile their requests with operational prudence, Zhilinskii simply told the French what they wanted to hear. At the 1911 meeting, although he told the French that the reform of the Russian army was far from complete, he nonetheless agreed that the Russians would try to attack in force on M+15. The protocols of this meeting were given legal force by the signature of Sukhomlinov and the approval of the tsar.[86]

As a way of excusing the disaster at Tannenberg, Russian and Soviet historians have frequently contended that this promise was extorted in exchange for French loans to improve Russian strategic railways.[87] Danilov, too, suggests in a vague way that Russian war planners were unable to ignore French financial pressure.[88] But this factor was not decisive in shaping either specific decisions or general policy. The Russians, for example, gave first priority to the rail lines serving the Austrian front. Only occasionally did they follow French suggestions, and even then no evidence suggests that their choices resulted from coercion.[89] More fundamentally, the thesis of French pressure fails to recognize that the dependence of France and Russia was mutual. The French could not afford to withhold the financing for Russian strategic railways even if Russia's strategy was not exactly to their liking. French diplomatic cables show that the French, at least, were acutely aware of the weakness of their bargaining position with the Russians.[90] Finally, the thesis does not explain why the Russians chose to honor an allegedly extorted promise. It is possible that in 1911 Zhilinskii had no intention of honoring his promise on M+15, or at least that he did not care whether Danilov and the operational planners took the promise seriously. Moreover, the promise would be irrelevant if the Germans attacked first. Three years later the Russians *did* honor their promise to the French, but only after improvements in Russia's position made the duty less onerous. Indeed, in 1914 Russia overfulfilled its promise to come to France's aid. The Russians can hardly have felt that Zhilinskii's undertaking obliged them both to attack East Prussia and to improvise a new strike force on the left bank of the Vistula. Only Russia's own interest in saving France can explain this decision.[91]

Let us return to the context of Russian war planning in 1912. Zhilinskii's promises obviously conflicted with Alekseev's original scheme, which would have left only a light defensive screen on the German front. Danilov's plan, as amended in February 1912, fitted this obligation much better, despite its defensive aspects. It is clear that Zhilinskii opposed the intrusion of the military districts into the process of strategic planning.[92] Alekseev's disregard of Zhilinskii's apparent commitment to an offensive against Germany may have helped to determine Zhilinskii's view in this regard.[93]

In sum, Plan A of 1912 may be seen as a compromise among three competing sets of strategic concerns, each promoted by important and partially independent elements within the military: first, Alekseev's concern for operational logic, widely shared among the military district staffs, and for Russian imperial goals in southeastern Europe, shared by most military and civilian circles; second, Danilov's and Kliuev's concern for the security of Russian deployments and operations, reflecting the views of the central General Staff and the Warsaw military district; and third, Zhilinskii's apparent concern about supporting France in the early days of the war, apparently shared by the tsar and Sukhomlinov and, more cautiously, by Danilov and the General Staff apparatus.

The aim of relieving German pressure on France played the smallest role in determining the actual deployments envisioned in Plan A of 1912. The zones of concentration of the First and Second armies were chosen to maximize security, not to facilitate an early offensive.

In 1913 and 1914, however, the goal of an early offensive would be given a higher priority.

THE HASTY ATTACK STRATEGY, 1913–1914

In 1913 the Russian war plan was changed to fit more closely with an early offensive. This alteration involved deleting late-arriving units from the complement of the armies that would fight the opening battles on the western front. Thus the first-line armies would be smaller, but ready to attack sooner. Railroad improvements also reduced by a day or two the time needed to concentrate the army. For the first time, the First Army was instructed to hold the Nieman River barrier against the expected German *attaque brusquée* at all costs, and objectives were specified for the offensives of the First and Second armies into East Prussia. According to the new plan, the second-line armies would form a strategic reserve to be used at the commander's discretion. Although these changes, labeled "Plan 20," were technically not supposed to go into effect until the fall of 1914, they were reflected in the actual concentration of August 1914.[94]

These changes occurred as the central General Staff reasserted their prerogatives as the primary war planning body. In January 1913 Zhilinskii wrote a memorandum to Sukhomlinov complaining of the disorganization and inconsistencies in strategic planning that had been caused by the erosion of the General Staff's authority. Sukhom-

Figure 4. Russia: Trading off speed versus size of concentration[a]

	Full infantry divisions 1912/1913	Completion of concentration, including logistical services (in days), 1912/1913
1st Army	15/15	36/26
2d Army	14/11	40/33
East Prussian front	29/26	
4th Army	11/10	38/26
5th Army	13/11	32/24
3d Army	21/11	36/23
8th Army	−/ 9	23/17
Galician front	45/41	

a. A. M. Zaionchkovskii, *Podgotovka Rossii k imperialisticheskoi voine* (Moscow: Gosvoenizdat, 1926), pp. 258ff, 302, 314ff. The Eighth Army was formed primarily from Third Army units. These units form the basis for the figures given for the "Eighth Army's" 1912 concentration.

linov agreed that the role of the military districts in laying down strategic policy should be strictly advisory, and primary responsibility should remain in the hands of the General Staff.[95] Thereafter, although the district commanders and staffs continued to play an important and partially independent role in making policy, there was at least no recurrence of the committee approach to strategic planning.

Several factors contributed to the General Staff's improved position over the districts. First, after 1912 the General Staff pursued their Germany-oriented strategy in a way that did not provoke the advocates of a major offensive against Austria. Of course, the 1913 decision favoring a smaller but earlier offensive primarily helped the French, not a high priority for Alekseev and other advocates of an Austria-oriented strategy. Nonetheless, the 1913 scheme left unchanged the proportion of forces allocated to the German and Austrian fronts. Thus was the chance of provoking significant opposition to the changes minimized.

Second, after 1912 the General Staff's strategy became less vulnerable to the allegation that it was too cautious. The plan changes of 1913 provided military district figures who believed that increased Russian strength should allow a more offensive strategy with an alternative to Alekseev's Austria-only strategy.

Third, Kliuev and perhaps other district figures found the case for early pressure on Germany to be convincing. Rethinking his earlier flirtation with the idea of shifting forces from his own East Prussian front to Alekseev's Galician front, Kliuev came to believe that Russia had to strike Germany in the early days of the war "to prevent Germany from finishing with France or so weakening her as to have the possibility of quickly turning a part of its corps against us. The depth of a possible French retreat is limited, and a prolonged retreat would demoralize their army."[96]

Fourth, a centralized bureaucracy has a natural advantage over regional staffs dispersed throughout an empire. In 1912 the military districts had a strong, unifying grievance to galvanize their common action. After 1913 these conditions no longer prevailed, and the initiative in planning tended to slip automatically back to the center.

Reasons for the General Staff's Change in Strategy

Perhaps more surprising than the reassertion of the power of the General Staff is the apparent change in the General Staff's strategic thinking. Before 1912 they advocated defensive deployments far from the frontiers; after 1912 they switched to advocating a hasty attack with diminished forces. Three hypotheses might account for this transformation.

The first is that the improvement in the Russian army was overestimated, causing a sudden surge of unwarranted optimism within the General Staff. On the one hand, it is true that Danilov's memoirs express considerable perplexity at the poor performance of the Russian forces invading East Prussia in August 1914. In particular, he claims to have been surprised by the extent of the disorganization of the supply service caused by the hasty advance. Similarly, General A. S. Lukomskii, who was responsible for rail transport planning, felt that preparations for mobilization were so well organized after 1912 that there was little left for him to do. He consequently applied for a command in the field, where he felt the real work of the coming war was to be done.[97] On the other hand, undercurrents of pessimism continued to influence Russian military thinking. During the Balkan Crisis of the autumn of 1912, the General Staff consistently advocated a nonprovocative policy, despite French prodding to countermobilize against the Austrians.[98] The conclusions of a December 1912 meeting of top military figures suggest the reason for this caution: Russian war stocks were still dangerously low. Until an emergency appropriation could build up these supplies, all steps had to be taken to delay the conflict. Although the supply situation improved considerably during 1913 and 1914, Danilov still exercised a cautionary influence on Russian policy. He argued against an adventure in the direction of Constantinople, since the adequacy of Russian forces in the main theater of war was in doubt.[99] During the July 1914 crisis deliberations, he claims to have emphasized Russian shortcomings and the risks of war.[100] Sukhomlinov likewise told a Foreign Ministry official on 23 July 1914 that Russian efforts to offset the German military program of 1913 would not be completed until 1917, especially in the area of artillery. "In these conditions, even with the support of France we would find ourselves until 1917, and perhaps even until 1918, in a position of indisputable inferiority with respect to the combined forces of Germany and Austria. Consequently, we should do everything in our power to avoid war." General Sergei Dobrorol'skii, the head of the mobilization section during August 1914, later claimed that this statement accurately reflected the views of the General Staff on the eve of the war.[101]

Such pessimism was also reflected in Russian war planning and intelligence estimates during 1913 and 1914. For example, the General Staff remained preoccupied with the danger of a preemptive attack that would disrupt the Russian concentration. One scenario envisioned an attack by four German infantry divisions as early as M+5.[102] Colonel Monkevitz, head of the General Staff's intelligence section and reportedly Danilov's "right hand," thought that an enemy *attaque brusquée* might develop into a successful Austro-German pincer attack on Brest-Litovsk between M+15 and M+20.[103] To hedge against this possibility, the 1913 draft plan shifted the center of gravity of the Russian deployments slightly to the rear. Whereas the 1912 plan had deployed 38 full divisions in the forward armies (the Second, Fourth, and Fifth) and 36 in the rearward armies, the 1913 ratio was 32 to 35.[104]

The General Staff's intelligence estimates also remained pessimistic in other respects. Even as late as the spring of 1914, the official Russian estimate of likely German strength in East Prussia continued at 16 to 25 divisions, figures that the French considered "exaggerated or alarmist."[105] Political estimates also continued to be moderately pessimistic. Sweden was still considered a possible enemy, although Rumania, it was now admitted, would probably be neutral at the outset. Most important, the General Staff were still not entirely confident of unconditional French support. "If, at the time of the collision between Germany and Austria-Hungary and us, this touches directly on French interests, then its participation in the struggle as our ally is assured; under other circumstances it is possible that France will assume a waiting position, which still will deflect from us part of Germany's attention. . . ."[106] Although the French were quite forthcoming in the 1912 Balkan Crisis, more recent socialist electoral advances and the challenge to the three-year law put the French commitment in a new light.

In sum, the General Staff's adoption of the hasty attack strategy in 1912 cannot be explained by an across-the-board tendency toward overoptimism. Although they may have underestimated the drawbacks of the East Prussia operation itself, they were quite pessimistic on most other questions.

A second hypothesis is that higher political authorities forced this hasty attack strategy on a reluctant General Staff. This line of speculation is, however, not very promising. All the participants have testified that nobody higher than Danilov played any significant role in operational planning. While the tsar, Sukhomlinov, and Zhilinskii all participated in making or approving promises to the French of an early offensive, there is no indication that they tied Danilov to any particular scheme or timetable. In fact, it is likely that the promises were primarily part of a public relations campaign aimed at convincing the French that Russia was a reliable and capable ally. Joseph Joffre's memoirs, for example, complain bitterly about misinformation provided by Sukhomlinov as to the state of Russian preparedness.[107] Moreover, the tsar, Sukhomlinov, and Zhilinskii were all reactionaries who felt an ingrained distaste for the French republic. They would hardly have felt bound to implement vague promises over the objections of Russian operations planners.

Danilov's attitude in August 1914 suggests that he was even more eager than Zhilinskii to press the attack as soon as possible. By that time, Zhilinskii had become the commander of the East Prussian front. From that vantage point, he suddenly discovered that it would be wise to delay the First Army's advance into East Prussia until M+20. In contrast, Danilov, at the Supreme Headquarters, pressed him for an earlier date. Danilov's memoirs make it clear that this order was not simply the wish of the Francophile commander-in-chief, Nikolai Nikolaevich, but that Danilov personally agreed with it (and perhaps was even primarily responsible for it).[108] Thus the explanation for Danilov's hasty attack strategy must reconcile it with the continuing strain of pessimism in his strategic outlook.

The third hypothesis attempts this reconciliation, holding that Danilov's support for a hasty attack into East Prussia was simply a new form of his longstanding pessimism about Russia's ability to compete with Germany. Before 1912 his pessimism expressed itself in a strategy of retrenchment: Russian military strategy, like Stolypin's political strategy, should avoid provocations and entanglements and prepare to concede losses at the margins. Russia conciliated Germany to buy time, as in the Potsdam diplomacy of 1910, and minimized the dangers of close ties with France, as in the tepid Russian policy during the Agadir Crisis. She also husbanded her limited military resources to deal with the principal threat to national security, from Germany, rather than squander those resources in expansionary schemes in the Far East, the Near East, or the Balkans.

After 1912 Danilov expressed his pessimism in mutual dependence with the French. Several interrelated changes in circumstances required this change in Danilov's strategy. One key development was the heightening of interbloc tensions. The Austrian confrontations with Serbia in 1912–13 and the simultaneous German arms buildup made it appear that Russian conciliatory diplomacy would be hard pressed to prevent war without making unacceptable concessions. (The July 1914 policy of the Austrians and Germans proved that this was in fact the case.) At the same time, growing Russo-French strength made it more difficult to rationalize appeasement: Russian military and economic strength had increased, and the French nationalist revival after Agadir had made France a worthier ally. Even if Danilov still personally preferred retrenchment, the attitude of the civilian press, the intelligentsia, and the military districts made retrenchment a dead option. As the foreign minister, Sergei Sazonov, remarked in 1914: "To feel at one's strongest and yet to go on giving way to an opponent whose superiority consists solely in his organization and discipline is not only a humiliating business but is dangerous because of the demoralization it brings in its train."[109]

Under the new circumstances, the best choice for a pessimist was the tightest possible alliance with France. If Russia could not appease the invincible Germans, she had at least to avoid fighting them alone. Thus Danilov urged Russian diplomats to strengthen the Triple Entente, making it a formal alliance. His assistants on the General Staff concurrently hinted to the French military attaché that the French should *not* hope for a localization of an Austro-Russian conflict in the Balkans. If Germany and France temporized, the bulk of Russia's forces would deploy against Austria. If Germany and France entered the war after that point, the Russians would not be able to carry out their pledge to press Germany in East Prussia. Instead, Russia and France should attack jointly at the outset of war.[110] This General Staff view directly opposed the views of Alekseev and Borisov, who, as we have seen, hoped for a localized Austro-Russian duel. The General Staff apparently cared more about avoiding the worst case—Austria and Germany against Russia alone—even if it meant entirely foresaking the best case—Russia against Austria alone.

If the Russian General Staff worried that France would leave them isolated to fight both Austria and Germany, they also worried that a rapid French defeat would have the same effect. Here is the crux of Danilov's hasty attack strategy and perhaps also the crucial difference between the Austria-oriented optimists and the Germany-oriented pessimists. Danilov, Stogov, and, to an extent, Kliuev suspected that the demise of France would bring about the demise of Russia. Thus it would be better to take some risks in order to help France at the outset than to face Germany alone in the second phase of the war. In contrast, optimists thought that Russia would be sufficiently strong to maintain a Russo-German condominium in Europe after the hypothesized defeats of Austria and France. In this sense, the hasty attack strategy was a pessimistic, security-driven strategy, whereas the Austria-oriented strategy was optimistic and driven by an interest in expansion.

Evaluating the East Prussia Operation

In adopting the hasty attack into East Prussia, Russian operations planners paid insufficient attention to two drawbacks. First, it was unlikely that the Russian invading forces would be able to achieve numerical superiority at the point of the engagement. Second, logistical shortcomings would have a debilitating effect on the vigor and mobility of the troops.

Neither difficulty was unforeseeable. The deputy war minister, General Polivanov, later told the commission studying the Tannenberg disaster that the Russians had obtained German war games prefiguring in every detail the actual course of the 1914 campaign.

> The very idea of the operation . . . did not sufficiently take into account the views on the defense of East Prussia that prevailed in the German General Staff. These views were known to us, because we obtained a report on an enemy war game of 1905 [as well as games of later years]. The report draws a conclusion that should have caught the attention of the planners and commanders of the ill-fated operation. Here is that conclusion: 'Almost everyone who has commanded the Russian side up to the present time has attacked with the Nieman army between Insterburg and Angerburg and with the Narew army around the Masurian Lakes from the south and then in a northerly or northwesterly direction, happily confident that the Germans, concentrated behind the Masurian Lakes or the Alle River, would be annihilated by this concentric attack. But their plan always miscarried: the Germans, not waiting for the pincer to close, retreated [toward the west] and used the opportunity presented to them to attack the left flank of the Narew army at its most vulnerable point.' Likewise, I cannot say how surprising it is that our staffs did not take into account the huge throughput capacity of the East Prussian railroads, which allowed the German corps to maneuver rapidly over long distances—facts that we were all apprised of in peacetime.[111]

In a general sense, Russian planners were aware of some of these difficulties and the opportunities they created for a successful German defense. The General Staff, Kliuev, and Zhilinskii all knew about the war games to which Polivanov refers.[112] Kliuev, in particular, seems to have devoted considerable attention to the problems of attacking East Prussia, but the conclusions he drew were rather arbitrary. He proposed that the danger of a German attack on the exposed left flank of the Narew army could be neutralized by an "energetic" attack by the Nieman army toward Allenstein, passing north of the lakes.[113] (This attempt at assistance would indeed have to be "energetically" carried out, since the marching distance from the Nieman to Allenstein was more than 250 kilometers, most of it through enemy territory.) However, Kliuev was more concerned about a passive German defense along the Lower Vistula than about an active defense using the lakes as a foil to the Russian pincer. Kliuev believed that three German corps on the Vistula could tie down nine Russian corps for a long time—"a situation that would be extremely unfavorable for us. For this reason, . . . it is necessary to assign to the East Prussian operations the First [Nieman] Army and not more than two corps of the Second [Narew] Army, the remaining three corps of the Second Army being transferred to the Austrian front."[114] Focusing on the Lower Vistula barrier, Kliuev failed to appreciate that if a large attacking force might be delayed by a stubborn defense, a smaller force might simply be destroyed.

The General Staff appear to have been equally casual in estimating how many troops to devote to the East Prussian operation. On completing their concentration, the First and Second armies would, according to the 1913 draft plan, contain the equivalent of 27 infantry divisions. This force would be nominally superior to the 16 to 25 German divisions that the General Staff expected to find in East Prussia.[115] However, this nominal superiority could for several reasons not be brought to bear on the battlefield. A war game of April 1914 shows that even before August 1914 the Russians intended to begin the East Prussia offensive long before these 27 divisions were fully concentrated. In that game, Zhilinskii ordered the First Army to attack a possibly superior German force on M+12.[116] In a hasty attack of this kind, the lack of rear services would further exacerbate the numerical inadequacy of the Russian forces. Most important, the separation of the First and Second armies by the Masurian Lakes would allow the rail-mobile Germans to achieve numerical superiority first on one front, then on the other. In this way, even 16 or fewer German divisions could achieve superiority at the time and place of battle.

One reason that the Russian General Staff overlooked these difficulties was their expectation that the German forces would launch a preemptive attack. Both the April war game, designed by Danilov, and a 1914 Danilov operational memorandum employ this assumption.[117] In this scenario, the Russians' hasty attack was in fact a counterattack, carried out near Russian railheads, fortresses, river barriers, supply depots, and reinforcements. From the standpoint of logistics and mobility, such an assumption was of course very favorable. By emphasizing an unsubstantiated German *attaque brusquée*, Danilov avoided considering the less favorable scenario in which the Germans allowed the Russians to make the first move.[118]

Pervasive inattention to logistical factors also helps to explain the Russians' failure to understand the dangers of a hasty attack into East Prussia. In an abstract, intellectual sense, the Russians seem to have understood logistical problems fairly well. Russian literature on logistics accurately assessed the logistical lessons of recent wars and appropriately emphasized the sometimes crucial influence of supply problems on the outcome of a military campaign.[119] One of the principal contributors to this literature was General N. N. Ianushkevich, a professor of military administration at the General Staff academy before he replaced Zhilinskii as chief of the General Staff in 1914.[120] Danilov's writings also demonstrate a basic awareness of the logistical facts of life—for example, the extreme difficulty of sustaining an offensive more than four days of marching from the railhead.[121]

It was no secret that the development of Russian logistical services lagged behind that of Russia's other military institutions. Blue-ribbon commissions repeatedly urged improvements and reforms, but the unglamorous auxiliary services continued to be shortchanged in the competition for scarce funds and the attention of the officer corps. Even the French had a very clear picture of the backwardness of the Russian supply services, as did the Russian Duma.[122]

The Russian military had at least as good an understanding of the shortcomings of its supply services as did these outsiders but found it difficult to overcome the habits of neglect and perhaps even more difficult to face its consequences. This ambivalence about logistical problems is evident in memoranda coauthored by Palitsyn and Alekseev. On theoretical questions, their insights were impeccable:

> On the map, as on the chess board, it is easy to move infantry and cavalry corps. In reality such movements are always difficult, sometimes impossible; they always entail strenuous effort and the wasting of the strength of the troops.
>
> Every operation has its limits of time, space, terrain, and the strength of the troops. Vigorous, continuous offensive operations . . . of contemporary armies usually cannot extend further than three to five days march, depending on administrative preparations, the wealth of the region, and the nature of communications.[123]

At the same time, however, they worried that the army would lose its mobility if it were tied to an extensive supply infrastructure. Their preferred solution—automobile transport—was in practice unobtainable because of Russia's financial and technical limitations.[124] Their discussion implied that supply difficulties inevitably put a major brake on military operations, but the tendency to let intractable problems of this kind dominate strategic calculations had nonetheless to be resisted.

Everyday habits reinforced this general attitude. The need to simplify operational calculations in training exercises made it convenient to underemphasize logistical factors. Staff officers would habitually skimp on the administrative section of staff ride reports. As a consequence, their tactical solutions frequently ignored considerations of logistical feasibility.[125] Similarly, to maximize simplicity and minimize expense, food and forage for large-scale maneuvers were dispensed from prepositioned caches on the battlefield, not brought up from the rear.[126]

The April 1914 war game assumed that transportation and supply would operate without delays or interruptions. Aside from the need to save time, another reason excluded logistical calculations from this game: participating luminaries from the military districts were afraid that the game would be used to demonstrate their incompetence in elementary staff work.[127] This inattention to logistics at the April war game had at least one notable consequence. At the game, the hypothetical advance of the Second Army remained to the east of the rail line running through Mlava, where it could stay in fairly close contact with the First Army. In August 1914, however, the poorly supplied Second Army was drawn further west in part by the need to make use of the rail lifeline. This movement exacerbated the lack of mutual support between the two armies.[128]

Kliuev's idea that the First Army could easily march to the Second Army's aid similarly indicated a considerable degree of logistical myopia. In 1914 P. K. Rennenkampf's First Army was slow in coming to the aid of A. V. Samsonov's Second Army not because of a purported grudge between the two commanders (the fabled fist-fight is mythical) but because Rennenkampf had outrun his supply lines.[129] In short, an accurate anticipation of the logistical aspects of the East Prussia operation would have forced the Russian high command to reevaluate not only their assumption that the First and Second armies could remain mutually supportive but also the logic of the East Prussia operation as a whole.

Inattention to logistical problems was not uniform. The commanders of the Galician front were much more realistic in this regard than were the proponents of a hasty attack into East Prussia. In reports preparatory to the April war game, Alekseev, Ivanov, and Dragomirov expressed the wish that the initial offensives not be hurried. They wanted the advance to take place only after the concentration of forces and rear echelons was essentially complete, around M+20 or 21. Moreover, they felt that there would have to be a break in operations after the initial contact, for the purpose of reorganizing the forces and ensuring the continuity of their supply, on which a successful penetration of Galicia would depend.[130]

Even this view was too sanguine. Accounts of the Galician campaign make it clear that the survival of the Austrian army was in large part due to the breakdown of the Russian supply system. Alekseev himself contended that "if we dared not storm the fortress of Przemysl, this was only because we were physically exhausted and had run out of supplies."[131] Detailed Soviet scholarship has shown that this breakdown was entirely predictable, given the extreme inadequacy of the Russians' horse-drawn convoys and narrow-gauge railways. After advancing for four days, the Russians knew they would be out of supply and traversing territory that the Austrians had already stripped.[132] In this sense, Alekseev was being true to the spirit of his memorandum of seven years earlier: be aware of logistical difficulties and minimize them as far as possible, but do not abandon great projects strictly on this account.

Much less information is available on logistical planning for the East Prussian campaign. It is clear, however, that the plans for a hasty attack into East Prussia received less logistical scrutiny than did Alekseev's plan for a more methodical invasion of Galicia. Histories and memoirs of the advance of the Second Army suggest that the hasty departure in essence left the troops with no system of supply other than requisitioning. Even this self-service system was hampered by a lack of wagons and, above all, the poverty of the land that the Second Army traversed in the first several days of its advance. Coupled with the forced pace of the march and the difficulty of transporting artillery on the sandy roads, this lack of logistical support left Samsonov's force in noticeably weakened condition on the eve of the battle of Tannenberg.[133]

The difference between the southern front commanders' conditional concern for logistics and the northern front's total disregard of it might be attributed in part to Alekseev's superior staff work. Kliuev and Zhilinskii were certainly not his equal in this regard. The more fundamental reason, however, is that the idea of a hasty advance into East Prussia to try to draw German forces away from France virtually presupposed that logistics would be ignored. If the "planners" of this operation had taken logistics at all seriously, they would have had to delay the advance by a week or more, by which time German forces would have been fully committed in the west.

Danilov's comment on this situation in his memoirs is difficult to evaluate:

> It must be admitted that the Second Army was not ready to march on the appointed day [M+20 for the frontier crossing, with the advance from initial concentration points preceding that by a few days], since the organization of its rear was still incomplete. History will have to judge whether this tardiness is to be attributed to a lack of energy on the part of that army's administrative organs, which did not complete their duties in time, or to errors in the peacetime calculations of the time needed to get organized.[134]

Since the 1913 draft plan had the Second Army completing the concentration of its rear echelons on M+33, this remark seems baldly disingenuous. But some units were scheduled to complete their concentration significantly before that date, and it may be to these units that Danilov is referring.

CREATING A THIRD FRONT: AUGUST 1914

The strategic circumstances of August 1914 were more favorable than the Russians had anticipated. Italy, Sweden, and Rumania remained neutral. The Austrians committed more forces against Serbia than the Russians had expected. Initial intelligence indicated that there were four active German corps in East Prussia, compared to an anticipated maximum of six or seven. (In fact, there were only three.)[135] At the same time, the initial news of the German attack on Liège led Danilov to believe that the maldeployed French army was in jeopardy.[136] As a result, Danilov believed that Russia had both an obligation to press Germany as soon as possible and the spare forces to do so successfully.

Danilov calculated that by M+12 the First and Second armies would have over 200 first-line battalions available. Facing this force, the Germans would only be able to muster four active corps (100 battalions) and "several reserve and Landwehr units."[137] In view of this correlation of forces, Danilov pressed Zhilinskii to begin his advance on M+14. He also concluded that a new army, the Ninth, should be created around Warsaw, with the aim of developing an offensive on the west bank of the Vistula. Included in this army were the First Corps and the Guards Corps, which otherwise would have been allocated to the East Prussia front. Supplemented by late-arriving units from the interior of the empire, the Ninth Army group would attack on two axes: toward the Lower Vistula, to take the formidable river defenses from behind and link up with the Russian forces operating in East Prussia, and toward Poznan and eventually Berlin.[138]

Actual operations dissipated the surfeit of Russian forces that Danilov calculated on paper. Although the German Eighth Army in East Prussia was composed of a mere three active corps and a total of only 13 field-grade divisions, the Russians were unable to achieve superiority on the battlefield. Several foreseeable factors prevented the Russians from turning their paper advantage into a real one: the hastiness of their advance; the diversion of forces to the left bank of the Vistula; the need to cover the gap between the First and Second armies; and above all, the disparity in mobility between the German and Russian forces.

At Gumbinnen, the Germans were able to engage 9 divisions against 6-1/2 divisions of the First Army. Partial Russian success resulted not from numerical advantage but from German error: the impending success of a German flank maneuver was nullified by a foolhardy German frontal assault that decimated the Germans' center and forced a general retreat. At Tannenberg, the Germans were also able to achieve a superiority of troops and firepower over those elements of the Russian Second Army that participated in the battle. The desire to amass a left-bank strike force kept the Russian First Corps and Guards Corps from joining in this engagement, although they were in the area.[139]

It is doubtful that Danilov anticipated the difficulties that the First and Second Armies might face. The only evidence that he thought the hasty offensive might entail some risk appears in a cable to Zhilinskii, explaining the transfer of units from the East Prussia front to the left bank. "A setback there [in East Prussia] could not have a decisive importance," Danilov said, since "the whole key to subsequent operations" lay on the left bank.[140] Even if Danilov was mildly concerned that a small Russian force might be defeated in East Prussia, he was more worried about the possibility that a large force could be bottled up there by the German defenses along the lower Vistula, which he believed had to be taken from the rear.[141] The partial Russian victory at Gumbinnen dissipated whatever doubts he may have entertained. At this point, Danilov thought the East Prussia campaign was all but over. Believing that the Germans intended to evacuate the province, he pressed Zhilinskii's chief of staff to complete the operations there quickly in order to free still more forces for the Ninth Army.[142]

According to Danilov, two factors influenced his desire to finish the East Prussia operation quickly: first, the need to take pressure off the French and second, the need to secure a strong position before the arrival of German reinforcements. "Given the importance for us of holding the Lower Vistula, we could not let pass the chance to profit from the relative weakness of our enemy on the northwest front."[143] In his concern to prepare for the hypothetical dangers of the second phase of the war, Danilov seriously underrated the immediate dangers of its opening phase.

CONCLUSIONS

This Russian case shows, better than the French and German cases do, that governmental decision making is a pluralistic political process as well as a unitary analytical one. In a sense, Russia's overcommitted offensives of 1914 were the active preference of no single individual but rather the political result of the competition between opposing factions. The absence of an authoritative arbiter produced a stalemated policy that was worse than either of the original positions. To the extent that this compromise came to be weighted in favor of Danilov and the General Staff, political and organizational factors were particularly important—for example, Kliuev's gradual defection from Alekseev's camp to protect the interests of the front that he would be commanding, and the natural advantages of the centralized General Staff over the dispersed military district staffs.

Nonetheless, the question of individual decision making does arise in connection with the dubious choices that Danilov made in his effort to accommodate Alekseev's priorities to his own. These errors, and especially Danilov's tendency to underestimate the dangers of the East Prussia operation, were fostered by cognitive biases, including the needs for simplification, for a parochial focus of attention, and for seeing the necessary as possible.

The need for cognitive and organizational simplicity, reinforced by bureaucratic political concerns, exerted an important influence on logistical assessments. In order to save time, expense, and reputations, planners habitually shortchanged the logistical element in war games, staff exercises, and maneuvers. These habits make it little wonder that logistical considerations were also underemphasized in actual war planning.

Another example of simplification is Danilov's tendency to "anchor" force-balance estimates on aggregate numbers of battalions or divisions.[144] In the complex and uncertain business of calculating the balance of forces, he tended to place disproportionate weight on a simple, salient indicator, such as the number of active units deployed on a given front. More complex, dynamic factors, such as the role of the German railroad as a force multiplier, he tended to underemphasize. This bias helps to explain Danilov's overestimate of Russia's useable strength in East Prussia. This is not to say, of course, that Danilov entirely ignored qualitative factors and dynamic operational effects but rather that he did not sufficiently adjust for them. Perhaps a motivational factor facilitated this bias: because the nominal force balance supported his preferred strategy, he may have been less inclined to examine the possibility that the dynamic force balance might be radically less favorable.

Perceptions were skewed by parochially focused attention. Where planners sat at least partially determined what they saw. In the governmental seat of St. Petersburg, Danilov and Zhilinskii were heavily influenced by the diplomacy of the Franco-Russian alliance, which favored the East Prussia operation. In contrast, the district commanders and staffs, who would take charge of field units in the event of war, tended to be more concerned with operational factors like terrain and logistics, which worked against the East Prussia plan.[145]

Further focus-of-attention effect may have influenced Russian decision making in a significant way. Danilov's inordinate preoccupation with the security of the Russian concentration led him to conceive of the opening engagement as an M+12 German attack on the Russian railheads. Focusing on the problems that this threat would entail, he was less attentive to the even greater difficulties that would result were the Germans to remain on the defensive.

General Lukomskii felt that Russia could face the coming war with confidence as long as her mobilization trains ran on time; this feeling suggests another cognitive bias. Indeed, this "illusion of preparedness" may constitute a general bias in balance calculations: military decision makers are swayed less by their view of the comparative military balance, which is difficult to calculate, than by their own absolute level of organizational or administrative preparedness. They are thus overconfident when their own house is in order and unwarrantedly pessimistic when it is in disarray. It follows that if the military establishments of two countries are in conditions of equal chaos, neither will want to challenge the other. But if both establishments operate with clockwork precision, both may risk confrontation with a sense of confidence. The existence of such a bias receives support from cognitive theory, which stresses the salience to decision makers of vivid, close-to-home impressions. In the French case, the illusion of preparedness can be found after 1911, when the French felt more confident because of their own improvements, despite the fact that the Germans had also improved their capabilities. This proposition helps to explain how both sides can start a war expecting to win it.[146]

A final source of bias was Danilov's denial of the grave risks inherent in the hasty attack strategy. On intelligence issues, however, it is difficult to find any strong, consistent relationship between preferred strategies and perceptions of reality. For example, Danilov consistently overestimated the likely number of German forces in East Prussia, despite the fact that his overestimate tended to contradict the strategy he adopted after 1912. He formed these estimates during his earlier, more defensive period and did not change them when he changed his preferences about strategy. Motivated bias may have occasionally led Russian planners to ignore the drawbacks of their preferred strategies, but no sustained, systematic skewing of perceptions matches what was apparent in the French case.

Perhaps the lack of an ingrained, institutionalized organizational ideology helps to account for the comparative weakness of motivated bias in the Russian case. As a result of the Russo-Japanese War, Russian doctrine remained in flux throughout the prewar period. Since doctrine tends to embody (and even magnify) motivated biases, the lack of a fixed doctrine may account for the absence of the sustained, cumulative type of motivated bias.[147]

[8]

The Determinants of Military Strategy

The choice of a military strategy is one of the weightiest tasks facing the modern nation-state. Strategy influences both the likelihood of war and the probability that, if war occurs, the state will achieve its aims. Before 1914 the continental European powers adopted offensive military strategies that increased the likelihood of war and decreased the probability of their success in war. These offensives not only defied the constraints of time, space, and technology, they also heightened the perceived advantage of preventive attacks and placed time pressures on crisis diplomacy. Strategy that goes this far awry demands explanation.

At the most general level, the period between 1870 and 1914 was conducive to offensive strategies. The Franco-Prussian War, although it demonstrated the devastating effect of defensive firepower, seemed superficially to show that modern wars could be short, offensive, and beneficial. At the same time, social Darwinist thinking made tests of military strength seem inevitable and "natural," and prevailing economic ideas suggested that these wars had necessarily to be short, decisive, and hence offensive. Finally, military doctrine and war planning were left almost entirely in the hands of military professionals, who usually incline toward the offensive but rarely have so free a rein to indulge their inclination.

Were we to compare the period 1870–1914 with other eras, such themes might warrant considerable attention. In this book, however, I have not emphasized these background factors. They may have operated as permissive causes of offensive bias, but in no case are they sufficient to explain a nation's offensive plans. In each of the three major continental powers, defensive or more limited offensive strategies prevailed at some point between 1870 and 1914. To explain the offensives of 1914, therefore, requires us to explain the specific circumstances of strategic policy making in each country.

DETERMINANTS OF STRATEGY: FIVE PATTERNS

Military strategy is shaped by the interaction of motivational biases, doctrinal simplifications, and rational calculations. These three general determinants are in turn shaped by organizational, cognitive, and strategic variables. For tracing the determinants of strategy in a particular case, it is easiest to begin with the foreign-policy goals of the state and the available evidence on the strategic implications of military technology, geography, and the military balance. Sometimes these variables may strongly favor—indeed, even require—offense or defense, but more often the constraints will be ambiguous, allowing a broad range of plausible strategies. The greater this degree of uncertainty, the greater is the role of motivational and simplification biases in shaping strategy.

The strength of the motivational bias depends primarily on the severity of the threat to the military's institutional interests and the degree of incompatibility between those interests and sound strategy. It might be argued that a motivated bias for offense is endemic to military institutions: although defense is usually easier than offense, militaries prefer offensive doctrines, which, so the argument runs, promote organizational autonomy, prestige, and budgets. But while this bias may be common, it is not universal, and in any particular case, therefore, the incompatibility between institutional interests and sound strategy must be treated as a variable, not a constant. The same is true for the degree of threat to military institutions. For example, the military's need to use operational strategy as a tool for promoting its autonomy will vary, depending on civilian attitudes.[1] Finally, motivational bias may occur when other core values are severely threatened, even if institutional interests are not at stake. People see the defense of core values as unconditionally necessary; therefore, the strategies needed to protect those values will be seen as feasible, whether they are or not. Strategists are biased toward seeing the necessary as possible.

Like motivational bias, the bias resulting from the simplification of strategic analysis should be treated as a variable. To some extent, of course, the arbitrary simplification and structuring of analysis is unavoidable, given all strategists' cognitive limitations and the complexity of the tasks they must perform. Even the most "objective" strategist has a limited focus of attention, adopts some kind of a priori doctrinal viewpoint, economizes on strategic calculations, and seeks to minimize uncertainty. Yet the degree of these biases may vary. Personal experience may make some strategists more dogmatic or narrowly focused than others. Organizational characteristics, such as the degree of centralization, may affect the extent to which prevailing doctrines are dogmatized. Even the tendency to take shortcuts in strategic calculations may vary, depending on the availability of information and the competence of the analyst. Furthermore, not only the degree but also the direction of the simplification may vary. Although the reduction of uncertainty and the parochial focus of attention may provide an endemic bias favoring the offense, strategists' doctrinal preconceptions will be strongly influenced by formative experiences at war college or in war itself, and these experiences may favor the offense, the defense, or some combination of the two.

Finally, doctrinal simplification and motivated bias inevitably interact. When motivated bias is strong, doctrinal simplifications will sooner or later tend to reinforce that bias. Conversely, doctrines spawn plans, force postures, and institutional structures, which generate a vested interest in self-perpetuation. Thus, unless the environment provides major disruptions, motivational bias and doctrinal predispositions will tend to converge.

These determinants produced five different patterns of strategic policy making in the European powers in the years before World War I.[2] Although the allegedly endemic biases in favor of offense are to be found in some cases, the most dramatic causes of offensive strategies prove to be motivational biases produced by circumstances peculiar to the individual case.

1. France before the Dreyfus Crisis

In the 1880s and 1890s the French military developed an organizational ideology centered around the concept of offensive operations carried out by well-trained, active-duty troops. The principal motive for this ideology was the need to forestall civilian desires for an army that would rely heavily on reservists. During these two decades, however, the military did not see this threat to traditional military structures as extreme or unmanageable, and its ideological bias toward the offense remained moderate.

Tactical doctrines largely reflected this motivational bias. Other potential sources of doctrinal simplifications, especially the experience of the Franco-Prussian War, had ambiguous implications for the choice between offense and defense. Initial lessons favoring the defense were easily reversed by reevaluations in the 1880s.

The moderately offensive doctrines of the period were disseminated through war college curricula, field regulations, and publications in unofficial journals. French military institutions were not highly centralized around the General Staff, however, and no single doctrinal school was able to impose a uniform dogma on the officer corps as a whole. The most influential approach was General Henri Bonnal's moderately offensive doctrine, based loosely on the practices of Napoleon.

Although doctrine was strongly influenced by motivational bias, strategy and war plans were constrained by unambiguous calculations of German capabilities. Actual war plans were consistently more defensive than doctrinal rhetoric suggested. Even on the sensitive issue of the value of reserve units, French strategists felt compelled to emulate Germany's clear intention to use reservists alongside active forces in the opening days of conflict.

2. *France after the Dreyfus Crisis*

The crisis in civil-military relations following the Dreyfus affair gave a new significance to the military's self-protective ideology of the offensive. Organizational ideology was more than ever needed to combat encroachments on military autonomy and institutional traditions. Yet this more extreme reassertion of traditional ideas did not triumph immediately. It first had to overcome a variety of obstacles: the legacy of Bonnal's "defensive-offensive" thinking, the tactical evidence from the Boer War, and the reformist officers that civilians had placed in key positions in the military hierarchy.

In 1911 the last and most important obstacle was surmounted, when the reformists discredited themselves by advancing an extreme plan. At the same time, French civilians learnt from the Agadir Crisis that pacifying their military had become more important than reforming it. The more traditional elements in the military took advantage of changed civilian attitudes to implement a program that reasserted the primacy of active-duty soldiers, offensive operations, and the role of morale in warfare.

The war plan that resulted can best be explained as a product of motivated bias. To justify the return to the three-year term of service, the French military overrated the offensive capabilities of active-duty soldiers, oversold the danger of a German *attaque brusquée* in Lorraine, and dismissed the danger that German reservists would be used in a flank march through northern Belgium. The strategic perceptions of the French General Staff were dominated not by the evidence but by the requirements of their program of institutional reconstruction.

Among the proponents of Plan 17 and the *offensive á outrance,* doctrine primarily reflected motivated bias. Among the more moderate officers, however, doctrinal preconceptions inculcated in the pre-Dreyfus era had a life of their own. People who had been schooled in the "defensive-offensive" did not readily change their doctrinal inclinations, regardless of motivational incentives for doing so.

Rational calculations played little role in shaping Plan 17, which defied strong strategic incentives to remain on the defensive. As a permissive factor, however, the ambiguity of some of the evidence bearing on French strategic calculations was important. Intelligence on the German war plan was just ambiguous enough that the French could continue in their erroneous view. Had the evidence been any clearer, the French might not have been able to maintain their preferred attitude, despite the strong parochial interests behind it.

3. Germany under the Elder Moltke

Doctrine and war planning under the elder Helmut von Moltke were influenced by parochial interests, pragmatic calculations, and an overly narrow conception of war. The German Wars of Unification had given the German army a towering reputation. From these short, beneficial wars, the General Staff had made the congenial deduction that the political problems of the German state could best be solved by decisive, preventive attacks, which incidentally would maintain the army's awesome prestige.

This motivated bias, rooted in parochial interests, was reinforced by a bias of simplification, rooted in the military's parochial focus of attention. As a consequence of their professional preoccupations, militaries tend to exaggerate military threats. Indeed, military officers often consider it their professional duty to assume the worst case. As Lord Salisbury put it, "If you believe the doctors, nothing is wholesome; if you believe the theologians, nothing is innocent; if you believe the soldiers, nothing is safe."[3] Moltke, suffering from the common perceptual bias of the military, overrated the inevitability of a Franco-Russian attack and consequently overrated the need for an offensive, preventive capability.

Moltke's broad experience of war had, however, made him above all a pragmatic realist. He understood that firepower, logistics, geography, and fortifications gave a considerable operational advantage to the defender. As a result, he devised an offensive doctrine, stressing flank maneuvers and limited aims, that minimized the disadvantages of the attacker. When circumstances made even this formula untenable, Moltke was willing to give up the initiative and contemplate a prolonged, positional defense.

4. *Germany under Schlieffen*

Alfred von Schlieffen inherited all of Moltke's biases but little of his pragmatic realism. He took Moltke's doctrine of encirclement, reduced it to a few simple deductive principles, and inculcated an entire generation of young staff officers with it. As a result, dogma replaced doctrine in German operational planning. Such an outcome was favored by Schlieffen's own theoretical bent, the long period of peace during which he presided, and the centralization of German military institutions under the General Staff.

Schlieffen was not the least rational of Europe's strategists. The encirclement doctrine that he had taken over from Moltke conflicted less with improvements in firepower than the French doctrine of frontal assault. Moreover, Schlieffen showed considerable realism in calculating how to implement his offensive strategy. But when evaluating defensive alternatives, Schlieffen employed double standards and logical inconsistencies to protect his preference for decisive, offensive operations. He arbitrarily assumed that attackers had greater mobility than defenders and that attackers could deplete the center of the front to strengthen the flanks, but defenders could not. The defensive options that he did consider used so few forces on the defensive front that they seem designed to fail.

Schlieffen's bolstering of his preferred strategy can be seen either as a motivated bias or as a doctrinal simplification. Parochial interest and operational dogma were so intertwined that it would be fruitless to try to separate them. Once in place, Schlieffen's operational dogma became a parochial interest in its own right and had to be protected against alternative views and disconfirming evidence. His dogma's career illustrates what may be a general characteristic of organizational ideologies: the biasing effects of motivation and simplification tend over time to be mutually reinforcing and ultimately indistinguishable.

5. *Russia*

Rational calculation played a major role in shaping the broad outline of Russian strategy. Between 1910 and 1914 Russia's relative power increased, the reliability of Russia's French ally became more certain, and Germany's intention to open the war with only a weak force on the eastern front became undeniable. As a result, Russian strategists calculated that offensive operations of some kind were both feasible and strategically desirable.

Beyond these general outlines, Russian calculations were less acute. Iurii Danilov, in the General Staff, was an inveterate pessimist about France's ability to hold out against the Germans and about Russia's ability subsequently to face Germany alone in a long war. He placed an absolute priority on saving France and if that failed, on putting Russia in the best possible position to meet the ensuing German attack. These deeply engrained concerns pointed toward an early attack on East Prussia in considerable force, but because of competing demands for forces for the Austrian front, the operation could not be carried out safely. Rather than rethink his strategic assumptions, Danilov pursued his dangerous East Prussia offensive, denying risks that should have been obvious. Ironically, his motivated optimism about the East Prussia operation was made necessary in part by his pessimistic preconceptions about French and Russian military weakness.

DETERMINANTS OF STRATEGY: COMPARISONS

These explanations of the determinants of strategy can be checked and reinforced by comparisons among the different cases. Such comparisons will highlight instances in which differences in the independent variables produced different patterns of strategic decision making. They will also point out those aspects of decision making that do not vary across the cases.

Motivation and Interests

Bias in strategic decision making was greatest when important parochial interests of the military were severely threatened. This proposition is most clearly shown by comparing French military policy before and after the Dreyfus crisis in civil-military relations. In the 1870s, when the threat to traditional military institutions was low, French military doctrine and war planning reflected relatively little bias. In the 1880s and 1890s, when the threat was somewhat greater, bias began to appear in the area of operational doctrine. In response to the still greater threats that the Dreyfus affair and the André ministry conjured up, doctrinal bias increased further among young officers. Eventually, biased assessments became pervasive among war planners and intelligence analysts as well.

In a superficial sense, the German military faced some of the same threats to traditional military institutions. The length of service, the value of reservists, and the democratization of the officer corps were issues in Germany as in France. The implications of these issues differed widely in the two countries, however, because of differences in the broader context of civil-military relations. In Germany, military reform occurred in a setting of high military prestige and cooperation between military officials and "militarized" civilian authorities. The German military was not particularly threatened by reform, because it could control the process.[4] In France, issues of reform arose against a backdrop of fundamental civil-military disputes, which were particularly divisive because they coincided with ideological and class cleavages in the society as a whole. Before 1898 the French miltary could more or less manage the reform process through the help of sympathetic civilian elites, but after that watershed year civilians sought to transform, not just reform, traditional military institutions.

Another important difference between the French and German cases was the absence of an opposition faction within the German military, as a consequence of which the German General Staff could afford a comparatively frank discussion of the shortcomings of their strategic plans. Realistic assessments of their preferred plans posed no threat as long as the General Staff maintained their faith in a few basic axioms. In contrast, the views of the French military were subjected to intense, hostile scrutiny. Constructive self-criticism of prevailing policies from inside the military would inevitably have played into the hands of unsympathetic critics both within the military and on the outside.

Yet there was also an important similarity in the way motivated bias operated in France and Germany. Both cases show that bias is greatest when central beliefs and values are in jeopardy; subsidiary beliefs are not similarly protected. Schlieffen, for example, committed numerous motivated errors when evaluating defensive strategies that could have undermined his whole strategic system, but his thinking was unbiased when he was choosing among alternative plans for a short, victorious war. Similarly, he resorted to misjudging French intentions only when he could rationalize his preferred short-war strategy in no other way. In Schlieffen's doctrinal system, core beliefs were expressed tautologically, so that no disconfirming evidence could possibly threaten them; lesser beliefs, which could be abandoned without threatening the integrity of the system, were pragmatically rooted in evidence and were not particularly resistant to change.

Between 1906 and 1914 the French estimated precisely as much of a German threat as could be managed by the preferred strategies and institutions of the observers. Reformists saw big threats that only the reforms they advocated could handle; moderates saw moderate threats that could be handled by incremental changes; opponents of widespread reservist use saw threats that the standing army could best handle. It is clear that estimates were determined by institutional preferences rather than vice versa, because the views on institutional questions were well established before biases in intelligence estimates began to occur. At least in these instances, decision makers only misperceived as much as was necessary to protect their core values or their basic orientations to questions of military policy.

A similar pattern prevailed when strategists saw the "necessary" as possible. Danilov did not generally succumb to optimistic misperceptions; he did so only when he felt that he had no choice but to pursue the risky course of invading East Prussia. German planners were likewise fairly realistic about the difficulty of implementing the Schlieffen Plan; undue optimism occurred only in connection with the *coup de main* against Liège, where realistic doubts would have called the whole strategy into question. In short, motivated optimism did not occur pervasively but only when the decision maker was somehow cornered by circumstances. Decision makers were "wishful" only when unbiased perceptions would have forced them to rethink core beliefs or sacrifice central values.

The Need to Simplify

Three sources of doctrinal simplification played a significant role in one or more of the cases: the parochial focus of attention, the formation of beliefs, and the dogmatization of beliefs.

German history offers the clearest example of what Huntington calls the military's "conservative realism," which is characterized by the belief that war is inevitable, natural, and must be won by a decisive victory.[5] Some of the German evidence suggests that this ethos is not just a function of the military's alleged interest in promoting international tension; rather, it is at least partly the result of the military's professional preoccupation with threats to national security and military means to counter them. As Bismarck discovered in dealing with his military commanders, the tendency of professional soldiers to ignore the political side of strategy does not make them politically neutral technicians, it makes them biased technicians who equate politics with armed struggle.

How widespread is this kind of Hobbesian "realism" among military professionals? The ethos of the imperial German military was certainly an extreme case, produced by the congenial views of militarized civilians, by Germany's vulnerable position in the center of Europe, and by the role of "blood and iron" in the unification of the German state. In France, the Hobbesian attitudes of the military were certainly less extreme and were obscured in policy making by other considerations. Nonetheless, Joseph Joffre sought permission to violate Belgian neutrality even if Germany did not, while Nöel Curières de Castelnau worked to provoke war in the Balkan Crisis of 1912 on the grounds that it was a favorable occasion.[6] The Russian military was likewise quick to perceive general war as inevitable in July 1914, whereas the Russian foreign minister sought to use an improvisation, a partial mobilization, as a way to prevent or limit it.[7]

The case studies, especially in the attitudes of moderate French officers of the Bonnal school, illustrate the persistence of early training. The formative impact of major historical events is, however, less clearly shown. In France, the "lessons" of 1870 were shaped and reshaped according to the needs and interests of the moment; at least on doctrinal questions, these lessons carried little autonomous, "formative" weight. Likewise, all the powers learned lessons very selectively from the Boer and Russo-Japanese Wars. A study of the interwar period might show that the lessons of World War I were so compelling that they submerged considerations of parochial interest, but in the period between 1870 and 1914 the reverse was the case.

Lastly, the degree of dogmatization was influenced by institutional factors, personalities, and the strength of motivational biases. In Germany under Schlieffen, the dogmatization of doctrine was facilitated by strong, centralized institutions and a long period free of domestic or international disruptions of organizational routine. In these circumstances, the German General Staff were able to educate new officers in a simple, standard doctrine and have them apply it to problems of war planning, training, and operational exercises. In contrast, France and Russia lacked strong, centralized institutions and undisrupted periods of organizational consensus. Dogmatization due to standardization did not occur in either country.

Still, French doctrine under Joffre and Loyzeaux de Grandmaison did become dogmatic by any definition of that term. Even more than German doctrine, the *offensive à outrance* was deductive, insensitive to circumstances, and impervious to evidence. This dogmatism was a relatively late development, however, and was caused by a strong motivation to be dogmatic, not by institutional or cognitive ossification.

The personality of the key military planner, especially his degree of open-mindedness and the breadth of his approach to strategic problems, also influenced the dogmatization of doctrine. Joffre and the elder Moltke provide examples of two very different kinds of open-mindedness.[8] Joffre was open-minded in the sense that he had no firm views on strategic issues before he became chief of the General Staff. As a military engineer, he had paid scant attention to operational matters. Lacking strong predispositions, Joffre was free to adopt the doctrine and strategy that motivational considerations dictated. In contrast, Joseph-Simon Gallieni had more fixed views and could not accept the *offensive à outrance.*

Moltke's open-mindedness came not from empty-mindedness but from a broad, practical experience of all kinds of strategic situations and expedients and from his pragmatic bent. He had predispositions, but not dogmatic ones. Therefore, unlike Schlieffen, he was not blind to the advantages of defensive strategies. Moltke's relative breadth of vision also helped him to see the plausibility of strategies of limited aims. His strategy encompassed, at least to some extent, the use of diplomatic as well as military means, a perspective that Schlieffen did not attain.

Rational Calculation

The plausibility of a given view is determined not only by the planner's cognitive preconceptions but also by the weight of the evidence itself. Sometimes facts are so clear that everyone, regardless of their preconceptions and interests, agrees about them. Conversely, the greater the ambiguity of the evidence, the greater is the influence that interests and preconceptions will exert on perceptions. This proposition is illustrated by the difference in the French response to public decisions around 1890 to increase the use of German reservists, compared to their reaction to later changes in German reserve policies about which French information was more ambiguous.

Biased assessments of concrete, tactical realities were less common than biased assessments at the more abstract level of strategic doctrine. After the Boer and Russo-Japanese Wars, almost no one denied that the increased firepower of modern weapons had made tactical frontal assaults more difficult. On that point, the facts left little room for interpretation. The strategic implications of these facts were, however, a matter of greater ambiguity. It could still be argued that flank attacks or breakthroughs in weak spots remained feasible and that the alleged strategic advantages of offense still obtained. Since the lessons of the Boer and Russo-Japanese Wars were inconclusive on this issue, biased assessments remained plausible.

The area of logistics shows that even a little ambiguity may be enough to allow free play for the planners' biases. Despite their rigid calculations of wagon loads of supplies that could be brought up from the rear, logistical planners could always use local requisitioning as an elastic clause, allowing them to establish the feasibility of the preferred strategy. In any case, it was the job of the logistics experts of the general staffs to implement the plans that were handed down by superiors, not to pass judgment on their advisability.

Synthesis: Organizational Ideology

In France and Germany, the military developed an organizational ideology—a coherent set of shared beliefs about the nature of war, the keys to success in combat, and the prerequisites for healthy military institutions. These ideologies became embodied in field manuals, war plans, and organizational structures, and they were perpetuated through the socialization of new officers.

The military ideology served three main functions. First, it promoted the military's interests, including parochial interests that might be unrelated or even negatively related to military effectiveness. Second, it simplified concepts and standardized procedures in order to facilitate training, planning, and implementation of policies. Third, it developed a plausible theory of victory to guide commanders to success on the battlefield.

The first two functions tended over time to reinforce each other. Doctrinal simplifications were more likely to survive and prosper if they coincided with organizational values and interests. Dogmatized and institutionalized, these doctrines themselves took on the status of institutional interests to be defended. In an organizational setting, simplifications and interests tended to coincide for yet another reason: the narrow focusing of attention on professional military concerns normally had the same effect on perceptions as did the rationalization of professional interests. In Germany, for example, both led to a view of war as an inevitable, normal means of resolving international disputes.

The third function, that of providing a plausible theory of victory, occasionally suffered when it conflicted with the other two. However, even in the worst cases, it was never completely eclipsed, as the brief rise of a defensive school in France after the Boer War demonstrates. The tendency even attracted some military traditionalists, despite the André ministry's concurrent attacks on traditional military institutions.

Organizational ideology developed differently from country to country, and in the Russian case, it failed to develop at all. These differences were caused in part by variations in the kinds of threats facing the military and the severity of those threats. They were also caused by variations in the degree of centralization of military institutions and in the personalities of the men at the top of those institutions—factors that affected the extent to which the ideology became standardized and dogmatized. Other causal factors included the presence or absense of external shocks, which could disrupt the process of institutionalizing the ideology. In the French case, the Dreyfus affair and its aftermath constituted such a shock, making the moderate doctrines of Bonnal inadequate to meet the new challenges to military interests. In the Russian case, defeat in the Russo-Japanese War constituted an even more disruptive shock, calling into question all of the previously accepted verities.

The determinants of military strategy are many, but they can all be considered under three headings: rational calculation, motivated bias, and doctrinal simplification. The explanation of strategic policy making, though beginning with the incentives and constraints that would shape the choice of any rational strategist in the given circumstances, must always consider the motivational, cognitive, and organizational biases that cause deviations from the rational path. The explanation will often culminate in the analysis of the military planners' organizational ideology, which melds rational, motivational, and doctrinal considerations into a stable, coherent, but biased belief system.

IMPLICATIONS FOR THEORY

For the past three decades, students of motivational biases in decision making have preoccupied themselves with one or another variation on the theme of wishful thinking. Those variations might be labeled "trade-off avoidance," "defensive avoidance," "avoidance of cognitive dissonance," or "images of transformation," but the essence of the theory remains the same: people tend to deal with painful problems by refusing to recognize that they exist.[9]

The first difficulty with this line of argument is the vast amount of evidence that people *can* deal forthrightly with painful problems, that they *can* make trade-offs, and that they even indulge in worst-case analysis, the very opposite of wishful thinking.[10] Obviously, the task for theoreticians is to specify the conditions under which decision makers are unwarrantedly optimistic, unwarrantedly pessimistic, and realistic. But attempts to define these conditions have not been particularly successful. Irving Janis and Leon Mann have proposed, for example, that "defensive avoidance" occurs "when a person has lost hope about finding a better solution than the objectionable ones he had been contemplating."[11] This formulation begs all of the interesting questions. What causes the loss of hope? Is the loss of hope simply a realistic response to the situation, or is it an unwarranted inference? How "objectionable" does the least objectionable option have to be before defensive avoidance will occur?

Another proposition holds that wishful thinking occurs when ambiguity is great.[12] Yet uncertainty is conducive to cognitive errors of *all* kinds, including unwarranted "worst-casing" as well as unwarranted wishfulness. Other propositions are obviously needed to specify when errors will tend in the direction of optimism rather than pessimism. One such notion is that ingrained preconceptions (about the "lessons of history," for example) bias some decision makers toward the former and others toward the latter. While probably true, this idea seems to rob the concept of wishfulness of all of its motivational content. Rather than responding to the need to reduce psychological stress, decision makers simply invoke long-standing beliefs to help them understand a complex, ambiguous situation. Calling the results of this process "wishful thinking" or "worst-casing" is an exercise in labeling, not explanation.

A final problem for theorists of wishful thinking is the fact that decision makers can be simultaneously wishful on one question while indulging in worst-case analysis on another. Schlieffen, for example, was pessimistic in believing that war was inevitable but optimistic in believing that Germany could win it in a short time and at a low cost.

We can overcome these theoretical difficulties by thinking not in terms of a generalized bias in favor of "wishfulness" but rather in terms of specific motives for bias and the specific circumstances in which they operate. (The clearest example is the motive to protect parochial interests that an accurate view of reality would jeopardize.)

Such an approach to explaining the degree and direction of bias focuses on motivational and situational specifics:

1. the degree of incompatibility between parochial interests and accurate perceptions. (How egregious must the misperception be in order to protect those interests?)

2. the severity of the threat to those interests. (How much will the interests suffer if reality is perceived accurately?)

3. the relative importance of the parochial interests and other interests at stake. (Are the parochial interests important enough to make a misperception worthwhile even though it may jeopardize other goals?)

4. the plausibility of the misperception to the decisionmaker. (Would unambiguous evidence or ingrained preconceptions rule out the desired rationalization?)

Focusing on the interests of the decision maker, the observer will find it easier to discover the specific circumstances and specific motives that sometimes lead to errors of optimism, sometimes to errors of pessimism, and sometimes to both kinds of errors simultaneously.

A second circumstance that produces motivated bias is a grave threat to core values and beliefs. When cornered, people tend to overestimate the prospects of strategies they need to save core values. Thus Danilov believed that the East Prussia operation was feasible because he thought it necessary to Russia's survival. Likewise, the younger Helmuth von Moltke glossed over the huge risks of the Liège operation, because he thought it necessary to Germany's survival. In both cases, these operations were "necessary" only because of the way Danilov and Moltke had defined their overall strategic problem. Had Danilov been less fundamentally pessimistic about Russia's strategic prospects and Moltke less biased regarding the feasibility of a defensive strategy, each might have found alternatives to his "necessary" gamble. However, they escaped the need to question their fundamental assumptions by seeing the "necessary" as possible. In this sense, the core values that were threatened were not only the survival of their countries but also the cognitive need to protect central beliefs.

This protective bias should not be confused with the indiscriminate notion of wishful thinking. Danilov was hardly wishful in his long-term view of Russia's strategic prospects, and Moltke was on the whole not particularly sanguine about the chances of the Schlieffen Plan. Their unwarranted optimism, that is to say, was not generalized. Rather, it occurred only in the face of threats so grave that their recognition would have required a fundamental reassessment of core values and beliefs. Thus both leaders saw not what they wanted to see but what they needed to see. If we must label this bias, we should call it not wishful thinking but "needful thinking."

The case studies have striking implications not only for our understanding of motivated bias but also for the close kinship between the cognitive and the organizational levels of analysis of public policy making. For individuals who operate in an organizational context, the decision-making process can be analyzed equally well as a cognitive or as an organizational phenomenon (true for motivational biases and for biases caused by the need to simplify). Both individuals and organizations pursue parochial interests but seek justifications expressed in terms of the public interest. Likewise, both individuals and organizations need to simplify and structure their tasks.

There are many similarities in the ways that individuals and organizations simplify the decision-making process. Both are biased in favor of the persistence and consistency of established beliefs and routines. Both prefer schemes that reduce uncertainty by imposing one's own plans on others. Both limit the scope of problems and solutions by defining them narrowly, disregarding links to other problems and overlooking types of solutions that lie outside their purview. Finally, both individuals and organizations simplify decision making by the use of "satisficing" criteria and by incrementalism. These similarities exist not just because organizations are made up of individuals but because individuals and organizations face the similar problem of decision making in a complex, uncertain environment, which requires a degree of arbitrary simplification and structuring. As John Steinbruner's "cybernetic theory" suggests, decision-making units of various types, from bees to bureaucracies, employ similar strategies to cope with complexity and uncertainty.[13]

OFFENSE AND THE SECURITY DILEMMA

"War is more likely, the stronger the offense relative to the defense." This proposition has been advanced in recent work by Robert Jervis, George Quester, and Stephen Van Evera. These authors suggest at the simplest level that when offense is relatively easy, war is more likely because conquest is feasible and cheap. "Defense-dominance converts aggressors into status-quo powers by making aggression too expensive," writes Van Evera, "while offense-dominance invites even mildly aggressive states to attack."[14]

More surprising is their argument that, when offense is easy, the search for security can itself lead to war. Jervis posits a "security dilemma," in which the efforts of one state to increase its security reduce the security of others, engendering a spiral of competition for security. Offense makes a cooperative solution to this dilemma harder to achieve. When offense is easy, even small shifts in the balance of power may make a state vulnerable to conquest, and as a result, states must compete intensely for strategic resources and give no quarter in the arms race. Making concessions for the sake of cooperation is dangerous if there is any chance that the opponent might cheat on the agreement, since even a small illicit gain might tip the balance. When strategic competition is this intense, war is a constant possibility. States, therefore, will consider starting war at a favorable moment, for when offense is easy, the side that strikes first may gain an advantage. Circumstances may also indicate the desirability of preventive attack, aimed at forestalling an unfavorable shift in the balance of power.[15]

In explaining the adoption of offensive or defensive strategies, both Quester and Jervis emphasize objective factors, especially technology and geographical factors such as terrain and distance. The case of World War I shows, however, that the offense-defense balance may be misjudged. Quester remarks: "For much of the analysis, our attention is directed toward the real impact of weapons, presuming that the generals and prime ministers have often judged these impacts correctly. At points, however, the contrast will have to be drawn between the real and expected impact, especially when technology begins to come along so rapidly that predictions of offensive or defensive superiorities become prone to error. How tragic that World War I was to be launched on the illusion of offensive advantage, and then was to be prolonged by the reality of defensive advantage!"[16]

In 1914 prevailing technologies and geographical circumstances should have mitigated the security dilemma. Each nation should have felt reassured by the strength of its own defenses and dissuaded from aggression by the inadequacy of its offensive capabilities. In fact, each underrated the advantages of the defense and adopted offensive military strategies that undermined stability. All of the symptoms of offense-dominance were present—preventive and preemptive war, unconditional alliances, time pressure on diplomacy, and expectations of a short, cheap war—not because offense was advantageous or necessary but because people thought it was.[17] In the years before World War II, military establishments, especially the French, tended to make the opposite error: they underestimated the offensive possibilities created by technical improvements in the tank after 1918.[18] Thus explanations of strategic stability and instability must not only identify technologies and geographical circumstances that favor the offense or the defense; they must also explain how such factors are perceived and misperceived.

In any specific case, the degree, direction, and cause of bias in thinking about offense and defense are likely to be shaped by a highly particular set of factors—that is, threats, predispositions, and strategic circumstances rooted in the peculiarities of the case. As a result, most of the hypotheses advanced in this book can make no prediction about bias for offense or defense until a great deal of case-specific information is supplied about threats to military autonomy, the centralization of doctrinal instruction, and so on. However, despite this emphasis on historical peculiarities, the World War I cases are certainly consistent with the general proposition that there is an endemic military bias in favor of offensive strategies, although it may be overruled by other factors. German history, in particular, suggests that the military's organizational interests and professional outlook make offense the "naturally" preferred strategy. An extremely useful contribution to the theory of the security dilemma would be to test this proposition in a wide range of cases, looking for double standards in military analysis and comparing civilian and military attitudes.[19]

For those who would try to foster strategic stability, the story of "the cult of the offensive" has two clear lessons. First, ideas count. Objectively, technology and geography may favor the defender (or the deterrer), but if the prevailing wisdom defies objective cirumstance and touts the offensive, the resulting security dilemma will be no less deadly. Second, the experts who shape the prevailing wisdom about offense and defense may pay no attention to the effect of their ideas on strategic stability. Indeed, their interests and outlook may lead them to exaggerate the advantages of offense and hence exacerbate the security dilemma. Certainly offensive capabilities and strategies are unavoidable in some circumstances or to some degree. But the decision for offense must be made in full view of the possible biases of the experts who favor it and with due consideration of its consequences for the likelihood of war.

Notes

1. Military Bias and Offensive Strategy

1. The consequences of offensive strategies and capabilities are discussed by Robert Jervis, "Cooperation under the Security Dilemma," *World Politics* 30 (January 1978), pp. 167–214; George Quester, *Offense and Defense in the International System* (New York: Wiley, 1977); Stephen Van Evera, "The Causes of War" (University of California at Berkeley dissertation, 1984); and Jack Snyder, "Perceptions of the Security Dilemma in 1914" (Paper delivered at the annual meeting of the International Society of Political Psychology, Washington, D.C., June 1982, revised for publication in Robert Jervis and Richard Ned Lebow, *Deterrence and Perceptions* [Baltimore: Johns Hopkins University Press, forthcoming]). It is important to distinguish between offensive capabilities (force posture) and offensive strategies (doctrine and plans). When the shortened term "offense" is used in this book, it refers to strategy unless the context clearly indicates another meaning.

2. The term "bias", as used in this book, means a nonrandom deviation from rationality, both in terms of the decision-making process and in terms of its substantive outcome. For further discussion, see the section "Method of Analysis" later in this chapter.

3. I use "least rational" in the sense of "most biased." There is no fully satisfactory treatment of French strategy; the best is probably Samuel Williamson, *The Politics of Grand Strategy* (Cambridge: Harvard University Press, 1969). The indispensable work on German strategy is Gerhard Ritter, *The Schlieffen Plan* (New York: Praeger, 1958). Norman Stone, *The Eastern Front* (New York: Scribner's, 1975), is seriously flawed but nonetheless the best treatment of Russian strategy in a Western language.

4. On motivational bias, see Irving Janis and Leon Mann, *Decision Making: A Psychological Analysis of Conflict, Choice, and Commitment* (New York: Free, 1977). On the need to simplify, see John Steinbruner, *The Cybernetic Theory of Decision* (Princeton: Princeton University Press, 1974). The outlooks of military planners in 1914 were pervasively influenced by the organizational setting in which they lived and worked. The values and motivations that they brought to strategic decision making were primarily those of the military profession and military institutions. Their perceptual biases were also organizational or professional in nature; for example, the doctrinal perspectives inculcated at the war college and the tendency to focus narrowly on military concerns. In this sense, these were the cognitive propensities not only of individuals but also of the organization.

5. Morton Halperin, *Bureaucratic Politics and Foreign Policy* (Washington, D.C.: Brookings, 1974).

6. In addition to Steinbruner, *Cybernetic Theory*, see Herbert Simon, *Administrative Behavior* (New York: Macmillan, 1957).

7. Paul Kennedy's overview article makes this connection in Kennedy, ed., *The War Plans of the Great Powers* (London: Allen & Unwin, 1979), p. 19, but the chapter specifically on France by Samuel Williamson in the same volume, "Joffre Reshapes French Strategy, 1911–1913," pp. 133–54, does not even mention the aim of revanche.

8. L. C. F. Turner, *The Origins of First World War* (London: Arnold, 1970), p. 36, quoting a General Staff memo of September 1912 in *Documents diplomatiques français* (hereafter *DDF*), 3d ser., vol. III, no. 359.

9. Williamson in Kennedy, *War Plans*, p. 144, discussing Colonel Grouard. Everyone in France assumed, correctly, that Germany would indeed attack France rather than Russia in the event of a general European war.

10. This is evident in the memoirs of the chief of the French General Staff from 1911 to 1914, Joseph Joffre, *The Memoirs of Marshal Joffre* (London: Bles, 1932), vol. 1.

11. This argument is implicit in Fritz Fischer, *War of Illusions* (New York: Norton, 1975), especially pp. 69 and 547–48. In this regard, note also Paul Kennedy, *Rise of the Anglo-German Antagonism* (London: Allen & Unwin, 1980).

12. Gerhard Ritter, The *Sword and Scepter: The Problem of Militarism in Germany*, 3 vols. (Coral Gables, Fla.: University of Miami Press, 1969–1972), vol. 2, p. 117. Material not footnoted in the following pages is discussed at length in the cases.

13. For a modern application of this idea, see John Mearsheimer, "Why the Soviets Can't Win Quickly in Central Europe," *International Security* 36 (Summer 1982), pp. 3–39.

14. Research on the causes of offense and defense is not sufficiently advanced to allow categorical judgments. Two recent studies have taken the first step toward answering this important question: Stephen Van Evera, "The Causes of War" (University of California at Berkeley dissertation, 1984) and Barry Posen, *The Sources of Military Doctrine: France, Britain, and Germany between the World Wars* (Ithaca: Cornell University Press, 1984).

15. Quoted by Van Evera from Ferdinand Foch, *Principles of War* (New York: Fly, 1918), p. 37.

16. On the officer corps, see Martin Kitchen, *The German Officer Corps, 1890–1914* (Oxford: Clarendon, 1968), pp. 115ff. Posen, chap. 2.

17. Quoted by Bernard Brodie, *War and Politics* (New York: Macmillan, 1973), p. 11.

18. Posen offers different arguments under the heading of autonomy.

19. The term is Halperin's, in *Bureaucratic Politics*.

20. On doctrine and strategy in the interwar period, see John Mearsheimer, *Conventional Deterrence* (Ithaca: Cornell University Press, 1983).

21. The problem of determining which interests are fundamental is examined in the "Method of Analysis" section later in this chapter.

22. "Decisional conflicts" is the term used by Janis and Mann in *Decision Making*. In addition, see Steinbruner, *Cybernetic Theory*, and Leon Festinger, *A Theory of Cognitive Dissonance* (Stanford: Stanford University Press, 1957).

23. Works discussing the need for cognitive simplification and the operation of belief systems in a policy-making context include Robert Axelrod, ed., *Structure of Decision: The Cognitive Maps of Political Elites* (Princeton: Princeton University Press, 1976); Robert Jervis, *Perception and Misperception in International Politics* (Princeton: Princeton University Press, 1976); Steinbruner, *Cybernetic Theory*; and Herbert A. Simon and James G.

March, *Organizations* (New York: Wiley, 1958), especially chap. 6, "Cognitive Limits on Rationality." See also the discussion of the "Cognitive Miser" model in Susan T. Fiske and Shelley E. Taylor, *Social Cognition* (Reading, Mass.: Addison-Wesley, 1984), chap. 9.

24. Jervis, *Perception and Misperception*, pp. 217–87.

25. Kenneth Waltz, *Theory of International Politics* (Reading, Mass.: Addison-Wesley, 1979), pp. 74–77, 127–28. Van Evera discusses the problem at length in "The Causes of War."

26. Quester, chaps. 11 and 12.

27. As the cases will show, there may also be motivational explanations for this bias.

28. Posen, chap. 2.

29. See the conclusion of this book for a fuller discussion of the independent and dependent variables in each case. These five patterns do not exhaust the list of logical possibilities. For an earlier study using a similar conception of organizational ideology, see Philip Selznick, *TVA and the Grass Roots* (Berkeley: University of California Press, 1953), especially pp. 47–50.

30. For a discussion of the characteristics of compromised policy, see Warner R. Schilling, "The Politics of National Defense: Fiscal 1950," in Schilling et al., *Strategy, Politics, and Defense Budgets* (New York: Columbia University Press, 1962), pp. 217–18.

31. See Alexander L. George, "Case Studies and Theory Development: The Method of Structured, Focused Comparison," in Paul Gordon Lauren, ed., *Diplomacy* (New York: Free Press, 1979), pp. 43–68.

32. Some methodologists would prefer to say there are actually several French cases in this study, divided by time period and by factional grouping, so that comparisons are being made among these minicases rather than "within" the French case as a whole. See Harry Eckstein, "Case Study and Theory in Political Science," in Fred Greenstein and Nelson Polsby, eds., *Handbook of Political Science* (Reading, Mass.: Addison-Wesley, 1975), vol. 8.

33. Janice Stein and Raymond Tanter have used similar criteria in *Rational Decision Making* (Columbus: Ohio State University Press, 1980).

34. Biased perceptions and choices need not seem completely implausible to neutral observers. Under uncertainty, there may be a number of ways to interpret reality that are all roughly consistent with the evidence. Even if plausible, a perception or choice can be considered biased if it is preferred to other plausible views for logically extraneous reasons (e.g., its implications for parochial interests).

35. See A. A. Ignat'ev, *Piat'desiat let v stroiu* (Moscow: Gosudarstvennoe izdatel'stvo khudozhestvennoi literatury, 1959), and Ian Hamilton, *A Staff Officer's Scrap Book during the Russo-Japanese War* (London: Arnold, 1908), vol. 1, p. v.

36. Jervis, *Perception and Misperception*, p. 297.

37. Since central causal beliefs usually have direct value implications, these can be included in the same rank listing. See Richard Nisbett and Lee Ross, *Human Inference: Strategies and Shortcomings of Social Judgment* (Englewood Cliffs, N.J.: Prentice-Hall, 1980), p. 180.

38. Axelrod, pp. 117–18, n. 2, and pp. 356–58.

39. Milton Rokeach, *The Open and Closed Mind* (New York: Basic, 1960), discusses the measurement of dogmatism.

40. Indeed, this was one reason that the war did not break out in 1910.

41. See Kennedy, *Rise*, pp. 12–19, and James Joll, "Unspoken Assumptions," in H. W. Koch, *The Origins of the First World War* (New York: Taplinger, 1972).

2. *France: Offensive Strategy as an Institutional Defense*

1. Joseph Jacques Joffre, *The Memoirs of Marshal Joffre* (London: Bles, 1932), vol. I, pp. 67–68. See also Eugen J. Weber, *The Nationalist Revival in France, 1905–1914* (Berkeley: University of California Press, 1959; Paul Lachance, "The Imagery of Generations in French Public Opinion on the Eve of World War I" (University of Wisconsin dissertation, 1971); Raoul Girardet, *Le nationalisme français, 1871–1914* (Paris: Colin, 1966).

2. Sewell Tyng, *The Campaign of the Marne, 1914* (New York: Longmans, Green, 1935), p. 23.

3. Ibid., pp. 24, 26–27.

4. On 1912 see Joffre, p. 62; on 1913, see David B. Ralston, *The Army of the Republic: The Place of the Military in the Political Evolution of France, 1871–1914* (Cambridge: MIT Press, 1967), pp. 249–53, and Samuel Williamson, *The Politics of Grand Strategy* (Cambridge: Harvard University Press, 1969), pp. 218, 226.

5. Etat-major de l'armée, service historique, *Les armées françaises dans la grande guerre*, 1st ser., vol. I, p. 30; Reichsarchiv, *Der Weltkrieg*, 3d ser.: *Kriegsrüstung und Kriegswirtschaft* (Berlin: Mittler, 1930), vol. III, p. 218.

6. Williamson, pp. 219–20. Gerd Krumeich, *Aufrüstung und Innenpolitik in Frankreich vor dem Ersten Weltkrieg* (Wiesbaden: Steiner, 1980), has attempted to argue that the tightening of the alliance with Russia after 1911 required the adoption of the offensive Plan 17 as the fulfillment of a mutual pledge to attack immediately and simultaneously (pp. 23–24 and *passim*). In fact, the Russians were convinced by this time that Germany would attack France first in any event, so that the mutual pledge was really a one-way obligation imposed on the Russians by the logic of the French offensive strategy. The Russians would have preferred the French to fight a defensive, delaying battle that would have mitigated the need for a premature attack in the east. See the authoritative article by A. Svechin, "Bol'shaia voennaia programma," *Russkaia mysl'* bk. 8, pt. 17 (1913), pp. 19–29.

7. General Noël Curières de Castelnau, Archives de Guerre, personal dossier, part 1, item 2, "Mémoire. Pour servir à l'établissement d'un plan de guerre" (January 1914).

8. Joffre, pp. 46–47.

9. Williamson, pp. 210–18; Joffre, pp. 74–80. The denial of permission to violate Belgium was one of two *direct* interventions by civilians in French war planning. The other was the ouster of General Michel, the commander-in-chief-designate in 1911, whose defensive war plan based on the intensive use of reservists was opposed by the General Staff and the Supreme War Council. The main issue in the civilians' eyes was not so much the substance of Michel's plan as the other chiefs' lack of confidence in him and his scheme (Ralston, p. 330). Aside from the question of the violation of Belgium, civilian authorities never seriously examined the assumptions or merits of Joffre's operational strategy (Williamson, p. 223). Civilians' *indirect* influence on war planning, through their institutional and personnel preferences, was considerable, however, as will be shown throughout the following narrative.

10. Williamson, p. 223.

11. Joffre, pp. 67–68 and, generally, pp. 66–82.

12. Ibid.; Tyng, pp. 16–17; Williamson, p. 224; *Armées françaises*, 1st ser., vol. I, pp. 52–53. Each of the 21 French army corps comprised about 44,000 men, totaling 940,000. Each of three separate active divisions and 25 reserve divisions comprised about 18,000 men, totaling 504,000. Some of the reserve divisions were used in the field armies, albeit in secondary roles, while others occupied fortresses or performed garrison duty

in the rear. For details on the older territorial reserves and other forces, see ibid., p. 32. For their respective armaments, see Tyng, pp. 26–31.

13. Sewell Tyng's *Campaign of the Marne* is the most useful account. Also, see below for more details on the numbers and deployment of the opposing forces.

14. Joffre, p. 145.

15. *Armées françaises*, 1st ser., vol. I, p. 39. All translations from French, German, and Russian throughout this book are mine unless otherwise noted.

16. Henri Contamine, *La revanche, 1871–1914* (Paris: Berger-Levrault, 1957), pp. 200ff, 235.

17. Barbara Tuchman, *A Distant Mirror* (New York: Knopf, 1978), p. 86. Even Douglas Porch, who is highly critical of the "nation-in-arms" school of historical analysis, admits that "reservists proved excellent when trained. . . . The poor performance of some reservist units in the opening weeks of war was due to a combination of poor training, which affected the entire army, poor cadres and unimaginative leadership from regular officers. Reservists proved able fighters once acclimatized to war. . . ." *March to the Marne* (New York: Cambridge University Press, 1981), p. 211, citing *Armées françaises*, 1st ser., vol. I, annex 4, p. 13, annex 942, pp. 768–69, and annex 1193, p. 937.

18. Jean Jaurès, *L'armée nouvelle* (1910; rpt. Paris: Editions sociales, 1977), and Gaston Moch, *L'armée d'une démocratie*, 2d ed. (Paris: Editions de la Revue Blanche, 1900), p. 21.

19. Georges Michon, *La préparation à la guerre: La loi de trois ans (1910–1914)* (Paris: Librairie des Sciences Politiques et Sociales, 1935), pp. 160 ff. See also Jaurès, *L'armée nouvelle*, and Porch, pp. 210, 246–49.

20. On Michel's background, see Ronald H. Cole, " 'Forward with the Bayonet!' The French Army Prepares for Offensive War, 1911–1914" (University of Maryland dissertation, 1975) pp. 31–32, 35. Michel's plan is reproduced in *Armées françaises*, 1st ser., vol. I, annex 3. Like Michel was General Maurice Sarrail, a "republican" who worked on upgrading the French reservists as the director of infantry. Sarrail, rumored in 1914 to be the replacement for Joffre in the event of a repeal of the three-year service law, believed that Germany would use reserve units in the initial attack. Unlike Michel, however, Sarrail seems to have preferred a preemptive attack in Lorraine. For both Michel and Sarrail, previous opinions and self-selection are probably a better explanation for their views than are their first-hand dealings with reserve troops. Jan Karl Tanenbaum, *General Maurice Sarrail, 1859–1929: The French Army and Left-wing Politics* (Chapel Hill: University of North Carolina Press, 1974), pp. 25, 34.

21. In fact, this was not true, because of the Germans' long march through northern Belgium.

22. Even Castelnau made this argument in his 1914 memoranda.

23. Williamson, pp. 219–20, citing Henri Bonnal, "Considérations sur la tactique actuelle," *Journal des sciences militaires* 5 (15 October 1912), pp. 380–81.

24. See the section in Chapter 3 on the intelligence failure.

25. Ferdinand Foch, *The Principles of War* (New York: Fly, 1918), p. 313. Foch became the commander of allied forces in 1918.

26. Ibid., p. 314.

27. Cole, pp. 148, 182–83. See also Richard D. Challener, *The French Theory of the Nation in Arms, 1866–1939* (New York: Columbia University Press, 1955), pp. 82–83, and Williamson, p. 128.

28. In this section, references are omitted when later sections discuss the material in greater detail. In general, see Ralston, *Army of the Republic*.

29. Porch, p. 41 and *passim*, provides a useful corrective to the tendency of some

authors to overdraw the picture of a hidebound traditionalist officer corps, pointing out that some officers actually sought reform and that many changed relatively gracefully. He also correctly observes that it is misleading to apply the term "professional army" to both the pre-1870 force and to the later three-year, universal-service regime.

30. See, for example, Ralston, pp. 249–53.

31. Challener, p. 83.

32. Joel A. Setzen, "The Doctrine of the Offensive in the French Army on the Eve of World War I" (University of Chicago dissertation, 1972), p. 182.

33. Williamson, p. 128, makes both points.

34. See Cole, p. 148, for Castelnau's February 1911 lecture at the Centre des hautes études militaires critiquing Jaurès's book. Castelnau contended that reservists, lacking cohesion, would dilute the offensive spirit of the active army.

35. L. Grandmaison, *Deux conférences faites aux officiers de l'état-major de l'armée (février 1911): La notion de sûreté et l'engagement des grandes unités* (Paris: Berger-Levrault, 1911), pp. 48–49.

36. Porch, p. 28, points out that recruits never served the full five-year term. They were usually released after between three and four years.

37. Ibid., p. 212.

38. Archives de Guerre, 5N2, letter of 24 February 1891, quoted by Allan Mitchell, "'A Situation of Inferiority': French Military Reorganization after the Defeat of 1870," *American Historical Review* 86 (February 1981), pp. 49–62.

39. It would be wrong to argue that the military faced no threat to its institutional interests after 1911, however. The military's attempt to make up lost ground provoked considerable resistance by the French left, and the results of the 1914 parliamentary election cast serious doubt on the viability of the three-year service law. See Weber, pp. 129–44; Krumeich, p. 219–71; and below.

3. *France: Du Picq, Dreyfus, and the Errors of Plan 17*

1. Charles Ardant du Picq, *Battle Studies* (New York: Macmillan, 1921). For background on this work and its influence, see Ronald H. Cole, "'Forward with the Bayonet!' The French Army Prepares for Offensive War, 1911–1914" (University of Maryland dissertation, 1975), p. 197.

2. Ardant du Picq, p. 96. See also Stefan T. Possony and Etienne Mantoux, "Du Picq and Foch: the French School," in Edward H. Earle, ed., *Makers of Modern Strategy* (Princeton: Princeton University Press, 1971).

3. Ardant du Picq, pp. 111, 110.

4. Ibid., p. 124. See also pp. 128–29.

5. Cole, pp. 195–97; Possony and Mantoux, pp. 207–8.

6. Michael Howard, *The Franco-Prussian War* (New York: Macmillan, 1961), pp. 29–34; Arpad Francis Kovacs, "French Military Legislation in the Third Republic, 1871–1940," *Military Affairs* 13 (Spring 1949), p. 3.

7. Raoul Girardet, *La société militaire dans la France contemporaine, 1815–1939* (Paris: Plon, 1953), pp. 87–93; Howard, pp. 15, 37; David B. Ralston, *The Army of the Republic: The Place of the Military in the Political Evolution of France, 1871–1914* (Cambridge: MIT Press, 1967), pp. 10–11, 21, 59; Pierre Chalmin, *L'officier français de 1815 à 1870* (Paris: Rivière, 1957), pp. 269–71.

8. See Possony and Mantoux, p. 208.

9. Ardant du Picq, p. 131.

10. See J. Revol, *Histoire de l'armée française* (Paris: Larousse, 1929), p. 215, on the

defensive plans between 1875 and 1884, based on the fortress line constructed under General Raymond Adolphe Séré de Rivières. See also Allan Mitchell, " 'A Situation of Inferiority': French Military Reorganization after the Defeat of 1870," *American Historical Review* 86 (February 1981), pp. 49–62.

11. Revol, p. 215; Howard, p. 7.

12. Lucien Cardot, "Ordre nouveau en tactique," *Revue militaire de l'étranger*, 16 November 1874, p. 276. See also Howard, pp. 181–82.

13. Charles de Gaulle, "Doctrine a priori ou doctrine des circonstances," *Revue militaire française*, 95th year (new ser.), no. 45 (March 1925), p. 313; Revol, p. 215.

14. See Robert Jervis, *Perception and Misperception in International Politics* (Princeton: Princeton University Press, 1976), pp. 226, 230, on the likelihood that the "lessons" of 1870 were determined more by the need to rationalize preferred strategies than by the historical facts.

15. Revol, p. 205.

16. Ralston, pp. 38–39; see also Revol, pp. 204–5, and Richard D. Challener, *The French Theory of the Nation in Arms, 1866–1939* (New York: Columbia University Press, 1955), pp. 10–90. For some qualifications, see Douglas Porch, *March to the Marne: The French Army, 1871–1914* (Cambridge: Cambridge University Press, 1981), pp. 1–44.

17. Jules-Louis Lewal, *Lettres à l'armée sur sa réorganisation* (Paris: Dumaine, 1872), vol. I, p. 81 and pp. 52, 82–83.

18. See Lewal, *La chimère du désarmement* (Paris: Baudoin, 1897), and compare Revol, p. 215, to Lewal, *Stratégie de combat*, vol. 1 (Paris: Baudoin, 1895), pp. 71, 73.

19. Girardet, pp. 198–99, and other works cited by Porch, pp. 16–18.

20. Noblemen and antirepublicans were also found to be disproportionately numerous in the central General Staff. For the 1878 data, see François Bédarida, "L'armée et la République: Les opinions politiques des officiers français en 1876–78," *Revue historique* 88 (July-September 1964), especially pp. 142–51. For data on social origins, see Porch, pp. 17–18, and Walter S. Barge, "The Generals of the Republic: The Corporate Personality of High Military Rank in France, 1889–1914" (University of North Carolina, Chapel Hill, dissertation, 1982).

21. Ralston, pp. 83–114; Challener, especially p. 46.

22. Adolphe Messimy, *Considérations générales sur l'organisation de l'armée: Extrait du rapport sur le budget de la guerre pour l'exercice 1907* (Paris: Charles-Lavauzelle, 1907), pp. 66–67.

23. Ralston, pp. 97–98.

24. See General Gallifet's comments in Conseil supérieur de la guerre (hereafter CSG), procès-verbal, 17 April 1883, Archives de Guerre, 1N3, p. 33 verso.

25. CSG, 21 March 1882, 1N3, p. 42.

26. CSG, 21 March 1882, 1N3, pp. 39–42.

27. An 1882 article cited by Emile Mayer, *Comment on pouvait prévoir l'immobilisation des fronts dans la guerre moderne* (Paris: Berger-Levrault, 1916), pp. 46–47.

28. Revol, p. 216.

29. Dallas D. Irvine, "The French Discovery of Clausewitz and Napoleon," *Military Affairs (Journal of the American Military Institute)* 4 (Fall 1940), p. 154.

30. Revol, p. 216.

31. CSG, July 2 1888, 1N4, pp. 44–46; see Revol, p. 216, on technological improvements.

32. On Gilbert's significance, see Juliette Adam, *Le Capitaine Georges Gilbert* (Paris: Berger-Levrault, 1929).

33. Gilbert, *Essais de critique militaire* (Paris: Nouvelle Revue, 1890), pp. 43, 47–48.

34. Quotation from Gilbert, *Lois et institutions militaires* (Paris: Nouvelle Revue, 1895), p. 175; see also pp. 22 and 229–31, and *Essais*, p. 271. For similar arguments by other French military writers, see Meredith P. Gilpatrick, "Military Strategy on the Western Front from 1871 to 1914 (University of Chicago dissertation, 1958), p. 510.

35. Gilbert, *Lois*, pp. 253–55; see also pp. 177, 182–83.

36. Revol, p. 354.

37. Also noteworthy is Gilbert's concern that the officer corps be a social elite and that the sense of hierarchy be reinforced. See *Lois*, p. 75; Gilbert, *Sept études militaires* (Paris: Nouvelle Revue, 1892), pp. 67–68.

38. General Bonnal, inspirer of French war plans of the 1890s, offers a similar interpretation. See Witold Zaniewicki, "L'impact de 1870 sur la pensée militaire française," *Revue de défense nationale* 26 (August-September 1970), pp. 1333–35.

39. Henry Contamine, *La revanche, 1871–1914* (Paris: Berger-Levrault, 1957), p. 68.

40. Gilpatrick, p. 319.

41. Etat-major général, Cabinet du chef d'Etat-major, "Note pour servir à l'étude d'un plan d'opérations offensives (1886)," Archives de Guerre, 7N1745, 13 August 1886. See also "Historique du Plan," 7N1737, p. 31; Revol, p. 216; and Mitchell, "'A Situation of Inferiority,'" *passim*.

42. CSG, 22 June 1882, 1N3, p. 107. For Plan 7 intelligence, see "Note pour servir à l'étude . . . ," 7N1745, especially p. 15.

43. Charles de Freycinet, *Souvenirs, 1878–1893* (New York: Da Capo, 1973), pp. 444ff, 469ff.

44. See the dispatch of the French military attaché in Berlin, 19 December 1892, Archives de Guerre, 7N1107. On German organizational reforms of this period and their political setting, see Gordon A. Craig, *The Politics of the Prussian Army, 1640–1945* (New York: Oxford University Press, 1964), pp. 238–50.

45. Generally, see CSG, 1888–1896, 1N4–1N7. On the numbers gap, see CSG, 13 January 1890, 1N5, and 5 February 1894, 1N5. On cannibalization and inspections, see CSG, 10 December 1888, 1N4; 22 August 1892, 1N5; 30 November 1896, 1N7; "Extrait du rapport de M. le General Billot, sur l'inspection des 3e et 10e corps en 1895," 7N1751, and Billot's "Inspection de la mobilisation des 1er, 2e, et 3e corps d'armée," 4 May 1889, 1N13, and Freycinet, p. 508. For backtracking in favor of active units, see CSG, 6 January 1890, 1N4.

46. Etat-major de l'armée, deuxième bureau, "Modifications à l'organisation de l'armée allemande à partir du 1er avril 1897," 15 March 1897, 7N655. See also Craig, *Politics*, and *Revue militaire de l'étranger*, June 1896, p. 510.

47. Alfred Schlieffen, *The Schlieffen Problems of 1891, 1896, 1901, 1903, 1904, and 1905* U.S. Army mimeo trans. (Ft. Leavenworth, Kans.: Command and General Staff School, 1935–36), problem no. 1 of 1896, p. 41; Gerhard Ritter, *The Sword and the Scepter: The Problem of Militarism in Germany*, vol. 2 (Coral Gables, Fla: University of Miami Press, 1970), pp. 212–13; Craig, *Politics*.

48. Etat-major de l'armée, deuxième bureau, "Plan général de mobilisation de l'armée allemande pour 1898–1899," January 1898, 7N666.

49. Regarding the golden age and military satisfaction, see Léon-Frédéric Metzinger, *La transformation de l'armée, 1897–1907* (Paris: Belleville, 1909), pp. 5–8; for antimilitia propaganda, see Lewal, *Chimère*; for French war plans, consult A. Marchand, *Plans de concentration de 1871 à 1914* (Paris: Berger-Levrault, 1926); Gilpatrick, p. 728; and Contamine, p. 80. A less sanguine view of French military capability and efficiency during this period is expressed by Allan Mitchell, "The Freycinet Reforms and the French Army, 1888–1893," *Journal of Strategic Studies* 4 (March 1981), pp. 19–28.

50. On the General Staff, for example, Michel was supported by Regnault and op-

posed by Dubail, although both were "republicans" who had risen under the André ministry. See André Morizet, *Le Plan 17* (Paris: Editions l'Humanité, 1919), pp. 62–65, for a classification of the political views of Dubail and other military figures; the CSG meeting of 19 July 1911 for Dubail's criticism of Michel; and below regarding Regnault.

51. See Georges Michon, *La préparation à la guerre: La loi de trois ans (1910–1914)* (Paris: Librairie des Sciences Politiques et Sociales, 1935), pp. 170ff. The same holds for the other principal military publicists arguing for the return of the three-year service, Maitrot, Cherfils, and Driant.

52. See Joel A. Setzen, "The Doctrine of the Offensive in the French Army on the Eve of World War I" (University of Chicago dissertation, 1972), p. 114; A. Maurice Selliers de Moranville, *Du haut de la Tour de Babel* (Paris: Berger-Levrault, 1925), p. 41; France, Assemblée nationale, Chambre des députés, Commission d'enquête sur le rôle et la situation de la métallurgie en France, *Procès-verbaux (Défense du Bassin de Briey)*, session de 1919 (hereafter cited as *Briey*), p. 105; CSG, *Procès-verbal*, 12 October 1908, 1N10; Etat-major de l'armée, service historique, *Les armées françaises dans la grande guerre*, 1st ser., vol. I, annex 3. Similarly, Percin, André's *chef de cabinet*, was at the same time a disciple of the artillery doctrine of the traditionalist Langlois, who urged light artillery for rapid offensive advances.

53. This is asserted by Gamelin, *Manoeuvre et victoire de la Marne* (Paris: Grasset, 1954), p. 42.

54. On Messimy's ostracism and his stress on modernization of the army, see, respectively, *Mes souvenirs* (Paris: Plon, 1937), pp. 11–14, and *Considérations*, p. 100. Generally, on the modernism of conservatives after the Dreyfus affair, see Michon, pp. 39ff.

55. On Grouard, see B. H. Liddell Hart, "French Military Ideas before the First World War," in Martin Gilbert, ed., *A Century of Conflict* (London: Hamilton, 1966), pp. 146–47. Comments at 19 July 1911 meeting, *Procès-verbal*, 1N10, pp. 209–11, juxtaposed against ratings reported by Morizet, pp. 62–65.

56. Porch, pp. vii–viii. His targets include Monteilhet, Michon, and Ralston.

57. Ibid., pp. 249–50.

58. Background information not specifically footnoted may be found in Girardet, chap. 7, "Crises de conscience," and Ralston, chap. 6. Gilbert's words are from Adam, pp. 51–53, letter of 9 November 1899.

59. Summarized by Setzen, pp. 68ff. Porch exaggerates only a little when he says that the André reforms "beat the dead horses of clerical reaction and military conspiracy. . . . The ancien regime no longer existed, so they had to invent it" (p. 73).

60. Ralston, pp. 289–97; Samuel R. Williamson, *The Politics of Grand Strategy: Britain and France Prepare for War, 1904–1914* (Cambridge: Harvard University Press, 1969), p. 119; Porch, p. 77; Eugen Weber, *The Nationalist Revival in France, 1905–1914* (Berkeley: University of California Press, 1959), p. 49; General Louis André, *Cinq ans de ministère* (Paris: Michaud, 1909) pp. 39, 45–46; 8 April 1903, 1N9, p. 36.

61. Messimy, *Souvenirs*, pp. 71–72; see also André, p. 27.

62. Mark Ira Kaplan, "The Radical Party and the Army in France, 1899–1905" (City Univeristy of New York dissertation, 1976), p. 143; Charles Humbert, *Sommes-nous défendus?* (Paris: Jouven, 1907), p. 22; Metzinger, p. 46.

63. On St. Cyr, see Gilpatrick, p. 786; generally, see Setzen, pp. 54, 57; Kaplan, pp, 119ff; Revol, pp. 208–9; Ralston, p. 356; André, pp. 98, 115; Metzinger, pp. 38–41.

64. Metzinger, p. 55, note 1.

65. Charles Kessler, *La patrie menacée* (Paris: Librairie académique Didier, 1906), p. 305.

66. Emile Driant, *Vers un nouveau Sedan* (Paris: Jouven, 1906), p. 126. Sedan was the crowning defeat of the French field army in 1870.

67. On the Midi incident, see Setzen, p. 53, and Guy Bechtel, *1907: La grande révolte du Midi* (Paris: Laffont, 1976).

68. On the socialist danger, see David L. Lewis, *Prisoners of Honor: The Dreyfus Affair* (New York: Morrow, 1973), pp. 183–85. On André's demise, see Kaplan, p. 198. For other points, see Henri Bonnal, *Questions militaires d'actualité*, 2d ser., *La première bataille* (Paris: Chapelot, 1908), p. 147; Metzinger, p. 3; Driant, p. 7.

69. Challener, p. 62.

70. André, pp. 177–78; Joseph Monteilhet, *Les institutions militaires de la France, 1814–1924* (Paris: Alcan, 1926), p. 235; Gustave Cognet, *Officers de réserve* (Paris: Chapelot, 1909), p. 130.

71. Monteilhet, p. 254.

72. Messimy, *Considérations*, pp. 278ff; Cognet, p. 111; Monteilhet, p. 254.

73. Setzen, p. 50.

74. Bonnal, p. 61.

75. CSG, 27 September 1907, 1N9, p. 209. This plan was approved by the vice-president, de la Croix, and the council on 27 September.

76. Ralston, pp. 344–45.

77. CSG, 12 October 1908, 1N10, pp. 74 verso and 75.

78. Ralston, pp. 344–45.

79. Setzen, pp. 45, 76–7, citing *Times*, 15 October 1910, p. 6, and *France militaire*, 2 December 1910, p. 1.

80. Setzen, pp. 48–49.

81. For background material on these wars, see Thomas Pakenham, *The Boer War* (New York: Random, 1979), and David Walder, *The Short, Victorious War: The Russo-Japanese Conflict of 1904–1905* (London: Hutchinson, 1973).

82. Kaplan, p. 110, citing *Le Matin*, 21 December 1899.

83. Emile Mayer, *Trois maréchaux: Joffre, Gallieni, Foch* (Paris: Gallimard, 1928), p. 137, quoting "Quelques idées françaises sur la guerre de l'avenir," *Revue militaire suisse* (May 1902); Mayer (pseud. Emile Manceau), *Notre armée: Essais de psychologie militaire* (Paris: Charpentier, 1901), for his views on institutional questions.

84. Contamine, p. 87 and *passim*; General Pierre Cherfils, *Pour l'armée* (Paris: Berger-Levrault, 1913), p. 321; Etat-major de l'armée, troisième bureau, "Envoi du projet du règlement d'infanterie modifié," Conseil supérieur de la guerre, 31 October 1904, 1N11; Stephen Ryan, *Pétain the Soldier* (New York: Barnes, 1969), pp. 19–32.

85. Henri Bonnal, *La récente guerre sud-africaine et ses enseignements* (Paris: Chapelot, 1903), p. 63.

86. Gilbert, *La guerre sud-africaine* (Paris: Berger-Levrault, 1902), especially pp. 477, 485, 497–98, 519.

87. Culmann, *Deux tactiques en présence* (Paris: Charles-Lavauzelle, 1904), pp. 24–26, 148, 184–86, 291.

88. General Marie Félix Silvestre, *Considérations sur la campagne de Mandchourie (1904–1905)* (Paris: Berger-Levrault, 1910), pp. 90–97; Etat-major de l'armée, deuxième bureau, "Enseignements de la guerre russo-japonaise," especially notes 2, 3 and 16 of 1905 and 1907, Archives de Guerre, 7N671.

89. "Enseignements," note 2, "Mitrailleuses," December 1905, 7N671, p. 18. These conclusions had an immediate, if inadequate, effect on French weapons procurement. See Messimy, *Considérations*, pp. 6–8; Humbert, pp. 101ff.

90. Culmann, *Etude sur les caractères généraux de la guerre d'Extrême-Orient* (Paris: Berger-Levrault, 1909), p. 7.

91. "Enseignements," note 16, p. 4; see also Silvestre, p. 83.

92. See Walder, chap. 11.

93. Silvestre, p. 100.

94. This is a quotation from Joseph de Maistre, cited in Foch, *The Principles of War* (New York: Fly, 1918). See also Ibid., pp. 310ff.

95. Ibid., pp. 370–71.

96. The views of contemporary observers in other European countries did not differ greatly from those of the French, however. They, too, had reasons to perceive the war as confirming their preferred offensive doctrines. See below.

97. For previous French estimates, see "Compte-rendu du Plan XV: Composition et répartition probable des forces allemandes," 7N1756. For the 1904 information itself, see Etat-major de l'armée, deuxième bureau, "Note au sujet des documents S. R. nos. 2474 et 2500 relatifs à la concentration allemand," January 1904, 7N1756. These archival sources do not square with the "Avenger" document discussed by Georges Maurice Paléologue, *The Turning Point* (London: Hutchinson, 1935), pp. 63–65. For the actual German plans, see Gerhard Ritter, *The Schlieffen Plan* (New York: Praeger, 1958), p. 42; Wolfgang Foerster, "Ist der deutsche Aufmarsch 1904 an die Französen verraten worden?" *Berliner Monatshefte* (November 1932), pp. 1060–62; Jean Charles Courbis, *Le comte Schlieffen* (Paris: Berger-Levrault, 1938), p. 70ff; Gilpatrick, p. 1071; Friedrich von Boetticher, "Der Lehrmeister des neuzeitlichen Krieges," in Friedrich von Cochenhausen, ed., *Von Scharnhorst zu Schlieffen, 1806–1906* (Berlin: Mittler, 1933), p. 266.

98. It also parallels the curvilinear response to threat outlined by Irving Janis and Leon Mann, *Decision Making* (New York: Free, 1977), which posits no change if the threat falls below a certain threshold, rational search for alternatives if the threat is manageable, and defensive denial that any adjustments must be made if the threat cannot be managed by acceptable means.

99. "Note au sujet . . . 2474 et 2500," 7N1756, pp. 1–4, 8–9. For details, see Snyder "Defending the Offensive: French, German, and Russian War Planning, 1870–1914," (Columbia University dissertation, 1981), pp. 128–30.

100. "Note au sujet . . . 2474 et 2500," 7N1756, pp. 8–9.

101. Etat-major de l'armée, troisième bureau, "Note au sujet du Plan de concentration allemande No. 1 présenté par le 2e Bureau de l'EMA," 29 January 1904, 7N1756, pp. 9–18; Ritter, *Schlieffen Plan*, pp. 41–42.

102. "Note au sujet de Plan de concentration allemande," 7N1756, pp. 5–9; Ritter, *Schlieffen Plan, passim*.

103. Etat-major de l'armée, deuxième bureau, "Suite à la Note du 12 Avril 1904 sur le document S. R. No. 2474, de 1904, relatif à la concentration allemande," 10 May 1904, 7N1756, p. 7 and *passim*.

104. Etat-major de l'armée, troisième bureau, "Note sur des renseignements récents relatifs à la concentration des armées allemandes: Etude de la violation de la neutralité de la Belgique par l'Allemagne," 13 August 1904, 7N1756, quoting General Saussier's remarks of 1889.

105. The quotation is from ibid., p. 28; for other points, see pp. 9, 23, 25–29, 32.

106. Letter to Etat-major de l'armée, troisième bureau, 27 September 1904, 7N1756.

107. The quotation is from a letter to Etat-major de l'armée, troisième bureau, 12 October 1904, p. 23; for other points, see pp. 3, 5–13, 30–32, 36–44, 21–22, 36.

108. Letter of 8 October 1904, 7N1756; see especially pp. 8–13, 21–22.

109. Boetticher, p. 267; Courbis, pp. 109–11; Gilpatrick, pp. 1091, 1094. See also Foerster, *Aus der Gedankenwerkstatt des deutschen Generalstabes* (Berlin: Mittler, 1931), p. 40. The more ambitious plans for the development of the reserve forces laid out in Schlieffen's December 1905 memorandum were not fully realized due to budgetary

limitations and opposition in the War Ministry. Despite this opposition, Schlieffen's successor as chief of staff, the younger Moltke, continued to seek ways to enhance the value of the reserves. Each year the number of reservists called up for exercises increased somewhat. (See the dispatch from the French military attaché in Berlin, Laguiche, 14 April 1907, 7N1108; *Revue militaire des armées étrangères* [September 1907], p. 219). In 1908 and 1909 Moltke unsuccessfully sought funds to improve the reserves' artillery and supply services so that they could function in exactly the same way as active field corps. By 1910, the revival of Russia's finances and army had become imminent, increasing the pressure on the German war planners to improve the reserves as the cheapest way to restore the balance. As a result, the army bill of 1911 finally began to improve the reserve forces, so that their fighting capabilities could be brought into line with the role they would be asked to play in the event of war. See Reichsarchiv, *Der Weltkrieg*, 3d ser.: *Kriegsrüstung und Kriegswirtschaft* (Berlin: Mittler, 1930), vol. I, appendix no. 34; Ritter, *Sword*, II, pp. 220–21; Erich Ludendorff, *The General Staff and Its Problems* (1920; rpt. Freeport, N.Y.: Books for Libraries, 1971), pp. 22–32.

110. See for example Capitaine Fournier, Etat-major de l'armée, deuxième bureau, "Les chemins de fer allemands à la fin de 1909," December 1909, 7N672.

111. General de Lacroix, CSG, 15 February 1908, 1N10, p. 57.

112. Etat-major de l'armée, deuxième bureau, "Note sommaire sur la couverture et la concentration allemande à la frontière française," May 1907, 7N672, especially pp. 7–8, and p. 10.

113. Gilpatrick, p. 1091; Courbis, pp. 109–11.

114. See for example CSG, 15 February 1908, 1N10, p. 57 verso; Etat-major de l'armée, "1er voyage d'Etat-major du 29 mai au 5 juin 1907: Journal des opérations du parti bleu (ennemi)," 7N1759.

115. This followed a series of modifications to Plan 15 that also moved in this direction. Williamson has a good discussion of Plan 16, pp. 122–25.

116. CSG, "Compte-rendu du Plan XVI," 15 May 1909, 1N10.

117. The Belgians themselves had been divided since 1905 between a "northern" and a "southern" school. Gilpatrick, pp. 739ff. For Regnault's background, see *Briey*, pp. 321ff.

118. Pellé dispatches, 23 January and 10 February 1910, 7N1109; Etat-major de l'armée, deuxième bureau, response dated 9 February 1910; Reichsarchiv, *Kriegsrüstung*, appendices, Table 13. See also a reiteration of Russian views in a report provided by the Russian attaché in Paris, "Note sur la mobilisation et le déploiement stratégique des forces armées de l'Allemagne," 7N1535.

119. April 27, 1910, 7N1109, and Etat-major de l'armée, deuxième bureau, "Note au sujet des mesures prises en Allemagne pour assurer le commandement et l'encadrement des formations de réserve," 21 March 1892, 7N665.

120. March 7, 1911, 7N1110. See also Charles E. Calwell, *Field-Marshal Sir Henry Wilson*, vol. 1 (New York: Scribner's, 1927), pp. 100, 104. This closely follows a plan outlined in a 1909 book by the influential German military writer, General Falkenhausen (Contamine, p. 174). Adding another British voice to this viewpoint, Repington noted that in the 1911 German maneuvers General von der Goltz deployed a single division over a 10 kilometer front. By extrapolation, the total German deployment would then stretch over 400 kilometers and cover much of Belgium (Contamine, p. 173).

121. Etat-major de l'armée, deuxième bureau, "Commentaires du document S. R. No. 1658 du 20 Avril 1911," June 1911, 7N1112.

122. Nikolai Nikolaevich Golovin, *The Russian Campaign of 1914* (Ft. Leavenworth, Kans.: Command and General Staff School Press, 1933).

123. "Commentaires."

124. Ecole supérieure de guerre, "Conferences d'organisation générale et de mobilisation, 1910–1911," 7N1766. Of course, Stirn may not have known about the latest information.

125. General Regnault, "L'échec du Plan XVII," *Revue de Paris*, 15 July 1920, pp. 369–70. It is somewhat difficult to square these postwar assertions with the much more modest analyses produced in the General Staff at the time. Probably Regnault exaggerated the extent of their knowledge, and possibly he was constrained from officially drawing the dramatic conclusions in which he personally believed. His chief at the General Staff, Laffon de Ladebat, was one of Michel's harshest critics at the 19 July 1911 session of the Supreme War Council. On his proselytizing, see pp. 370–71.

126. Cole, pp. 151–52, footnotes 21 and 22. It is interesting that Porch understands the role of offense as a cure for poor morale and also sees "political and social strife" related to the Dreyfus affair as the cause of poor morale (pp. 214, 224). Nonetheless, he fails to make the final connection between offense and the protection of threatened military institutions.

127. Loyzeaux de Grandmaison, *Dressage de l'infanterie en vue du combat offensif* (Paris: Berger-Levrault, 1908), esp. pp. 2–3, 24, 36–40, 47. Two historians have recently interpreted Grandmaison's tactical system as a solution for the problem of the two-year service. In a sense, they are right. In terms of the movement of larger tactical units, Grandmaison's formula of attacking straight ahead at every point on the front was much simpler than Bonnal's concept of Napoleonic maneuver. Still, almost everyone agreed that the tactical defense of prepared positions was the easiest task for poorly trained troops. Logically, the defensive was more compatible with a short term of service, which Jaurès understood perfectly in designing his six-month training system. Grandmaison's tactics, while purporting to be compatible with a short term of service, would always require more than six months training to instill military esprit, group coordination, and offensive technique, which is necessarily more complicated than shooting from a trench. Offensive tactics also could—and later did—serve as part of the rationale for a return to the three-year service. See Douglas Porch, "The French Army and the Spirit of the Offensive," in Brian Bond and Ian Roy, eds., *War and Society* (New York: Holmes & Meier, 1975), esp. pp. 135–36; Jonathan M. House, "The Decisive Attack: A New Look at French Infantry Tactics on the Eve of World War I," *Military Affairs* 40 (December 1976), pp. 164–69; and C. M. Lardemelle, *1914: Le redressement initial* (Paris: Berger-Levrault, 1935), pp. 23–24.

128. Grandmaison, pp. 68, 5.

129. Ibid., p. 31; above points on pp. 4, 8.

130. Ibid., p. 42–45.

131. Cole, p. 222; Setzen, p. 44.

132. Setzen, pp. 48–49; Alexandre Percin, *1914: Les erreurs du haut commandement* (Paris: Albin Michel, 1920), p. 82.

133. Lardemelle, pp. 4–5; Lieutenant Colonel d'Esclaibes, "La pensée militaire Grandmaison," *Revue militaire d'information* no. 196 (25 June 1952), pp. 19–26.

134. L. Grandmaison, *Deux conférences faites aux officiers de l'état-major de l'armée (février 1911): La notion de sûreté et l'engagement des grandes unités* (Paris: Berger-Levrault, 1911), pp. 23, 28, 25.

135. Ibid., pp. 48–49.

136. Ibid., pp. 40–42, 47, 57.

137. Gilpatrick, p. 827; Selliers de Moranville, p. 35.

138. Etat-major de l'armée, "Note du 1er bureau au sujet des propositions de M. le Général Michel," 1911, 7N1766.

139. Etat-major de l'armée, troisième bureau, "Etude d'un projet de plan," 1911, 7N1766.

140. Gilpatrick, p. 826, citing Selliers de Moranville, p. 53.

141. CSG, 19 July 1911, 1N10, pp. 214 verso, 215; for other points, pp. 209 verso and ff.

142. See for example Etat-major de l'armée, deuxième bureau, "Extrait du rapport annuel de l'attaché militaire à Berlin du 17 février 1909," 7N672; CSG, 18 February 1905, 1N9, pp. 89–91; Commandant Stirn, "Conférences d'organization générale et de mobi-lization, 1910–1911," Ecole supérieure de Guerre, 7N1766, pp. 66–72; Henri Langlois, *Questions de défense nationale*, (Paris: Berger-Levrault, 1906) p. 11.

143. Joseph Joffre, *The Memoirs of Marshal Joffre* (London: Bles, 1932), vol. I, pp. 26ff.

144. As Joffre's principal deputy, General Castelnau, put it, "an army uncertain of its doctrine . . . is not in a state to meet the challenges of the field of battle victoriously: it lacks a primordial quality, faith—faith in its methods of combat." (Castelnau, person-al dossier, "Conférences faites par le Général de Castelnau," Centre des hautes études militaires, no. 1, "Doctrine.") Pétain took a more skeptical view of such matters, saying that "the three cardinal virtues of the Young Turks" like Grandmaison are "guts, confidence, and the taste for risk. We put the confidence between the other two for fear that it might escape" (Lardemelle, p. 26 note 1).

145. See Porch, p. 172, and Ralston, pp. 332–34.

146. Joffre, p. 45; Revol, p. 228; Porch, pp. 191ff; Etat-major de l'armée, troisième bureau, "Bases du Plan 17," 1912, 7N1171, pp. 6–18.

147. Sewell Tyng, *The Campaign of the Marne, 1914* (New York: Longmans, Green, 1935), p. 376. On the skeptical reaction of Berthelot and the rest of the French opera-tions staff to intelligence indicating the true strength of the German force west of the Meuse, see Revol, p. 230, and Gamelin, pp. 63–66.

148. Joffre, p. 86, citing his draft Plan 16, variant 2, written during the debate on the three-year law in April 1913.

149. Joffre, p. 68.

150. See especially Cole's discussion of the 1913 infantry field regulations, p. 287. For additional examples and citations, see Snyder, pp. 165–66.

151. Porch, p. 133, quoting *France militaire*, 24 October 1913. On the mutinies, Porch, p. 189, and Gerd Krumeich, *Aufrüstung und Innenpolitik in Frankreich vor dem Ersten Weltkrieg* (Wiesbaden: Steiner, 1980), pp. 95, 109ff.

152. Weber, p. 110.

153. Monteilhet, pp. 332, 394; Michon, p. 94. The quotation is from Monteilhet, p. 297.

154. Remarks by Reinach, Driant, and Lefebre, cited by Ralston, p. 352; Cole, pp. 173–74; Michon, pp. 106, 151, 156; and Monteilhet, p. 269.

155. Ralston, pp. 352–53.

156. Joffre and the General Staff seem to have been concerned about a hasty German attack in Lorraine, but only in the sense that military planners are always concerned about conceivable but improbable threats. The document "Plan 17: Bases du Plan" concluded that "the prudent and methodical Germans will not want to expose their advance corps to the risks [of an *attaque brusquée*], which would not be compensated by

the results which might be achieved" (pp. 83–85, 7N1171). See also Ralston, p. 355. The Liège *coup de main* shows that concern about small-scale *attaques brusquées* against specific targets was not totally unwarranted. Castelnau was seriously worried about a grab for Nancy, while the General Staff's Belin worried about the Hauts-de-Meuse. See Ferdinand Engerand, *La bataille de la Frontière (Août 1914): Briey* (Paris: Bossard, 1920), pp. 20–21. Pau seems to have been genuinely concerned about the *attaque brusquée* scenario on a larger scale. See the Supreme War Council session of 4 March 1913, 1N10, p. 56.

157. Krumeich, p. 50 and *passim*. One parliamentarian came up with the grand synthesis, arguing that offense was needed to respond to an *attaque brusquée!* Michon, p. 151.

158. The views of Gallieni and Lanrezac might be explained either in terms of self-interest, as commanders of the Fifth Army, or as part of their moderate views on doctrine and institutions. See below.

159. Contamine, p. 235.

160. Tyng, pp. 354–60.

161. Ibid., pp. 61–62, 145, 62.

162. Testimony of General Percin, *Briey*, p. 128; see also *Briey*, pp. 181, 194; Joffre, p. 64.

163. Contamine, p. 202.

164. Joffre, p. 164; Gamelin, p. 63. Lanrezac understood the situation in August 1914 better than Joffre did, but this fitted his prewar expectations of a major German attack through Belgium and thus is no test of what an "objective observer" should have been able to perceive. The most detailed source on the August intelligence errors is Lardemelle, *Redressement initial*.

165. Tyng, pp. 367–68.

166. Joffre, pp. 179–80, and Tyng, p. 366.

167. Joffre, pp. 18, 64.

168. *Armées françaises*, 1st ser., vol. I, p. 39.

169. Ibid.

170. Ibid.

171. Joffre, pp. 143ff.

172. These facts were reported in General Staff studies (Etat-major de l'armée, "Renseignements sur l'armée allemande," 3 July and 20 October 1913, 14N38); dispatches from the French military attachés in Berlin (especially Pellé, *Documents diplomatiques français [DDF]*, 2d ser., vol. III, no. 392, 28 April 1912, p. 403; Serret, *DDF*, 3d ser., vol. VI, no. 123, 30 March 1913, p. 159); and the press (*Revue militaire des armées étrangères* [July-December 1911], p. 195). See also Gustave Cognet, *Le problème des reserves* (Paris: Chapelot, 1914), pp. 136–37.

173. *DDF*, 3d ser., vol. VI, no. 123, 30 March 1913, p. 159.

174. Garros, "Prélude," p. 40; Etat-major de l'armée, "Etude relative au théâtre d'opérations russo-allemand," May 1914, 7N1538.

175. Cole, p. 153; *Armées françaises*, 1st ser., vol. I, p. 40; *DDF*, 3d ser., vol. VI, pp. 156–60; Joffre, p. 62.

176. *DDF*, 3d ser., vol. V, no. 210, 5 April 1913, pp. 256ff.

177. Buat's "plan" used only actives in the first line. The German right extended into southern Belgium. Setzen, p. 182.

178. Gallieni, *Mémoires du Maréchal Gallieni: Défense de Paris* (Paris: Payot, 1926), p. 10. Gallieni's comments on war games at the Centre des hautes études militaires appear in

"Critique: hypothèse générale," 1914, 6N44; Gallieni, "Considérations générales. Le théâtre d'opérations et les mouvements de l'ennemi," April 1911, 6N42.

179. Henry Charbonnel, *De Madagascar à Verdun* (Paris: Karolus, 1962), p. 247.

180. Georges Beau and Leopold Gaubusseau, *En août 1914 Lanrezac a-t-il sauvé la France?* (Paris: Presses de la Cité, 1964) pp. 68–69.

181. For Gallieni's defensive prescription for the Fifth Army, see "Critique: Conclusions," 6N44, p. 2.

182. In fact, the Germans sent two corps from the right wing to the eastern front, which would have eliminated their superiority on the right had Gallieni's plan been adopted.

183. Recall Duchesne's arguments of 1904, discussed above.

4. Germany: The Elusive Formula for Decisive Victory

1. See Gerhard Ritter, *The Schlieffen Plan* (New York: Praeger, 1958), pp. 100–103, for Schlieffen's assessment of the threat to German security as expressed in "Der Krieg in der Gegenwart," *Deutsche Revue* (1909), which is reproduced in Schlieffen's *Cannae*, 3d ed. (Berlin: Mittler, 1936), pp. 273–85.

2. James E. Edmonds, *A Short History of World War I* (1951; rpt. New York: Greenwood, 1968) p. 9. Qualitative differences were reflected not only in matériel but also in the skills and aptitudes of officers and troops. It should be noted that a few of these Russian divisions were deployed in the Far East and others were initially designated for the Turkish front, the protection of St. Petersburg, and the observation of the Rumanian frontier.

3. These figures are based on the May 1912 plan. A. M. Zaionchkovskii, *Podgotovka Rossii k imperialisticheskoi voine* (Moscow: Gosvoenizdat, 1926), p. 266. See chapter 7 for details.

4. On the advantages of the "interior line of operations," see Crane Brinton, Gordon A. Craig, and Felix Gilbert, "Jomini," in E. M. Earle, ed., *Makers of Modern Strategy* (Princeton: Princeton University Press, 1971), pp. 86–87.

5. The first quotation is from Schlieffen's comments on a 1905 war game; I adapt the U.S. Army War College translation of Wilhelm Groener, *Commander against His Will* (Washington D.C., 1943), originally *Der Feldherr wider Willen* (Berlin: Mittler, 1931), p. 379. The second quotation is from Schlieffen's "Der Krieg in der Gegenwart," quoted by Hajo Holborn, "Moltke and Schlieffen," in Earle, p. 187.

6. See Hermann von Kuhl, *The Marne Campaign* (Ft. Leavenworth, Kans.: Command and General Staff School Press, 1936), pp. 17–23, and Ritter, *The Sword and the Scepter* (Coral Gables, Fla.: University of Miami Press, 1970), vol. II, pp. 152–53.

7. On the Russian wartime economy, see Norman Stone, *The Eastern Front, 1914–1917* (London: Hodder & Stoughton, 1975). On the Germans' misunderstanding of their own argicultural problem, see Joe Lee, "German Agricultural Policy in the First World War," in J. N. Winter, ed., *War and Economic Development* (New York: Cambridge University Press, 1975).

8. See Ritter, *Schlieffen Plan*.

9. Ibid., pp. 42, 46. The parting memorandum, usually referred to as *the* Schlieffen Plan, is reproduced in Ritter, *Schlieffen Plan*, pp. 134–48. See also Sewell Tyng, *The Campaign of the Marne, 1914* (New York: Longmans, Green, 1935), pp. 1–10.

10. Ritter, *Schlieffen Plan*, p. 166.

11. The comparison is detailed in Tyng, pp. 353–55. On the Ersatz Corps, see Ritter,

Schlieffen Plan, pp. 62–63, 66–67. So-called Reserve units were manned by the most recent veterans of active service. Landwehr units were formed by somewhat older veterans. Ersatz units were composed of young men who had received brief military training instead of serving a full two-year tour of active duty.

12. Ritter, *Schlieffen Plan*, pp. 54, 61, 65, and Wilhelm Groener, *Das Testament des Grafen Schlieffen* (Berlin: Mittler, 1927), translated by W. P. Papanforth as *The Testament of Count Schlieffen*, mimeo (Ft. Sherman, Kans., 1931).

13. See Tyng, pp. 6–10, and Groener, *Das Testament*.

14. Ritter, *Schlieffen Plan*, covers all of these arguments.

15. Ibid., p. 66. On the forces engaged in 1914, see Tyng, pp. 358–60; on earlier periods, see Henri Contamine, *La revanche, 1871–1914* (Paris: Berger-Levrault, 1957), especially pp. 62ff, 91ff.

16. From the 1905 memorandum, Ritter, *Schlieffen Plan*, p. 141. On the logistics of the Schlieffen plan, which will be discussed in greater detail in chapter 5, see Martin van Creveld, *Supplying War* (New York: Cambridge University Press, 1977), pp. 113–41.

17. Ritter, *Schlieffen Plan*, p. 67 note 48. On balance, strengthening the right wing at the expense of the left might have marginally improved the 1914 war plan, but it would have further complicated an already difficult logistical problem and would have allowed the French to shift more troops from their right in Lorraine to their left around Paris.

18. Holborn, p. 192, citing Schlieffen's comments on a 1901 staff exercise.

19. A 1905 staff ride, reported by Friedrich von Boetticher, "Der Lehrmeister des neuzeitlichen Krieges," in Friedrich von Cochenhausen, ed., *Von Scharnhorst zu Schlieffen, 1806–1906* (Berlin: Mittler, 1933), pp. 310–11.

20. Ritter, *Schlieffen Plan*, pp. 149–50, 64.

21. Ibid., pp. 64, 140; p. 45.

22. On the reinforcement of the Paris garrison and the formation of the Sixth Army, see Tyng, pp. 131, 199–200.

23. Cited by Ritter, *Schlieffen Plan*, p. 60 note 34.

24. Jehuda Wallach, *Das Dogma der Vernichtungsschlacht* (Frankfurt: Bernard & Graefe, 1967), pp. 162–64.

25. Boetticher, pp. 310–11.

26. Ritter, *Schlieffen Plan*, pp. 67–68.

27. Ronald L. Ernharth, "The Tragic Alliance: Austro-German Military Cooperation, 1871–1918" (Columbia University dissertation, 1970), p. 118, citing the memoirs of Count Franz Conrad von Hötzendorff, *Aus meiner Dienstzeit* (Vienna: Rikola, 1921–1925), vol. III, pp. 667ff.

28. Cable to Ambassador Bertie in Paris, quoted in Luigi Albertini, *The Origins of the War of 1914* (London: Oxford University Press, 1952), vol. III, p. 383. For the nuances of this idea, see Harry F. Young, "The Misunderstanding of August 1, 1914," *Journal of Modern History* 48 (December 1976), pp. 644–65. For a general discussion of British wavering during this period, see Samuel R. Williamson, *The Politics of Grand Strategy: Britain and France Prepare for War, 1904–1914* (Cambridge: Harvard University Press, 1969), pp. 343–61.

29. Paul Kennedy, *Rise of the Anglo-German Antagonism, 1860–1914* (London: Allen & Unwin, 1980), pp. 425, 465. Zara Steiner, *Britain and the Origins of the First World War* (New York: St. Martin's, 1977), pp. 211, 228–37. See also Kennedy, ed., *The War Plans of the Great Powers, 1880–1941* (London: Allen & Unwin, 1979), pp. 12–13.

30. In 1909 he had asked Kuhl to reconnoiter the Franco-German frontier to determine whether an alternative to the violation of Belgium could be devised. Ritter, *Sword*,

vol. II, pp. 216–19 and notes 34–38 on p. 305; see also Ritter, *Schlieffen Plan*, pp. 68–69 note 50.

31. Moltke's statement to the Austrian chief of staff, General Beck, 8 September 1888, cited from Austrian Kriegsarchiv by Ernharth, pp. 30–31.

32. For Moltke's operation plans, see Ritter, *Schlieffen Plan*, pp. 17–27, and Helmuth Karl Bernhard von Moltke, *Die deutschen Aufmarschpläne, 1871–1890*, ed. Ferdinand von Schmerfeld (Berlin: Mittler, 1929).

33. Louis Garros, "Préludes aux invasions de la Belgique," *Revue historique de l'armée* 5 (March 1949), pp. 37–38; report of the French military attaché in St. Petersburg, Laguiche, to the second bureau, 12 April (Russian style) 25 April (Western style) 1913, Archives de Guerre, 7N1478; Etat-major de l'armée, "Etude relative à l'importance, à la répartition et à l'emploi des forces allemandes sur le théâtre d'opérations russo-allemand," May 1914, 7N1534.

34. Egon von Gayl, *General von Schlichting und sein Lebenswerk* (Berlin: Stilke, 1913), p. 367.

35. Stone, pp. 93, 185.

36. Staabs suggested deploying 19 corps plus 6-1/2 Ersatz divisions defending in the west and about 20 corps pursuing a limited offensive in the east: *Aufmarsch nach zwei Fronten* (Berlin: Mittler, 1925), pp. 57–63. For Beck's various hypotheses, see Ludwig Beck, *Studien* (Stuttgart: Koehler, 1955), pp. 143–89.

37. David B. Ralston, *The Army of the Republic: The Place of the Military in the Political Evolution of France, 1871–1914* (Cambridge: MIT Press, 1967), pp. 370–71.

38. Tyng, p. 380.

39. Van Creveld, p. 140.

40. L. L. Farrar, *Arrogance and Anxiety* (Iowa City: University of Iowa Press, 1981), pp. 24, 23.

41. See Alfred Graf von Waldersee, *General-Feldmarschall Alfred Graf von Waldersee in seinem militärischen Wirken*, ed. Hans Mohs, vol. II (Berlin: Eisenschmidt, 1929), p. 348, and Meredith P. Gilpatrick, "Military Strategy on the Western Front from 1871 to 1914" (University of Chicago dissertation, 1958), p. 652.

42. See Norman Rich, *Friedrich von Holstein* (Cambridge: Cambridge University Press, 1965), 1, pp. 302–5, and Rich, ed., *The Holstein Papers* (Cambridge: Cambridge University Press, 1955–1963), vol. III, pp. 347 note 1 and 352–55.

43. The 1899 quotation is from Ritter, *Schlieffen Plan*, pp. 91–92; on 1912 see Fritz Fischer, *War of Illusions: German Policies from 1911–1914* (New York: Norton, 1975), p. 390.

44. Making a similar argument is John C. Rohl, *Germany without Bismarck* (Berkeley: University of California Press, 1967).

45. Martin Kitchen, *The German Officer Corps, 1890–1914* (Oxford: Clarendon, 1968), chap. 4.

46. See the section on Schlieffen's views on politics in chapter 5 below.

47. Ritter, *Sword*, vol. II, pp. 247–63.

5. Germany: The "Necessary" Is Possible

1. Moltke, quoted by Jehuda Wallach, *Kriegstheorien* (Frankfurt: Bernard & Graefe, 1972), p. 74.

2. Eugene Carrias, *La pensée militaire allemande* (Paris: Presses universitaires de

France, 1948), p. 250; Larry Addington, *The Blitzkrieg Era and the German General Staff* (New Brunswick, N.J.: Rutgers University Press, 1972), p. 4.

3. Quotation adapted from Meredith P. Gilpatrick, "Military Strategy on the Western Front from 1871 to 1914" (University of Chicago dissertation, 1958), p. 239, citing F. Schmerfeld, ed., Moltke's *Ausgewahlte Werke* (Berlin: Hobbing, 1925).

4. Martin van Creveld, *Supplying War* (New York: Cambridge University Press, 1977), p. 88, citing Moltke's *Militärische Werke*, vol. IV, p. 210.

5. Addington, p. 9.

6. On 1870, see Michael Howard, *The Franco-Prussian War* (New York: Macmillan, 1961), especially pp. 82–83. Generally, Moltke's mode of operations is discussed by Dennis E. Showalter, *Railroads and Rifles: Soldiers, Technology, and the Unification of Germany* (Hamden, Conn.: Archon, 1975), chap. 3; Addington, chap. 1, and Hajo Holborn, "Moltke and Schlieffen," in E. M. Earle, ed., *Makers of Modern Strategy* (Princeton: Princeton University Press, 1971), pp. 172–205.

7. Gerhard Ritter, *The Sword and the Scepter* (Coral Gables, Fla.: University of Miami Press, 1969–72), vol. I, p. 213 (for similar views held by other German officers, see Roger Chickering, *Imperial Germany and a World without War* [Princeton: Princeton University Press, 1975], pp. 293–94); and Moltke, *Essays, Speeches, and Memoirs* (New York: Harper, 1893), vol. II, p. 116.

8. Adolf Lasser, *Das Kulturideal und der Krieg* (1868), excerpted in Adolf Gasser, "Deutschlands Einschluss zum Präventivkrieg," *Discordia concors: Festgabe für Edgar Bonjour* (Basle: Helbing & Lichtenhann, 1968), pp. 221–24. For a general overview of this strain in civilian philosophy and culture, see Ritter, *Sword*, vol. I, pp. 206–7 and *passim*.

9. Ritter, *Sword*, vol. I, p. 236.

10. Ibid., p. 315 note 73; Helmuth von Moltke, *Die deutschen Aufmarschpläne, 1871–1890*; ed. Ferdinand von Schmerfeld (Berlin: Mittler, 1929), p. 5; Alfred Vagts, *The Military Attaché* (Princeton: Princeton University Press, 1967), p. 243.

11. Ritter, *Sword*, vol. I, pp. 217–18.

12. Moltke's arguments about the Luxembourg fortress, which contradict his general views on the role of fortresses, would tend to indicate a cognitive bias, if they reflected Moltke's sincere assessment. However, the evidence is mute on this point.

13. Ritter, *Sword*, vol. I, p. 245 (for Moltke's memoranda, see *Aufmarschpläne*, pp. 137ff, 143ff; for other generals' views, see Norman Rich, ed., *The Holstein Papers* [Cambridge: Cambridge University Press, 1955–1963], vol. II, pp. 332–33; and vol. I, p. 314 note 63).

14. Ibid., p. 216; his 1860 words are quoted by Frederick E. Whitton, *Moltke* (Freeport, N.Y.: Books for Libraries, 1972), p. 85. On the need to avoid a defensive, attritional campaign against Austria, see Whitton, p. 88.

15. Quoted by Gordon Craig, *Germany, 1866–1945* (New York: Oxford University Press, 1978), pp. 34–35.

16. Ritter, *Sword*, vol. I, p. 305 note 21, letter of 1 January 1852.

17. Ibid., pp. 222–26.

18. Translated by Ronald L. Ernharth, "The Tragic Alliance: Austro-German Military Cooperation, 1871–1918" (Columbia University dissertation, 1970), p. 15.

19. Karl Justrow, *The Commander and Military Science* (Washington, D.C.: U.S. Army War College, 1943), English translation of *Feldherr und Kriegstechnik* (Oldenburg, 1933), p. 18, quoting Bismarck, *Gedanken und Erinnerungen*, vol. II, pp. 92–93.

20. Ritter, *Sword*, vol. I, p. 237.

21. See Gilpatrick, pp. 215ff, and Moltke, *Aufmarschpläne*, pp. 4–67. For other consid-

erations and details, see Snyder, "Defending the Offensive: French, German, and Russian War Planning, 1870–1914" (Columbia University dissertation, 1981), pp. 233–34.

22. For the plan of 1879 and reasons for attacking first in the east, see Moltke, *Aufmarschpläne*, pp. 77–83, Gilpatrick, pp. 516, 526, 533–34. On the Russian build-up of 1877–79, see *Aufmarschpläne*, p. 80, and Eberhard Kessel, *Moltke* (Stuttgart: Koehler, 1957), p. 651. For the particularly exposed Russian deployment of 1883, see Ernharth, p. 35. For more details and considerations, see Snyder, p. 235.

23. For Moltke's last memorandum for a two-front war of February 1888, see *Aufmarschpläne*, pp. 150–56, and Graydon A. Tunstall, "The Schlieffen Plan: The Diplomacy and Military Strategy of the Central Powers in the East, 1905–1914" (Rutgers University dissertation, 1974), p. 71. Regarding Russian improvements, see *Aufmarschpläne*, p. 141.

24. Gilpatrick, pp. 580–86; and *Aufmarschpläne*, pp. 122ff. On the Belgian contingency, see Hermann von Kuhl, *Le grand Etat-major allemand avant et pendant la guerre mondiale*, trans. François Douchy (Paris: Payot, 1922), originally *Der deutsche Generalstab in Vorbereitung und Durchführung des Weltkrieges*, 2d ed. (Berlin, Mittler, 1920), p. 77.

25. Quoted in Holborn, p. 180.

26. From a 1912 memorandum, quoted by Gerhard Ritter, *The Schlieffen Plan* (New York: Praeger, 1958), p. 103. For other points, see pp. 100–103, and Ritter, *Sword*, vol. II, pp. 106–7.

27. Ritter, *Schlieffen Plan*, p. 100. Unlike Moltke, Schlieffen did not advocate preventive war in his official capacity as chief of the General Staff. On a personal level, however, he tended to favor preventive wars in 1867 and probably in 1905 on the grounds that war was inevitable sooner or later and that the present was a favorable moment. Although some historians have attempted to prove that Schlieffen actively lobbied for preventive war in 1905 and designed the Schlieffen plan of 1905 expressly for this end, this view has not stood up to historical scrutiny. The final word on the long, detailed debate is Albrecht Moritz, *Das Problem des Präventivkrieges in der deutschen Politik während der ersten Marokkokrise* (Frankfurt: Lang, 1974), esp. pp. 216–17, 221.

28. See Walter Görlitz, *History of the German General Staff* (1953; rpt. New York: Praeger, 1962), p. 140, and Frank M. Laney, "The Military Implementation of the Franco-Russian Alliance, 1890–1914" (University of Virginia dissertation, 1954).

29. On Schlieffen's view of the inevitability of a two-front war, see Tunstall, p. 84; Edmund Glaise von Horstenau, *Franz Josephs Weggefährte* (Vienna: Amalthea, 1930), p. 246; and Reichsarchiv, *Der Weltkrieg*, vol. I (Berlin: Mittler, 1930), and vol. II (Berlin: Mittler, 1931), p. 3.

30. On this subject, see the views of the elder Moltke and Colmar von der Goltz, quoted in Ritter, *Sword*, vol. I, pp. 194–96. Bernard Brodie, *War and Politics* (New York: Macmillan, 1973), p. 58, reports a perhaps apocryphal statement by Schlieffen that if his plan failed to achieve decisive results, then Germany should negotiate an end to the war. Even if he did say this, the possibility of negotiations had no effect on his war planning, in contrast to that of the elder Moltke.

31. Görlitz, p. 129. See also Ritter, *Sword*, vol. II, pp. 201–2, and Raymond Aron, *Penser la guerre* (Paris: Gallimard, 1976), vol. II, p. 45.

32. On the difference between Moltke's and Schlieffen's outlooks in this regard, see Holborn, pp. 175 and 186–87.

33. Ritter, *Schlieffen Plan*, p. 51.

34. From Schlieffen's 1901 eastern staff ride, quoted by Jehuda L. Wallach, *Das Dogma*

der Vernichtungsschlacht: Die Lehren von Clausewitz und Schlieffen und ihre Wirkungen in zwei Weltkriegen (Frankfurt: Bernard & Graefe, 1967) p. 89.

35. Schlieffen, quoted by Theodore Ropp, *War in the Modern World* (1959; New York: Collier, 1962), p. 224. Generally, on the essential features of Schlieffen's doctrine, see Wallach, *Vernichtungsschlacht*, especially pp. 65, 71; Alfred von Schlieffen, *Die taktisch-strategischen Aufgaben aus den Jahren 1891–1905* (Berlin: Mittler, 1937), esp. pp. 86–87; *The Schlieffen Problems of 1891, 1896, 1901, 1903, 1904, and 1905*, U. S. Army translation (Ft. Leavenworth, Kans.: Command and General Staff School, 1935–36), p. 71, 130; Schlieffen, "Der Krieg in der Gegenwart," in his *Cannae*, 3d ed. (Berlin: Mittler, 1936), pp. 273–85; Bernhardi, *On War of Today* (London-Rees, 1912), vol. 2, pp. 156–60; Ritter, *Schlieffen Plan*, pp. 49ff; Kuhl, *Le grand Etat-major*, p. 97; Lothar Burchardt, *Friedenswirtschaft und Kriegsvorsorge* (Boppard am Rhein: Boldt, 1968), pp. 42–44. It should perhaps be mentioned that Schlieffen did *not* argue that the stronger enemy had to be attacked first as a matter of principle. In a critique of a 1905 war game, he explicitly stated that in abstracto a case could be made for attacking either the weaker or the stronger side first. Friedrich von Boetticher, "Der Lehrmeister des neuzeitlichen Krieges," in Friedrich von Cochenhausen, *Von Scharnhorst zu Schlieffen, 1806–1906* (Berlin: Mittler, 1933), p. 280.

36. See Ritter, *Schlieffen Plan*, p. 50; Schlieffen, *Aufgaben*, p. 87; Wallach, *Vernichtungsschlacht*, p. 74; *The Schlieffen Problems*, p. 32; and Kuhl, p. 103.

37. Students of cognitive psychology may see in this the effects of the"representativeness heuristic", which "involves the application of relatively simple resemblance . . . criteria to problems of categorization." See Richard Nisbett and Lee Ross, *Human Inference* (Englewood Cliffs, N.J.: Prentice-Hall, 1980), esp. pp. 115ff.

38. Ritter, *Schlieffen Plan*, p. 49. See also Wallach, *Vernichtungsschlacht*, pp. 86–87. For those who wish to consider a link between Schlieffen's dogmatism and his hubris, see the evidence presented by Nisbett and Ross, pp. 98–101, regarding the cautiousness of data-driven estimates (Moltke) and the boldness of theory-driven estimates (Schlieffen). In laboratory experiments, subjects were found to be overconfident of their judgments when they were deduced from a general theory but less confident when their estimates were ad hoc.

39. Ritter, *Schlieffen Plan*, p. 50, quoting Schlieffen's letter to Freytag-Loringhoven of 14 August 1912; Wallach, *Vernichtungsschlacht*, pp. 55–56.

40. Egon von Gayl, *General von Schlichting und sein Lebenswerk* (Berlin: Stilke, 1913), p. 339.

41. Groener, *The Testament of Count Schlieffen*, trans. W. P. Papanforth (mimeo, Ft. Sherman, 1931), p. 176; the imagery is Goethe's.

42. Wallach, *Kriegstheorien*, pp. 91–92; see also Wallach, *Vernichtungsschlacht*, p. 104.

43. On opposition to Schlieffen, see Görlitz, p. 136; on the standardization of doctrine through regulations, see Wallach, *Vernichtungsschlacht*, pp. 119ff; on the General Staff socialization process, see Gilpatrick, pp. 188ff.

44. Schlieffen, *Briefe*, ed. Eberhard Kessel (Gottingen: Vandenhoeck & Ruprecht, 1958), pp. 15, 21.

45. Colmar von der Goltz, *The Nation in Arms* (1883; rpt. London: Rees, 1914), p. 112.

46. Jean Courbis, *Le comte Schlieffen: Organisateur et stratège* (Paris: Berger-Levrault, 1938), pp. 84–86. Note also that, in the same year, Schlieffen's critique of a staff problem on the defense of East Prussia envisioned rapid changes of front and maneuvers by the German defenders, prefiguring the essential features of the victory of Tannenberg. See *The Schlieffen Problems*, p. 64. In this context note Goltz's view that

"since . . . the speed of the railway trains makes little of detours, . . . we may always reckon confidently upon our ability of moving large masses of troops in an emergency. The defender naturally reaps the greatest benefit in this respect on his own ground" (p. 141).

47. Carrias, p. 318, and Bernhardi, vol. II, p. 44.

48. *The Schlieffen Problems*, p. 49. See also pp. 65, 68, for other kinds of "friction."

49. Ritter, *Schlieffen Plan*, p. 59, and Hugo Friedrich Freytag-Loringhoven, *The Power of Personality in War* (Harrisburg, Penn.: Military Service Publishing, 1955), p. 62.

50. From "Krieg in der Gegenwart," quoted by Bernhardi, vol. II, p. 155.

51. Wallach, *Vernichtungsschlacht*, p. 79.

52. Quoted by Ropp, p. 224 note 33.

53. From an 1893 comment on an operational exercise, quoted by O. von Zoellner, "Schlieffens Vermächtnis," *Militarwissenschaftliche Rundschau* (Supplementary issue, 1938), p. 18.

54. On this question, see Burchardt, p. 15, and Schlieffen's utterances on the economic consequences of a long war in 1902 (*Aufgaben*, pp. 86–87), 1905 (Reichsarchiv, *Kriegsrüstung*, vol. I., p. 328), and 1909 ("Krieg in der Gegenwart"). Aron, vol. II, p. 40, argues that Schlieffen's economic arguments were mere rationalizing after the fact.

55. Burchardt, pp. 163–64.

56. Ritter, *Schlieffen Plan*, pp. 41–46; Courbis, pp. 50–51; Zoellner, p. 49. Ritter notes that Schlieffen expressed many doubts and reservations in the early drafts of his 1905 memorandum but removed them from the final version. *Schlieffen Plan*, p. 52.

57. A. M. Zaionchkovskii, *Podgotovka Rossii k imperialisticheskoi voine* (Moscow: Gosvoenizdat, 1926), pp. 36–39.

58. This document is reproduced in Alfred Graf von Waldersee, *General-Feldmarschall Alfred Graf von Waldersee in seinem militärischen Wirken*, ed. Hans Mohs, vol. II (Berlin: Mittler, 1929), pp. 327–30; for this quotation, see Ernharth, p. 54.

59. Ritter, *Schlieffen Plan*, p. 25, and Courbis, p. 26, quoting a memorandum of December 1892.

60. The April 1891 memorandum, quoted by Ritter, *Schlieffen Plan*, p. 22.

61. Ibid., p. 23. As early as October 1883, German engineers had proposed the construction of a fortress line linking Metz and Strasbourg along the Saar, which was promised to be strong enough to allow a force of 300,000 to hold out indefinitely against a force twice that size. See Waldersee, vol. II, pp. 271–72.

62. Zoellner, pp. 34–35, citing a *Schlussaufgabe* of 1892 and a 1900 staff ride.

63. Schlieffen's 1894 memo, quoted in Courbis, pp. 36–37, Gilpatrick, p. 1050, and Wolfgang Foerster, *Aus der Gedankenwerkstatt des deutschen Generalstabes*, (Berlin: Mittler, 1931), p. 26. It is difficult to see how the French could develop an overwhelming superiority at the point of their main assault and still be superior in the other sectors of the front, unless Schlieffen is assuming a very small German defending force.

64. The 1894 memo, quoted by Ritter, *Schlieffen Plan*, p. 38.

65. Courbis, p. 36; Boetticher, pp. 262, 309–10.

66. Moltke, *Aufmarschpläne*, p. 150.

67. Zoellner, pp. 46–48.

68. Courbis, pp. 115–117.

69. This and following quotations from Kuhl, *Grand Etat-major*, pp. 100–101; German ed., pp. 162ff.

70. Ritter, *Schlieffen Plan*, p. 39, 153–54. It might be argued, however, that these scenarios are not strictly comparable, since the former envisioned a long defense with a moderate-sized force and the latter envisioned a brief defense with a small force.

71. Ibid., pp. 135–41, quoting the final memorandum of 1905, and Courbis, p. 93.
72. Ibid., p. 93, and Ritter, *Schlieffen Plan*, p. 23.
73. Ritter, *Schlieffen Plan*, p. 78. This belief could be the result either of a motivated rationalization of Germany's plan or of unmotivated mirror-imaging.
74. See Ritter, *Sword*, vol. II, pp. 195–96; Gilpatrick, pp. 1055, 1071; Zoellner, p. 41.
75. Kuhl, *Grand*, French ed., pp. 23–30; Kuhl, *The Marne Campaign, 1914* (Ft. Leavenworth, Kans.: Command and General Staff School Press, 1936), p. 28.
76. Samuel R. Williamson, *The Politics of Grand Strategy: Britain and France Prepare for War, 1904–1914* (Cambridge: Harvard University Press, 1969), pp. 209ff.
77. Ritter, *Schlieffen Plan*, pp. 22–23; see also p. 26 note 19.
78. Tunstall, p. 89, and Kuhl, *Grosser Generalstab*, p. 164.
79. Kuhl, *Grand Etat-major*, pp. 103–5.
80. Waldersee, vol. II, pp. 331–33, for an 1890 Schlieffen memorandum, and Ritter, *Schlieffen Plan*, pp. 38–39, for similar ideas in 1894.
81. See the final version of the 1905 memorandum, Ritter, *Schlieffen Plan*, pp. 135–36.
82. Ibid., p. 55, and Boetticher, p. 311.
83. Ritter, *Schlieffen Plan*, pp. 51, 146.
84. See Ritter, *Schlieffen Plan*, pp. 57–58; Wallach, *Vernichtungsschlacht*, p. 131; and the following section on the younger Moltke.
85. Helmut Haeussler, *General William Groener and the Imperial German Army* (Madison: State Historical Society of Wisconsin, 1962), p. 50.
86. Correlli Barnett, *The Swordbearers* (New York: Morrow, 1964), pp. 44–45.
87. Volker R. Berghahn, *Germany and the Approach of War in 1914* (London: Macmillan, 1973), p. 97.
88. Ibid., p. 172. For more details on Moltke's attitude toward preventive war, see Moritz, pp. 224–26; Ritter, *Sword*, vol. II, pp. 249ff; Rich, vol. II, p. 768 note 1; and Berghahn, p. 169.
89. Alfred Vagts, *History of Militarism* (New York: Norton, 1937), p. 385.
90. The quotation is from Haeussler, pp. 17–18, citing *The Papers of William Groener*, U.S. National Archives, roll 16. See also Haeussler, pp. 19, 29; Burchardt, p. 33; and Wilhelm Groener, *Lebenserinnerungen* (Gottingen: Vandenhoek & Ruprecht, 1957), pp. 107–9.
91. Haeussler, pp. 44–45, citing *Papers*, roll 13, piece 132. In 1905, Groener seems to have hoped for a preventive war (Haeussler, p. 32).
92. Haeussler, p. 72, citing *Papers*, roll 3, piece 13-1, and roll 5, piece 23, i-iv.
93. Ernharth, pp. 93–94, quoting a 21 January 1909 letter from Moltke to Conrad, citing the Austrian Kriegsarchiv and Franz Conrad von Hötzendorff, *Aus meiner Dienstzeit* (Vienna: Rikola, 1921), vol. I, pp. 382–84. Groener's views were the same (*Lebenserinnerungen*, pp. 102, 146).
94. This document is paraphrased in Ritter, *Schlieffen Plan*, pp. 68–69 note 50, and *Sword*, vol. II, pp. 216–19, 305 note 34; see also Kuhl, *Grand Etat-major*, p. 126 note 3.
95. Van Creveld, especially pp. 122ff; Major Daniel Noce, *Strategic Demolitions in Front of the German Right Wing, August-September 1914*, Occasional Paper no. 72 (Washington, D.C.: U.S. Army Engineering School, March 1940), p. 18.
96. General Paul Bronsart von Schellendorf, *The Duties of the General Staff*, 4th ed., rev. by Major Bronsart von Schellendorf (London: Harrison, 1905), p. 494, and p. 501; 3d ed., rev by Colonel Meckel, trans. by W. A. H. Hare (London: HMSO, 1983), pp. 414–15.
97. Bronsart, 4th ed., pp. 525, 494, and 3d ed., p. 403.
98. Groener, *Papers*, roll 18, piece 168, p. 2; Haeussler, p. 140 note 10.

99. Haeussler, p. 34.

100. *Papers*, roll 18, piece 168, p. 5.

101. See van Creveld; also Generals Hermann von Kuhl and Walter von Bergmann, *Movements and Supply of the German First Army during August and September, 1914* (Ft. Leavenworth, Kans.: Command and General Staff School Press, 1929).

102. Kuhl and Bergmann, pp. 180–81. Sometimes improvisation was done only in the unit's narrow self-interest and at the expense of the general supply effort. See Haeussler, p. 63.

103. Noce, p. 21. For the argument that reconstruction would have been more rapid, see General Gérard Leman, *La rapport du général Leman sur la défense de Liège en août 1914* (Brussels: Palais des Académies, 1960), pp. 88–89.

104. Leman, p. 173 note 14 and Wilhelm Groener, article in the journal *Wissen und Wehr*, 1927, p. 532.

105. Ritter, *Schlieffen Plan*, p. 166.

106. Sewell Tyng, *The Campaign of the Marne, 1914* (New York: Longmans, Green, 1935), p. 56.

107. It is also possible that they believed that the Schlieffen Plan might succeed even without immediate access to the north Belgian rail system. See Groener, *Lebenserinnerungen*, p. 149, and *Testament*, p. 161.

108. Burchardt, pp. 51–52.

109. Barnett, p. 34, quoting Moltke's letter to his wife of 29 January 1905; also found in the French ed. of Moltke's memoirs, p. 185, and the German ed., p. 308.

110. Haeussler, p. 50, citing *Kriegsrüstung*, vol. II, p. 349.

111. On the "windpipe," see Ritter, *Sword*, vol. II, p. 152, and Haeussler, p. 49. For other points, see Burchardt, pp. 56, 172.

112. Burchardt, p. 147.

113. Erich Ludendorff, *Ludendorff's Own Story* (Freeport, N.Y.: Books for Libraries, 1971), p. 31.

114. Haeussler, pp. 45–46. On German financial limitations, see Fritz Fischer, *War of Illusions: German Policies from 1911 to 1914* (New York: Norton, 1975), p. 121.

115. Haeussler, p. 49; Burchardt, p. 25; Groener, *Lebenserinnerungen*, p. 135.

116. See especially Arthur Dix, "Deutschlands Zukunft in Krieg und Frieden," *Jahrbücher für Nationalökonomie und Statistik*, 3rd ser., 40 (August 1910), p. 480; see also Fischer, pp. 11, 200.

117. See L. L. Farrar, *The Short-War Illusion* (Santa Barbara: ABC-Clio, 1973).

118. Richard Neustadt, *Alliance Politics* (New York: Columbia University Press, 1970), p. 62, commenting on U.S. and British decision making during the Suez crisis.

6. Russia: Bureaucratic Politics and Strategic Priorities

1. For these arguments, see General M. V. Alekseev's "Obshchii plan deistvii" of February 1912, discussed by A. M. Zaionchkovskii, *Podgotovka Rossii k imperialisticheskoi voine* (Moscow: Gosvoenizdat, 1926), pp. 236–37; Iu. N. Danilov, *Rossiia v mirovoi voine, 1914–1915* (Berlin: Slovo, 1924), pp. 88–89, of which there is an expanded French version, *La Russie dans la Grande Guerre, 1914–1917* (Paris: Payot, 1927); V. I. Bovykin, *Iz istorii vozniknoveniia pervoi mirovoi voiny: Otnosheniia Rossii i Frantsii v 1912–1914 gg.* (Moscow: Moskovskii Universitet, 1961), pp. 96–97; and also chap. 7 below.

2. For details, see V. A. Emets, *Ocherki vneshnei politiki Rossii v period pervoi mirovoi voiny: Vzaimootnosheniia Rossii s soiuznikami po voprosam vedeniia voiny* (Moscow: Nauka,

1977), pp. 46–49; Norman Stone, *The Eastern Front, 1914–1917* (New York: Scribner's, 1975) pp. 54–58, 84; and below.

3. Stone, p. 84.
4. Ibid., pp. 44–69.
5. Ibid., pp. 70–91.
6. Ibid., p. 66. N. N. Golovin, *The Russian Campaign of 1914* (Ft. Leavenworth, Kans.: Command and General Staff School Press, 1933), pp. 324–25, argues for somewhat lower figures.

7. Russia: The Politics and Psychology of Overcommitment

1. A. M. Zaionchkovskii, *Podgotovka Rossii k imperialisticheskoi voine* (Moscow: Gosvoenizdat, 1926), pp. 140, 183–230, 301. In addition to the forces deployed on the main fronts, eight divisions were designated to protect the coasts near St. Petersburg from Swedish or German sea-borne attack and six divisions were assigned to observe the Rumanian border. The westernmost force in Danilov's scheme was the Second Army, deployed from Bielostok to Brest-Litovsk. Of the forces deployed north of the Pripiat marsh barrier (i.e., those blocking the path of a German attack toward St. Petersburg and Moscow), the 32 divisions of the First and Second armies formed the first line of defense with the 21 divisions of the Fourth and Fifth armies deployed behind them.

2. Finance Minister Kokovtsov's 1906 report in K. F. Shatsillo, *Russkii imperializm i razvitie flota* (Moscow: Nauka, 1968), p. 205. A. A. Manikovskii, *Boevoe snabzhenie russkoi armii, 1914–1918* (Moscow: Vysshii voennyi redaktsionnyi sovet, 1923), vol. III; A. S. Lukomskii, *Vospominaniia* (Berlin: Kirscher, 1922), vol. 1, especially pp. 29–30.

3. P. A. Zaionchkovskii, *Rossiiskoe samoderzhavie v kontse XIX stoletiia* (Moscow: Mysl', 1970), p. 34; K. F. Shatsillo, *Rossiia pered pervoi mirovoi voinoi: Vooruzhennye sily tsarizma v 1904–1914 gg.* (Moscow: Nauka, 1974), p. 15; Iu. N. Danilov, *Velikii kniaz' Nikolai Nikolaevich* (Paris: Imprimerie de Navarre, 1930), p. 62, trans. and abridged as *Le Grand-duc Nicolas* (Paris: Berger-Levrault, 1932); A. A. Polivanov, *Iz dnevnikov i vozpominanii po dolzhnosti voennogo ministra i ego pomoshchika, 1907–1916 gg.* (Moscow: Vysshii voennyi redaktsionnyi sovet, 1924), p. 42.

4. On these developments, see especially I. I. Rostunov, *Russkii front pervoi mirovoi voiny* (Moscow: Nauka, 1976). Previously, power and responsibility had been divided among three independent bodies: the General Staff, the War Ministry, and the State Defense Committee, a commission of notables dominated by the grand dukes.

5. See especially Polivanov's remarks at a 1908 "war council," M. N. Pokrovskii, "Tri soveshchaniia," *Vestnik Narodnogo Komissariata Inostrannykh Del* no. 1, 20 June 1919, p. 22; published separately in German as *Drei Konferenzen* (Hamburg: Hoym, 1920).

6. A. A. Brusilov, *Moi vospominaniia* (Moscow: Voenizdat, 1963), pp. 9–10.

7. K. Ushakov, *Podgotovka voennykh soobshchenii Rossii k mirovoi voine* (Moscow: Gosizdat, 1928), pp. 54, 93; A. M. Zaionchkovskii, pp. 156–57. Note especially Alekseev's critique in A. M. Zaionchkovskii, pp. 348–54.

8. A. M. Zaionchkovskii, pp. 159–63.

9. A. M. Zaionchkovskii, pp. 185–95, citing a 30 June 1910 document, "Sily, sredstva i veroiatnie plany nashykh zapadnykh protivnikov." For details, see Jack Snyder, "Defending the Offensive: French, German, and Russian War Planning, 1870–1914" (Columbia University dissertation, 1981), pp. 313–14.

10. A. M. Zaionchkovskii paraphrases these arguments on pp. 184 and 190.

11. A. V. Ignat'ev, *Russko-angliiskie otnosheniia nakanune pervoi mirovoi voiny (1908–1914 gg)* (Moscow: Izdatel'stvo sotsial'no-ekonomicheskoi literatury, 1962), p. 97. For other material on the Russian view of French reliability and the chance of a large-scale German attack during this period, see for example *Documents diplomatiques français* (DDF), 2d ser., vol. XII, no. 453, 10 February 1910, pp. 690ff. Here Pellé, the French attaché in Berlin, reports that his Russian colleague Mikhelson informed him that "the Russian government cannot entirely abstain from considering the hypothesis in which, in a European conflict that seriously engages Russian interests, a strong current hostile to war would appear in France and perhaps force the hand of the government" (p. 696). Mikhelson says at one point that the contingency of Germany attacking first in the east is the "less probable" alternative, but his other statements seem to belie this view. He asks Pellé, for example: "If the war had broken out last year, during the Serbian crisis, you do not contest that we would have had the bulk of the German forces against us?" (pp. 692–93). In another dispatch (no. 399, 23 January 1910, pp. 609–11), Pellé says Mikhelson argued that Balkan turmoil made the eastern alternative more likely for 1910, too. Mikhelson worried that Germany could defend against France with only a handful of forces (the covering forces, the Bavarian and reserve units), while having a free hand against Russia. See also V. A. Sukhomlinov, *Vospominaniia* (Moscow: Gosizdat, 1926), p. 160; A. A. Svechin's article in *Voina i revoliutsiia*, 1926, no. 5, p. 10; A. M. Zaionchkovskii, p. 212; Ushakov, pp. 94–95; A. P. Izvolskii, *The Memoirs of Alexander Iswolsky* (London: Hutchinson, 1920), p. 132.

12. A. M. Zaionchkovskii, pp. 183–85. See also Alfred Vagts, *Military Attaché* (Princeton: Princeton University Press, 1967), p. 228.

13. A. A. Kersnosvkii, *Istoriia russkoi armii* (Belgrade: Tsarskii Vestnik, 1933–35), part III *(1881–1917)*, p. 621.

14. A. A. Ignat'ev, *Piat'desiat let v stroiu* (Moscow: Gosudarstvennoe izdatel'stvo khudozhestvennoi literatury, 1959), vol. I, pp. 457–58.

15. *DDF*, 2d ser., vol. XII, no. 187, pp. 234–38, Delavaud to Pichon, 12 May 1909.

16. A. M. Zaionchkovskii, p. 348. For force allocations to secondary fronts, compare Alekseev's, pp. 352–53, to Danilov's 1908 draft, p. 162.

17. Ibid., pp. 350–52.

18. Ibid., pp. 351.

19. Ibid.

20. Ibid., p. 75. This earlier memo dates from Alekseev's tenure as deputy quartermaster of the central General Staff. It may therefore reflect the influence of corporate judgments. The December 1908 document was written after Alekseev became chief of staff of the Kiev military district, in which capacity he was almost certainly an intellectual free agent.

21. Nicholas Daniloff, "How Russia's Military Tried to Undermine Lenin's Separate Peace," *Foreign Service Journal*, June 1980, pp. 19–20. Roger Haydon correctly points out that the engineer Joseph Joffre, French chief of staff after 1911, was not "painstakingly technical" in his approach to strategy; rather, he promoted a doctrine based in part on "dash and heroics" and morale (personal communication, January 1984). Thus Joffre was like Danilov in personality and background, but he supported an opposite strategy. Joffre's deviation from the expected pattern can be explained in terms of the pressing institutional needs of the French military, which overrode the lesser impact of Joffre's taciturn nature and engineering background. Even Danilov eventually took up the offensive, when pressed by circumstances. Still, the comparison with Joffre does suggest that the connection between Danilov's personal style and his strategy may simply be spurious.

22. Etat-major de l'armée, deuxième bureau, dispatch from a French attaché in St. Petersburg, Wehrlin, 12/25 October 1913.

23. F. F. Palitsyn, chief of the main directorate of the General Staff, and M. V. Alekseev, first oberquartermaster, *Svod ukazanii dannykh nachal'nikom General'nogo Shtaba vo vremia voennoi igry ofitserov General'nogo Shtaba v 1907 godu* (St. Petersburg: Voennaia tipografiia, 1908), pp. 5–7; Alekseev, *Voina 1877–1878 gg. na aziatskom teatre: Deistviia otdel'nogo kavkazkogo korpusa* (St. Petersburg: Tipografiia shtaba voisk gvardii, 1892), pp. 9, 13, 32–33; Alekseev, *Voina 1877–1878: Shturm Karsa* (St. Petersburg: Ekonomicheskaia tipografiia, 1903 ed.), p. 38; V. Borisov, "General M. V. Alekseev," *Voennyi sbornik* (Belgrade), bk. 2, 1922, p. 9.

24. Norman Stone, *The Eastern Front, 1914–1917* (New York: Scribner's, 1975), p. 111. It should be noted, however, that Danilov's postwar writings point out several theoretical disadvantages to defensive strategies. See *Rossiia*, p. 88, and *Velikii kniaz'*, p. 92. Generally speaking, Russian conclusions on offense and defense after the Russo-Japanese War were similar to those of the French and Germans: increased firepower made frontal assaults extremely difficult, but offensive strategies were nonetheless preferred to defensive strategies on other grounds. See A. A. Strokov, *Vooruzhennye sily i voennoe iskusstvo v pervoi mirovoi voine* (Moscow: Voenizdat, 1974).

25. Danilov, "Na puti krusheniiu: Ocherki iz poslednogo perioda russkoi monarkhii," unpublished manuscript written in Paris, 1926 (in the possession of Nicholas Daniloff and Houghton Library, Harvard University), pp. 38, 61–62, 105ff, abridged and published in German as *Dem Zusammenbruch entgegen* (Hannover: Hahnsche, 1928). See also *Rossiia,* pp. 25–26. Alekseev's and Danilov's experiences during the Russo-Japanese War do not seem to have been an important determinant of differences in their views on offense and defense. Danilov spent the war in St. Petersburg in the General Staff; Alekseev spent it in the headquarters of the Russian viceroy in Manchuria, far to the rear of the battle area. The quotation is from *Velikii kniaz'*, pp. 25–26; also p. 92.

26. *Rossiia*, pp. 2–3, 67–68; *Mezhdunarodnoe otnoshenie v epokhe imperializma* no. 295, 8/21 February 1914; Danilov, "Na puti krusheniiu," p. 41; V. A. Emets, *Ocherki vneshnei politiki Rossii v period mirovoi voiny: Vzaimootnosheniia Rossii s soiuznikami po vedeniia voiny* (Moscow: Nauka, 1977), p. 67. This is not to say that Danilov was incapable of jingoistic sentiment. See, for example, *Rossiia*, pp. 3–4, 25. For Danilov's view that Nicholas II was prone to adventurism, see Danilov, "Moi vospominaniia ob Imp. Nikolae II i Vel. Kn. Mikhaile Aleksandroviche," *Arkhiv russkoi revoliutsii* (Berlin), vol. 19 (1928), p. 215. Complementing these doubts about Russian capabilities was Russian awe at German accomplishments. For the argument that this biased Russian military intelligence estimates, see William Fuller, "The Russian Empire and Its Potential Enemies, 1909–1914" (Colgate University, unpublished manuscript, 1981).

27. M. V. Alekseev, *Voina 1877–1878 gg.: Shturm Karsa* (St. Petersburg: Ekonomicheskaia Tipografiia, 1903); A. Samoilo, *Dve zhizni* (Moscow: Voenizdat, 1958), p. 56.

28. Polivanov, p. 18.

29. A. L. Sidorov, "Zheleznodorozhnyi transport v pervoi mirovoi voine i obostrenie ekonomicheskogo krizisa v strane," *Istoricheskie zapiski* no. 26 (1948), p. 13; A. M. Zaionchkovskii, p. 80.

30. A. M. Zaionchkovskii, pp. 166–67; Beryl J. Williams, "The Revolution of 1905 and Russian Foreign Policy," in C. Abramsky and B. Williams, eds., *Essays in Honour of E. H. Carr* (London: Macmillan, 1974); Rostunov, pp. 88–91; *DDF*, 2d ser., vol. XI, nos. 68 and 442; Pokrovskii, pp. 19, 24; Shatsillo, p. 31; K. F. Shatsillo, "Razvitie vooruzhennykh sil Rossii nakanune pervoi mirovoi voiny" (Institut Istorii of Moscow dissertation,

1968), pp. 52–55. F. F. Palitsyn and M. V. Alekseev, "Doklad o meropriiatiiakh po oborone Gosudarstva, podlezhashchikh osushchestvleniiu v blizhaishee desiatiletie," marked top secret, 1907 or 1908, especially pp. 48–49, 53, 58–59.

31. N. N. Golovin, *The Russian Campaign of 1914* (Ft. Leavenworth, Kans.: Command and Staff School Press, 1933), pp. 53–54. Although Sukhomlinov supported Danilov's 1910 plan against its critics, when Sukhomlinov was for a short time Alekseev's commander in Kiev, he went on record that he "completely agreed" with Alekseev's December 1908 draft plan. Thus it is difficult to interpret Danilov's plan as primarily reflecting Sukhomlinov's preferences. A. M. Zaionchkovskii, p. 348.

32. A. M. Zaionchkovskii, p. 87; Danilov, *Rossiia*, p. 40.

33. A. M. Zaionchkovskii, pp. 84–86; Polivanov, pp. 61, 94; Rostunov, p. 47. Palitsyn, "Desiatiletie," p. 33; Sergei Oldenburg, *The Last Tsar: Nicholas II, His Reign and His Russia* (Gulf Breeze, Fla.: Academic Press International, 1977), vol. III, p. 72.

34. V. A. Melikov, *Strategicheskoe razvertyvanie* (Moscow: Voenizdat, 1939), pp. 238–39; A. M. Zaionchkovskii, pp. 117, 266; Kersnovskii, pp. 602–3; Vasilii Iosifovich Gurko, *War and Revolution in Russia* (New York: Macmillan, 1919), p. 5.

35. Shatsillo, "Razvitie," p. 219 note. Also compare K. F. Shatsillo, "Podgotovka tsarizmom vooruzhennykh sil k pervoi mirovoi voine," *Voenno-istoricheskii zhurnal* (September 1974), p. 93, and A. Kavtaradze, "Iz istorii russkogo general'nogo shtaba," ibid. (July 1974), p. 91.

36. Generally, see I. V. Bestuzhev, *Bor'ba v Rossii po voprosam vneshnei politiki, 1906–1910* (Moscow: Akademiia Nauk, 1961), p. 315; Bestuzhev, "Bor'ba v Rossii po voprosam vneshnei politiki nakanune pervoi mirovoi voiny (1910–1914 gg.)," *Istoricheskie zapiski* 75 (1965), pp. 46–47; I. I. Astaf'ev, *Russko-germanskie diplomaticheskie otnosheniia 1905–1911 gg.* (Moscow: Moskovskii Universitet, 1972), pp. 90–94; Astaf'ev, "Potsdamskoe soglashenie 1911g," *Istoricheskie zapiski* no. 85 (1970), p. 157. It is certain that Danilov's motives, to the extent they had a political component, were similar to Stolypin's "breathing spell" concept, discussed by Anatolii Vasil'evich Nekliudov [A. Nekludoff], *Diplomatic Reminiscences before and during the World War, 1911–1917* (London: Murray, 1920), pp. 32–33. They had nothing in common with Rosen's desire for outright, open-ended appeasement of Germany. Roman Romanovich Rosen, *Forty Years of Diplomacy* (New York: Knopf, 1922), vol. II, pp. 88ff. For Danilov's positive view of Stolypin see *Puti,* pp. 95, 105ff. For his negative evaluation of appeasement, *Rossiia,* pp. 23, 25. Sukhomlinov, however, may have flirted with the appeasement viewpoint (see *Vospominaniia,* p. 152).

37. A. M. Zaionchkovskii, pp. 206–7.

38. J. D. Walz, "State Defense and Politics under the Last Tsar" (Syracuse University dissertation, 1967), pp. 138–40, 149; E. Z. Barsukov, *Artilleriia russkoi armii* (Moscow: Voenizdat, 1948), vol. I, p. 79; W. Thomas Wilfong, "Rebuilding the Russian Army: The Question of a Comprehensive Plan for National Defense" (Indiana University dissertation, 1977), p. 136. The earlier reform plan authored by Palitsyn and Alekseev intended to eliminate specially trained, immobile fortress troops, but it did not intend to eliminate the fortresses themselves (Shatsillo, "Razvitie," pp. 206, 216–17). The Duma seems to have been generally favorable to the fortress-razing idea and to the rearward deployment of the field army (Walz, pp. 188–89). In particular, the Octobrists, the key moderate-conservative group allied tacitly with Stolypin, seems to have taken this view (Ben-Cion Pinchuk, "The Octobrists in the Third Duma" [University of Washington dissertation, 1969], p. 93).

39. A. M. Zaionchkovskii, pp. 209–10; Danilov, *Rossiia,* pp. 41–44; Polivanov, pp. 70–73.

40. A. F. Rediger, "Iz zapisok A. F. Rediger," *Krasnyi arkhiv* no. 60, 1933, p. 119; Polivanov, p. 62; Lukomskii, p. 24.

41. Polivanov, p. 97.

42. A. M. Zaionchkovskii, pp. 235, 243.

43. Ibid., pp. 236–37, 238–43.

44. Kersnovskii, pp. 622–23.

45. Ignat'ev, *Russko-angliiskie otnosheniia*, p. 115. Sukhomlinov was speaking to the French in terms of cautious optimism as early as November 1910. See Georges Louis, *Les carnets de Georges Louis* (Paris: Rieder, 1926), vol. I, p. 151. French observers tended to agree that the Russian army (and economy) was very much improved and basically sound. See Louis Garros, "En marge de l'alliance franco-russe, 1902–1914," *Revue historique de l'armée* (June 1950), p. 33; "Rapport du Capitaine Perchenel à la suite du stage accompli dans la circonscription de Vilna d'avril à octobre 1912," 21 December 1912, Archives de la guerre, 7N1486.

46. These fears lingered to a lesser degree until 1914, however. Ushakov, pp. 47–48, 58 note 3.

47. P. fon Lang, year-end-review editorial, *Ofitserskaia zhizn'* no. 300, 30 December 1911, p. 2969. E. Krivtsov, "Neumerennyi optimizm," *Russkii invalid* no. 263, 9 December 1911, p. 5.

48. A. J. P. Taylor, *The Struggle for Mastery in Europe, 1848–1918* (London: Oxford University Press, 1971), pp. 468, 488; French attaché Laguiche, dispatch of 18-31 January 1912, Archives de Guerre, 7N1478; *DDF*, 2d ser., vol. XIV, no. 201, p. 257, Georges Louis dispatch of 22 August 1911; Frank M. Laney, "The Military Implementation of the Franco-Russian Alliance, 1890–1914" (University of Virginia dissertation, 1954), pp. 263, 351–52.

49. A. M. Zaionchkovskii, pp. 297, 306; Manikovskii, vol. III, pp. 7–8 and *passim;* V. I. Bovykin, *Iz istorii vozniknoveniia pervoi mirovoi voiny: Otnosheniia Rossii i Frantsii v 1912–1914 gg.* (Moscow: Moskovskii Universitet, 1961), p. 136.

50. This is explicitly asserted by V. A. Emets, "O roli russkoi armii v pervyi period mirovoi voiny 1914–1918 gg.," *Istoricheskie zapiski* no. 77 (1965), p. 67.

51. General Dobrorol'skii, Glavnoe upravlenie general'nogo shtaba, mobilizatsionnyi otdel, "Nastavlenie okruzhnym shtabam po sostavleniiu novogo mobilizatsionnogo raspisaniia i po vvedeniiu ego v deistvie," document no. 54, 1913 (Lenin Library, Moscow).

52. Astaf'ev, *Russko-germanskie diplomaticheskie otnosheniia*, p. 4; F. Ogorodnikov, "Kritike sosredotocheniia russkikh armii v 1914 godu," *Voina i revoliutsiia* no. 9, September 1926, p. 28; Ignat'ev, *Russko-angliiskie otnosheniia*, p. 116; Samoilo, p. 126; Bovykin, p. 72; S. Dobrorol'skii, "Bibliografiia," *Voennyi sbornik* no. 5, 1912, p. 181.

53. A. V. Ignat'ev, *Russko-angliiskie otnosheniia*, p. 112, citing a General Staff estimate of December 1911. See also Vagts, *Military Attaché*, p. 379, and Emets, *Ocherki*, p. 36.

54. See, for example, Ignat'ev's 1912 reports from Paris (A. A. Ignat'ev, *Piat'desiat let*, vol. I, pp. 522–23, 531) and Sazonov's December 1912 remarks to the Council of Ministers (A. V. Ignat'ev, *Russko-angliiskie otnosheniia*, p. 155).

55. *DDF*, 2d ser., vol. XII, no. 453, p. 695, Pellé's paraphrase of Mikhelson. Samoilo also uses the concept of a German "Pyrrhic victory" over France, adding that "I never had any doubt about the victory of the Russian army over Austria-Hungary" (p. 129). In the spring of 1914, the tsar told Ignat'ev: "Let God grant that the French hold out for a few weeks while we succeed in getting fully mobilized" (A. A. Ignat'ev, *Piat'desiat let*, vol. I, p. 576).

56. A. M. Zaionchkovskii, p. 240; Ogorodnikov, p. 27; General'nyi shtab RKKA, 10-i

otdel, *Vostochno-prusskaia operatsiia: Sbornik dokumentov* (Moscow: Voenizdat, 1939), documents no. 4 (Colonel Stogov of the central General Staff), no. 5 (Kliuev), and no. 8 (staff of the Second Army).

57. For the poverty of Russian intelligence on Germany, see Boris Mikhailovich Shaposhnikov, "V varshavskom voennom okruge," *Voenno-istoricheskii zhurnal* no. 1, 1967; Shaposhnikov, *Vospominaniia, Voenno-nauchnye trudy* (Moscow: Voenizdat, 1974), p. 215. The Russians did acquire a 1912 German war game showing that the Germans thought a major attack on Russia would lead to disaster, but this was almost certainly obtained long after the Russian plan changes of 1912 were completed. See chaps. 3 and 5. On the alleged influence of French estimates, see A. M. Zaionchkovskii, p. 243. On Russian views of French estimates, see K. K. Zvonar'ev, *Agenturnaia razvedka*, vol. 1: *Russkaia agenturnaia razvedka vsekh vidov do i vo vremia voiny 1914–1918 gg.* (Moscow: Izdanie IV upravleniia shtaba RKKA, 1929), p. 118.

58. A. M. Zaionchkovskii, pp. 238–39.

59. Whereas the Russians apparently used a rule-of-thumb calculation based on the nominal capacity of the Austrian lines, the French took into account the overlap of lines and other sources of friction (Etat-major de l'armée, deuxième bureau, "Observations sur la note russe au sujet de la concentration autrichienne en Galicie," Summer 1911, Archives de Guerre, 7N1538).

60. A. M. Zaionchkovskii, p. 241. The operational arguments for Galicia and against East Prussia are laid out in Golovin, pp. 63–66.

61. A. M. Zaionchkovskii, pp. 244, 277, 354, and 272.

62. Shatsillo, *Russkii imperializm i razvitie flota*, especially p. 100, presents Russian documents from 1911–1912 that on their face amount to a blueprint for forcibly changing the status quo of the Straits by 1917 or 1918. For other background, see Edward C. Thaden, *Russia and the Balkan Alliance of 1912* (University Park: Pennsylvania State University Press, 1965), especially pp. 65ff; Laney, pp. 23–24; Sergei Sazonov, *Fateful Years, 1909–1916* (New York: Stokes, 1928), p. 78; I. V. Bestuzhev, "Russian Foreign Policy, February–June 1914," *Journal of Contemporary History* 1 (July 1966), pp. 93–112.

63. The quotation is from "Obzor vneshnei politiki," *Ofitserskaia zhizn'* no. 269, 20 May 1911, p. 2558. See Vagts, pp. 333, 374ff; "Rapport de M. le capitaine brêveté Maurice Fournier, . . . stagiaire dans l'armée russe du 1e avril au 1e octobre 1913," 30 October 1913, Archives de Guerre, 7N1486; Wehrlin dispatch, 8-21 November 1912, 7N1478; Laguiche dispatch, 18-31 January 1912, 7N1478.

64. Fournier report, 7N1486.

65. See Nekliudov's characterization of Stolypin's views, pp. 32–33.

66. Emets, "O roli," p. 63.

67. See P. N. Durnovo's memo to the tsar, translated in Frank A. Golder, *Documents of Russian History, 1914–1917* (Gloucester, Mass.: Smith, 1964), pp. 20–22.

68. G. P. Morozov, "Russko-frantsuzskoe sblizhenie, 1885–1887 gg." (Leningrad State University abstract [*avtoreferat*] of a candidate dissertation, 1954), p. 11, attributes this view to the war minister, General Vannovskii.

69. Garros, p. 37, citing a dispatch by Laguiche from early 1913. Sukhomlinov hoped to couple this with improved relations with Germany and perhaps a Franco-Russo-German alliance offering benefits to all three members. Sukhomlinov's failure to object to the foreign minister's idea of a partial mobilization in 1914 against Austria alone might also be seen as evidence of this kind of thinking, but it may simply reflect ignorance (as Danilov charges) or a habitual desire to go along with the tsar's wishes (Danilov, *Rossiia*, p. 12). For similar Sukhomlinov remarks, see Matton's dispatch, 13/26 June 1909, 7N1535; Wehrlin dispatch, 8/21 December 1912, 7N1478. Despite this,

Sukhomlinov appears to have normally backed Danilov's strategic conceptions rather than Alekseev's. More generally, Russia's failure to develop serious plans for war against Austria alone is a reflection of both Danilov's influence and Germany's strong support for Austria in the 1909 Bosnia Crisis, which made a localized war seem unlikely.

70. A. M. Zaionchkovskii, pp. 103, 350; Borisov, "Alekseev," pp. 5–6. Borisov implies that Palitsyn shared this view, although it was in part his plans they were critiquing.

71. Stone, p. 111.

72. A. M. Zaionchkovskii, p. 241.

73. Pre-positioning of supplies was to be done according to Plan A. See Russia, 10-i otdel General'nogo shtaba RKKA, *Vostochno-prusskaia operatsiia: Sbornik dokumentov,* hereafter *VPO* (Moscow: Gosvoenizdat, 1939), pp. 32, 36.

74. "Otchetnaia rabota po operativnoi chasti 2-i armii," undated in *VPO*, p. 57; see also p. 35, and F. Ogorodnikov, "K kritike sosredotocheniia russkikh armii v 1914 godu," *Voina i revoliutsiia* (September 1926), p. 27.

75. Danilov, *Rossiia*, p. 88.

76. A. M. Zaionchkovskii, pp. 237, 258–59.

77. Ibid., pp. 244, 246, 256, 260–61, 278. The I. I. Rostunov dissertation, "Russkii front pervoi mirovoi voiny" (Moscow: Institut Voennoi Istorii, 1974), p. 57, indicates that all or part of this change from the district quartermasters' March draft took place not in May but in December 1912. (Also compare Rostunov, *Russkii front*, p. 93, and Zaionchkovskii, pp. 259–60.) If so, it may have been influenced by the acquisition of intelligence that the Austrians planned to deploy more of their forces in Eastern Galicia. There is no particular reason why this news should have favored the eastern frontal attack over the western flank envelopment idea, however. Indeed, it could be argued that an Austrian deployment shifted toward East Galicia would have been even more vulnerable to a blow to its left flank.

78. For Kliuev's views see *VPO*, pp. 29–33, 37–39, 48–59, and A. M. Zaionchkovskii, pp. 249–50. Despite his cautiousness in this regard, Kliuev was generally a proponent of offensive operations and tactics. Varshavskii voennyi okrug, shtab (signed by Kliuev), "Otchet o dvukhstoronnei polevoi poezdke ofitserov General'nogo Shtaba Varshavskogo voennogo okruga, proizvedennoi v iule 1909g." (Warsaw: Tipografiia okruzhnogo shtaba, 1909); Varshavskii voennyi okrug, shtab, "Nekotoryia takticheskiia polozheniia vyrabotannyia na s"ezde starshikh pekhotnykh i artilleriiskikh nachal'nikov pri Shtabe Varshavskogo voennogo okruga v fevrale 1910g." (Warsaw: n.d.).

79. A. M. Zaionchkovskii, pp. 236, 263.

80. Ibid., p. 254; *VPO*, pp. 34–37. Note also the November 1912 "northern front" meeting of Stogov, Kliuev, and Przhentsev of the Vilna district, discussed in Zaionchkovskii, p. 269, and Gunther Frantz, *Russlands Eintritt in den Weltkrieg* (Berlin: Deutsche Verlagsgesellschaft für Politik und Geschichte, 1924), p. 300.

81. A. M. Zaionchkovskii, p. 254, quoting a report of 25 September 1912.

82. As early as March 1912, Alekseev recognized that there were logistical limits to the size of the Fourth Army, which may also have influenced this decision. Ushakov, p. 100. Note also Zaionchkovskii, p. 278.

83. N. Valentinov [N. V. Vol'skii], "Voennye soglasheniia Rossii s inostrannymi gosudarstvami do voiny," *Voenno-istoricheskii sbornik* (Moscow), 1919 no. 2, p. 111.

84. On Zhilinskii's rise to the top, see A. I. Denikin, *The Career of a Tsarist Officer: Memoirs, 1872–1916* (Minneapolis: University of Minnesota Press, 1975), p. 232.

85. Danilov, *Velikii kniaz'*, p. 105.

86. This meeting is extensively examined in Carol H. Wilcox, "The Franco-Russian Alliance, 1908–1911" (Clark University dissertation, 1969), pp. 216ff. See E. M. Rozental', *Diplomaticheskaia istoriia russko-frantsuzskogo soiuza v nachale XX veka* (Moscow: Sotsial'no-ekonomicheskaia literatura, 1960), p. 228.

87. This is asserted by A. M. Zaionchkovskii and essentially all Soviet historians other than Emets.

88. Iurii Nikiforovich Danilov, *La Russie dans la Grande Guerre Mondiale (1914–1917)* (Paris: Payot, 1927; French ed. of *Rossiia*), p. 117.

89. Ushakov, pp. 110–11 and *passim.*

90. Garros, p. 33.

91. This is argued by Emets, *Ocherki*, pp. 25–67, especially p. 52.

92. A. M. Zaionchkovskii, p. 201.

93. However, although the obligation to help France influenced Zhilinskii and perhaps Danilov, this argument was not used by Stogov in his critique of Alekseev's plans.

94. A. M. Zaionchkovskii, pp. 302–20. Previously, Russian forces deployed on the Nieman would presumably have fallen back in the event of a German *attaque brusquée.*

95. A. M. Zaionchkovskii, pp. 201–2; see also pp. 319–20.

96. Emets, *Ocherki*, p. 47, citing the Central State Military History Archive.

97. Lukomskii, vol. I.

98. Laney, p. 402; *DDF*, 3d ser., vol. V, nos. 52 and 61; Garros, pp. 35–36; Laguiche dispatches of 27 November/4 December and 30 November/13 December 1912, Archives de Guerre, 7N1478; A. A. Ignat'ev, *Piat'desiat let*, vol. I, pp. 505ff. The standard historical literature has portrayed Sukhomlinov as advocating at this time a relatively large-scale partial mobilization against Austria, based on a misleading account in the memoirs of the chairman of the Council of Ministers, V. N. Kokovtsov, *Out of My Past* (Stanford: Stanford University Press, 1935), pp. 344ff. According to documents discovered by Soviet historians, Sukhomlinov requested (1) reinforcement of cavalry on the Austro-Hungarian border, using the internal resources of the Warsaw and Kiev military districts, (2) the movement of two cavalry brigades from the Moscow district to the southern part of the Warsaw district, (3) calling up an unspecified number of reservists for trial maneuvers in the Warsaw and Kiev districts, and (4) some minor security measures. Bovykin, *Iz istorii*, pp. 151–53. Minutes of a Council of Ministers meeting make it clear that the motive for these precautions was defensive, arising from the fear that Austria's preparations might allow her to "force war upon us at an unfavorable moment." They specifically cited the fact that the "concentration of the Russian army requires a very long time." Bestuzhev, "Borba v Rossii." It also should be noted, however, that the Russians had already taken several military measures in response to the Balkan events including the temporary retention of some 350,000 soldiers who had been scheduled to leave active duty. E. C. Helmreich, *The Diplomacy of the Balkan Wars, 1912–1913* (Cambridge: Harvard University Press, 1938), pp. 158–59, 257–58.

99. Laney, pp. 457–58.

100. Danilov, *Rossiia*, p. 63.

101. The quotation is from Nicholas de Basily, *Diplomat of Imperial Russia, 1903–1917: Memoirs* (Stanford: Hoover Institution Press, 1973), p. 90. On its accuracy, see S. Dobrorol'skii, "La mobilisation de l'armée russe en 1914," *Revue d'histoire de la guerre mondiale* 1 (April–July 1923), p. 161.

102. *VPO*, document 9, p. 69.

103. Report by Alfred Knox, British military attaché in St. Petersburg, 10 December 1913, Archives de la Guerre, 7N1538. Samoilo, p. 114.

104. Compiled from A. M. Zaionchkovskii, pp. 258ff, 314ff.

105. *VPO*, no. 9; Laguiche dispatch, 30 January/12 February 1913, Archives de la Guerre, 7N1478.

106. *VPO*, no. 9; pp. 60–61.

107. Joffre, p. 59. For evidence of Zhilinskii's untruthfulness in dealing with the French, see *DDF*, 3d ser., vol. II, no. 90, p. 85, and Garros, p. 39, compared to A. M. Zaionchkovskii, p. 307.

108. On Danilov's major personal role in Russian war planning and the minor role of formally higher figures, see Danilov, *Velikii kniaz'*, p. 105; Danilov, *Rossiia*, p. 13; Samoilo, p. 144; Laguiche dispatch, 29 March/11 April 1914, 7N1478.

109. A 1914 letter to the ambassador to Britain, published in *Mezhdunarodnye otnosheniia v epokhe imperializma*, 3d ser., vol. I, cited by Samantha Kazarinov, "Russian Foreign Policy on the Eve of World War One" (Columbia University unpublished manuscript, 1977). Note also Danilov's remarks about the influence *inter alia* of "the prevailing 'psychology' of the country" on strategy (*Velikii kniaz'*, pp. 104–5).

110. Laney, pp. 416–17; Delcassé regarding Wehrlin's report, 12 April 1913, during the Scutari Crisis, *DDF*, 3d ser., vol. VI, no. 284, p. 341; Emets, *Ocherki*, p. 67.

111. Polivanov, article in the journal *Voennoe delo* no. 14, 1920, p. 421, quoting his own testimony of the autumn of 1914. See *VPO*, no. 9, p. 69, for evidence that the Russians had information about a similar German war game of 1913.

112. A. M. Zaionchkovskii, pp. 420, 422; *VPO*, p. 10, 38; V. M. Dragomirov, "Podgotovka russkoi armii k velikoi voine," *Voennyi sbornik* no. 4, 1923, p. 110; V. Fuks, "Kratkii ocherk operatsii Narevskoi armii," ibid., p. 131.

113. *VPO* no. 5, p. 38.

114. *VPO* no. 2, p. 30.

115. In terms of quality and firepower, an average Russian division could be fairly judged the equal of an average German division, since the superiority of the German active units was offset by the inferiority of the Landwehr brigades that the Germans would have to employ.

116. Melikov, p. 257. However, it was subsequently decided to delay the attack to M+14 to coordinate the First Army's offensive with that of the slower-mobilizing Second Army. A. N. Suvorov, "Voennaia igra starshikh voiskovykh nachal'nikov v aprele 1914 goda," *Voenno-istoricheskii sbornik* no. 1, 1919, p. 17.

117. A. M. Zaionchkovskii, p. 9; Golovin, p. 36. See also K. Adaridi, "27'ia pekh. divisiia v boiakh 4 (17) avgusta 1914g. pod Stalupenenom i 7 (20) avgusta pod Gumbinnenom," *Voennyi sbornik* no. 9, 1928, p. 164. The April war game assumed 21 German divisions attacking the Nieman on M+9 (Suvorov, p. 15).

118. According to the war game's scenario, shortly after the initial German attack and Russian counterattack, the Germans learned that the British army had landed on the continent. To meet this force, the Germans pulled three active corps out of their East Prussian force and transported them to the west. Thereupon, the remaining German forces fell back on the defensive as the Russians pursued them around both sides of the lakes. Zhilinskii treated this stage of the campaign as a routine mop-up and siege operation, despite the fact that the German force still presumably numbered 15 divisions. See Suvorov, pp. 17, 23.

119. See, for example, *Voennyi sbornik* no. 1, 1909, pp. 161–62, no. 5, 1910, pp. 288ff, no. 3, 1914, pp. 117–18; *Intendantskii zhurnal* no. 5, 1911, pp. 7–10, no. 6, 1911, p. 16; F.

A. Maksheev, *Voennoe khoziaistvo: Kurs Intendantskoi Akademii* (St. Petersburg: USOV, 1912); A. Ageev, "Ofitsery russkogo general'nogo shtaba ob opyte russko-iaponskoi voiny," *Voenno-istoricheskii zhurnal* no. 8, 1975, p. 102.

120. Rostunov, *Russkii front*, p. 100; N. N. Ianushkevich, *Organizatsiia i rol' intendant-stva v sovremennykh armiiakh na voine* (St. Petersburg: Skachkov, 1910).

121. Danilov, "K voprosu o podgotovke gosudarstva k sovremennoi voine: Po opytu voiny 1914–1918 gg." (Paris, unpublished manuscript, 1925), chap. 7; see also his early book on on the mechanics of the mobilization process, *Posobie mestnym uchrezhdeniiam ministerstva vnutrennykh del dlia sostavleniia mobilizatsionnykh soobrazhenii i dlia vypolneniia ikh v sluchae mobilizatsii armii* (Kiev: Tipografiia okruzhnogo shtaba, 1897).

122. E. F. Nikitin, "Russkaia armiia nakanune pervoi mirovoi imperialisticheskoi voiny" (Vysshii Voenno-pedagogicheskii institut of Leningrad candidate dissertation, 1949), p. 157; A. M. Zaionchkovskii, pp. 89, 281–301; Samoilo, p. 57. For French views, see Etat-major de l'armée, deuxième bureau, "La physionomie de l'armée russe," July 1913, 7N673; "Rapport du capitaine Marchal, stagiaire dans l'armée russe en 1912," 7N1486; Polivanov, *Iz dnevnikov*, pp. 99–100.

123. *Svod*, p. 7.

124. "Desiatiletie," p. 32.

125. Varshavskii voennyi okrug, shtab, reports on exercises of May 1909, p. 7, July 1909, p. 12. Ironically, one of the officers most critical of this habit was General Postovskii, who, as the Second Army's chief of staff, presided over the worst logistical debacle of the war in August 1914 (June 1910, pp. 9, 12, 24).

126. L. Radus-Zenkovich, "Nashi dol'shie manevry," *Voennyi sbornik* no. 6, 1910, pp. 76–77. See also *Intendantskii zhurnal* no. 1, 1912, pp. 11ff; *Voennyi sbornik* no. 12, 1911, p. 21; M. Bonch-Bruevich, "Dve privychki," *Razvedchik* no. 1152, 27 November 1912, pp. 801–2; M. Gareev, "Iz istorii razvitiia metodov provedeniia takticheskikh uchenii i manevrov v russkoi armii," *Voenno-istoricheskii zhurnal* no. 2, 1972, p. 100.

127. Melikov, pp. 249, 251; Suvorov, pp. 15, 23; Golovin, pp. 38–39; Polivanov, p. 99; Danilov, *Rossiia*, p. 147.

128. Suvorov, pp. 25–26; Golovin, pp. 179–80; Danilov, *Rossiia*, pp. 145–46.

129. Uncertainty regarding the direction of the German retreat was also a factor. See I. I. Vatsetis, *Operatsii na vostochnoi granitse germanii v 1914g. Chast' 1-ia:Vostochno-prusskaia operatsiia* (Moscow: Gosvoenizdat, 1929), p. 139, citing the report of General-Major Baiov, quartermaster general of the First Army, to his chief of staff, 12/25 August 1914, stressing the urgent need to break off operations and set up working lines of communications. See also Golovin, p. 286.

130. Suvorov, pp. 16, 20–22; Melikov, pp. 251–52.

131. M. V. Alekseev, *Rech' 8 avgusta 1917 Gen. M. V. Alekseeva na moskovskom so-veshchanii obshchestvennykh deiatelei* (Moscow: Moskovskii Listok, 1917), pp. 1–2. Generally, see Stone, pp. 70–91, esp. p. 90; M. Bonch-Bruevich, *From Tsarist General to Red Army Commander* (Moscow: Progress, 1966), p. 23; I. Trutko, "Podgotovka tyla iugo-zapadnogo fronta (1914g.)," *Voenno-istoricheskii zhurnal* no. 3, 1939; Brusilov, pp. 33–34, 51–52; Bernard Pares, *Day by Day with the Russian Army, 1914–1915* (London: Constable, 1915), p. 206; A. Beloi, *Galitsiiskaia bitva* (Moscow: Gosizdat, 1929), pp. 140, 346.

132. Beloi argues that "the supply crisis of the Fourth and Fifth Armies was foreseen already in peacetime" (p. 109 note 1). Generally, see Ushakov, pp. 94–101; Trutko; N. Vasil'ev, *Transport Rossii v voine 1914–1918 gg.* (Moscow: Voenizdat, 1939), pp. 54–60; Denikin, p. 225. On the four-day limit, see Beloi, pp. 73–74. For the Fifth, it was 2-1/2 days (p. 109).

133. Golovin, esp. pp. 179–88, but also pp. 94–95, 101–2, 129, 156–60, 166, 169, 220; Fuks, pp. 126–27; *VPO*, pp. 513–20. 547; Denikin, p. 231; N. F. Evseev, *Avgustskoe srazhenie 2-i russkoi armii v Vostochnoi Prussii (Tannenberg) v 1914 godu* (Moscow: Gosizdat, 1936), pp. 70, 87; A. Rosenchild-Paulin, "Prichiny neudach II armii generala Samsonova v Vostochnoi Prussii v avguste 1914g.," *Voennyi sbornik* no. 4, 1923, pp. 155–56; I. Patronov, "Destviia VI korpusa i glavniia prichiny neudachy II armii v Vostochnoi Prussii," *Voennyi sbornik* no. 4, 1923, pp. 165–66.

134. Danilov, *La Russie*, p. 182.

135. *VPO* no. 32, p. 85; no. 39, pp. 89–91.

136. According to his memoirs, *Rossiia*, pp. 64, 133.

137. *Rossiia*, p. 135; *VPO* no. 32, p. 85. At this time, Postovskii at the Second Army thought the German reserve units would amount to about ten divisions. *VPO* no. 39, pp. 90–91.

138. Danilov, *Rossiia*, pp. 135–36; *VPO* no. 20, p. 80, no. 37, p. 89; Emets, *Ocherki*, pp. 74–75; Golovin, pp. 91, 177. The idea of operating on the left bank had been tentatively raised before August 1914, but only as an objective for the future. Ushakov, pp. 57–59.

139. At the point of the encirclement of the central Russian corps, the Germans' numerical advantage was about 3 to 2; overall in the sector it was about 8 to 7. On the forces engaged, see Stone, pp. 55, 58, 60. Also see Vatsetis, pp. 18, 27, 52; "Dokumenty i materialy," *Voenno-istoricheskii zhurnal* no. 7, 1965, which counts the equivalent of 14-1/2 German divisions in East Prussia; Golovin, p. 177, on the effect of the diversion of forces to the left bank.

140. Jean Savant, *Epopée russe* (Paris: Calmann-Levy, 1945), pp. 19–20. According to Paléologue, a not always reliable source, Sazonov told Paléologue on 26 August that "General Jilinsky, who is commanding the north-western front, considers that an offensive in East Prussia is doomed to certain defeat, because our troops are still too scattered and their concentration is meeting with many obstacles. . . . Janushkevitch . . . shared Jilinsky's views and is protesting strongly against the offensive. But Danilov, the Quartermaster General, is insisting, not less forcibly, that we have no right to leave our ally in danger and ought to attack at once, *notwithstanding the indubitable risks* of the plan. The Grand Duke Nicholas has just ordered an immediate attack. . . ." Georges Maurice Paléologue, *An Ambassador's Memoirs* (London: Hutchinson, 1923–1925), vol. 1, p. 104, my emphasis.

141. *Rossiia*, p. 90.

142. Savant, p. 38; Emets, p. 76; Evseev, p. 59; *VPO*, no. 374, pp. 280–81.

143. *Rossiia*, p. 132.

144. On the role of the anchoring bias in statistical estimates, see Richard Nisbett and Lee Ross, *Human Inference* (Englewood Cliffs, N.J.: Prentice-Hall, 1980).

145. It is noteworthy that the central General Staff and the district staffs had similar backgrounds and that there was continual rotation between them (e.g., Alekseev and Danilov themselves). Hence, the most likely explanation for their differing views is the difference in their temporary vantage points.

146. On this latter point, see Geoffrey Blainey, *The Causes of War* (New York: Free, 1973).

147. There was some bias due to parochial interests in the case of Kliuev, for example. However, if parochial interests affected preferences, they did not greatly affect perceptions. Perhaps the weakness of this effect is due to the relative frequency of job rotation.

8. *The Determinants of Military Strategy*

1. For a more contemporary case showing the link between autonomy and preferred strategy, see Perry M. Smith, *The Air Force Plans for Peace* (Baltimore: Johns Hopkins University Press, 1970), especially chaps. 2, 3, and 4.

2. A second Russian pattern, the defensive plan of 1910, could have been added, but the unmistakeable fact of Russian weakness so dominates the period that there would be little more to say about it.

3. For the quotation and a discussion of the general point, see Samuel P. Huntington, *The Soldier and the State* (New York: Vintage, 1957), p. 66.

4. There were civil-military squabbles and resistance to reform did exist, but there was never any risk that the military would be forced to sacrifice its autonomy or "essence." See Gordon Craig, *The Politics of the Prussian Army, 1640–1945* (London: Oxford University Press, 1964), and B. F. Schulte, *Die deutsche Armee: Zwischen Beharren und Verändern* (Düsseldorf: Droste, 1977).

5. Huntington, pp. 59–79.

6. Williamson, *The Politics of Grand Strategy: Britain and France Prepare for War, 1904–1914* (Cambridge: Harvard University Press, 1969); L. C. F. Turner, "The Edge of the Precipice," *Royal Military College Historical Journal* (Canberra) 3 (1974).

7. L. C. F. Turner, "The Russian Mobilization in 1914," in Paul Kennedy, ed., *The War Plans of the Great Powers* (London: Allen & Unwin, 1979).

8. For an attempt to identify the characteristics contributing to open-mindedness, see Milton Rokeach, *The Open and Closed Mind* (New York: Basic, 1960), especially chaps. 3 and 4.

9. John Steinbruner, *The Cybernetic Theory of Decision* (Princeton: Princeton University Press, 1974), pp. 103–9, 116–117; Irving L. Janis and Leon Mann, *Decision Making: A Psychological Analysis of Conflict, Choice, and Commitment* (New York: Free, 1977), pp. 45–80, 107–34; Leon Festinger, *A Theory of Cognitive Dissonance* (Stanford: Stanford University Press, 1962).

10. Robert L. Jervis has shown that there is little reason to believe that on balance wishfulness is more common than its opposite. See Robert L. Jervis, *Perception and Misperception in International Politics* (Princeton: Princeton University Press, 1976), pp. 356–81.

11. Janis and Mann, p. 73.

12. Steinbruner, pp. 104–5.

13. See especially ibid., pp. 47–139.

14. Robert Jervis, "Cooperation under the Security Dilemma," *World Politics* 30 (January 1978), pp. 167–214; George Quester, *Offense and Defense in the International System* (New York: Wiley, 1977); Stephen Van Evera, "The Causes of War," (University of California at Berkeley dissertation, 1984), from which the quotations come.

15. Jervis, "Cooperation," and Van Evera, "Causes of War," explore these as well as other reasons that offense promotes war.

16. Quester, p. 11. Jervis, "Cooperation," makes a similar point on p. 191.

17. For a more nuanced discussion of offense as a cause of World War I, see Jack Snyder, "Perceptions of the Security Dilemma in 1914," in Robert Jervis and Richard Ned Lebow, eds., *Deterrence and Perception* (Baltimore: Johns Hopkins University Press, forthcoming), and Stephen Van Evera, "The Cult of the Offensive and the Origins of the First World War," *International Security* 38 (summer 1984).

18. Quester, chaps. 11 and 12.

19. Two excellent first steps in this direction have been taken by Van Evera, "Causes of War," and Barry Posen, *The Sources of Military Doctrine: France, Britain, and Germany between the World Wars* (Ithaca: Cornell University Press, 1984).

Selected Bibliography

GENERAL WORKS

Albertini, Luigi. *The Origins of the War of 1914.* 3 vols. London: Oxford University Press, 1952–57.

Axelrod, Robert, ed. *Structure of Decision: The Cognitive Maps of Political Elites.* Princeton: Princeton University Press, 1976.

Creveld, Martin van. *Supplying War: Logistics from Wallenstein to Patton.* Cambridge: Cambridge University Press, 1977.

Garros, Louis, "En marge de l'alliance franco-russe (1902–1914)." *Revue historique de l'armée,* June 1950, pp. 29–46.

Gilpatrick, Meredith P. "Military Strategy on the Western Front from 1871 to 1914." University of Chicago dissertation, 1958.

Janis, Irving L., and Leon Mann. *Decision Making: A Psychological Analysis of Conflict, Choice, and Commitment.* New York: Free, 1977.

Jervis, Robert L. *Perception and Misperception in International Politics.* Princeton: Princeton University Press, 1976.

Kennedy, Paul M., ed. *The War Plans of the Great Powers, 1880–1914.* London: Allen & Unwin, 1979.

Laney, Frank M. "The Military Implementation of the Franco-Russian Alliance, 1890–1914." University of Virginia dissertation, 1954.

Neustadt, Richard. *Alliance Politics.* New York: Columbia University Press, 1970.

Nisbett, Richard, and Lee Ross. *Human Inference: Strategies and Shortcomings of Social Judgment,* Englewood Cliffs, N.J.: Prentice-Hall, 1980.

Posen, Barry R. *The Sources of Military Doctrine: France, Britain, and Germany between the World Wars.* Ithaca: Cornell University Press, 1984.

Rokeach, Milton. *The Open and Closed Mind.* New York: Collier, 1962.

Steinbruner, John D. *The Cybernetic Theory of Decision.* Princeton: Princeton University Press, 1974.

Tyng, Sewell. *The Campaign of the Marne, 1914.* New York: Longmans, Green, 1935.

Vagts, Alfred. *The Military Attaché.* Princeton: Princeton University Press, 1967.

Van Evera, Stephen. "The Causes of War." University of California at Berkeley dissertation, 1984.

FRANCE

André, Louis, *Cinq ans de ministère.* Paris: Michaud, 1909.

Ardant du Picq, Charles. *Battle Studies.* Trans. from the 8th ed. in French by Colonel John N. Greely and Major Robert C. Cotton. New York: Macmillan, 1921.

Beau, Georges, and Leopold Gaubusseau. *En août 1914 Lanrezac a-t-il sauvé la France?* Paris: Presses de la Cité, 1964.

Carrias, Eugene. *La pensée militaire française.* Paris: Presses Universitaires de France, 1960.

Challener, Richard D. *The French Theory of the Nation in Arms, 1866–1939.* New York: Columbia University Press, 1955.

Cole, Ronald H. "'Forward with the Bayonet!' The French Army Prepares for Offensive War, 1911–1914." University of Maryland dissertation, 1975.

Contamine, Henri. *La revanche, 1871–1914.* Paris: Berger-Levrault, 1957.

Driant, Emile. *Vers un nouveau Sedan.* Paris: Jouven, 1906.

d'Esclaibes, Lieutenant Colonel. "La pensée militaire Grandmaison." *Revue militaire d'information,* 25 June 1952, pp. 19–26.

Foch, Ferdinand. *The Principles of War.* Trans. by J. de Morinnio New York: Fly, 1918.

France, Assemblée nationale. Chambre des députés. Commission d'enquête sur le rôle et la situation de la métallurgie en France. Procès-verbaux. (*Défense du Bassin de Briey.*) Paris: Chambre des députés, 1919.

France. Etat-major de l'armée. Service historique. *Les armées françaises dans la Grande Guerre.* Paris: 1922.

France. Ministère des affaires étrangères. Commission de publication des documents relatifs aux origines de la Guerre de 1914. *Documents diplomatiques français. (1871–1914).* Paris: 1929–1936.

Freycinet, Charles de. *Souvenirs, 1878–1893.* New York: Da Capo, 1973.

Gallieni, Joseph-Simon. *Mémoires du Maréchal Gallieni: Défense de Paris.* Paris: Payot, 1926.

Gamelin, Maurice. *Manoeuvre et victoire de la Marne.* Paris: Grasset, 1954.

Grandmaison, L. *Deux conférences faites aux officiers de l'état-major de l'armée (février 1911): La notion de sûreté et l'engagement des grandes unités.* Paris: Berger-Levrault, 1911.

Grandmaison, L. *Dressage de l'infanterie en vue du combat offensif.* 3d ed. Paris: Berger-Levrault, 1908.

House, Jonathan M. "The Decisive Attack: A New Look at French Infantry Tactics on the Eve of World War I." *Military Affairs* 40 (December 1976), pp. 164–69.

Jaurès, Jean. *L'armée nouvelle.* 1910; rpt. Paris: Editions Sociales, 1977.

Joffre, Joseph Jacques Césaire. *The Memoirs of Marshal Joffre.* London: Bles, 1932.

Krumeich, Gerd. *Aufrüstung und Innenpolitik in Frankreich vor dem Ersten Weltkrieg.* Wiesbaden: Steiner, 1980.

Lardemelle, C. M. de. *1914: Le redressement initial.* Paris: Berger-Levrault, 1935.

Liddell Hart, B. H. "French Military Ideas before the First World War." In Martin Gilbert, ed. *A Century of Conflict, 1850–1950.* London: Hamilton, 1966.

Marchand, A. *Plans de concentration de 1871 à 1914.* Paris: Berger-Levrault, 1926.

Mayer, Emile. *Comment on pouvait prévoir l'immobilisation des fronts dans la guerre moderne.* Paris: Berger-Levrault, 1916.

Messimy, Adolphe. *Considérations générales sur l'organisation de l'armée.* Paris: Charles-Lavauzelle, 1907.

Messimy, Adolphe. *Mes souvenirs.* Paris: Plon, 1937.

Metzinger, Léon-Frédéric. *La transformation de l'armée, 1897–1907.* Paris: Société d'Edition Belleville, 1909.

Michon, Georges. *La préparation à la guerre: La loi de trois ans (1910–1914).* Paris: Librairie des Sciences Politiques et Sociales, 1935.

Selected Bibliography

Mitchell, Alan. "'A Situation of Inferiority': French Military Reorganization after the Defeat of 1870." *American Historical Review* 86 (February 1981), pp. 49–62.

Monteilhet, Joseph. *Les institutions militaires de la France, 1814–1924*. Paris: Alcan, 1926.

Paléologue, Georges Maurice. *The Turning Point: Three Critical Years, 1904–1906*. London: Hutchinson, 1935.

Porch, Douglas. *March to the Marne: The French Army, 1871–1914*. Cambridge: Cambridge University Press, 1981.

Porch, Douglas. "The French Army and the Spirit of the Offensive, 1900–1914." In Brian Bond and Ian Roy, eds. *War and Society*. New York: Holmes & Meier, 1975.

Possony, Stefan, and Etienne Mantoux. "Du Picq and Foch: The French School." In Edward M. Earle, ed. *Makers of Modern Strategy*. Princeton: Princeton University Press, 1971.

Ralston, David B. *The Army of the Republic: The Place of the Military in the Political Evolution of France, 1871–1914*. Cambridge: MIT Press, 1967.

Regnault, General. "L'échec du Plan XVII." *Revue de Paris*, 15 July 1920, pp. 355–91.

Revol, J. *Histoire de l'armée française*. Paris: Larousse, 1929.

Ryan, Stephen. *Pétain the Soldier*. South Brunswick and New York: Barnes, 1969.

Selliers de Moranville, Antonin Maurice de. *Du haut de la Tour de Babel: Commentaire sur la préparation de la guerre et la situation stratégique de la Belgique en 1914*. Paris: Berger-Levrault, 1925.

Setzen, Joel A. "The Doctrine of the Offensive in the French Army on the Eve of World War I." University of Chicago dissertation, 1972.

Silvestre, F. *Considérations sur la campagne de Mandchourie (1904–1905)*. Paris: Berger-Levrault, 1910.

Tanenbaum, Jan Karl. *General Maurice Sarrail, 1856–1929: The French Army and Left-Wing Politics*. Chapel Hill: University of North Carolina Press, 1974.

Weber, Eugen J. *The Nationalist Revival in France, 1905–1914*. Berkeley: University of California Press, 1959.

Williamson, Samuel R. *The Politics of Grand Strategy: Britain and France Prepare for War, 1904–1914*. Cambridge: Harvard University Press, 1969.

GERMANY

Addington, Larry H. *The Blitzkrieg Era and the German General Staff, 1865–1941*. New Brunswick: Rutgers University Press, 1971.

Bernhardi, Friedrich von. *Germany and the Next War*. New York: Longmans Green, 1914.

Bernhardi, Friedrich von. *On War of Today*. London: Rees, 1912.

Bronsart von Schellendorff, Paul. *The Duties of the General Staff*. London: Harrison, 1905.

Burchardt, Lothar. *Friedenswirtschaft und Kriegsvorsorge: Deutschlands wirtschaftliche Rüstungsbestrebungen vor 1914*. Boppard am Rhein: Boldt, 1968.

Carrias, Eugène. *La pensée militaire allemande*. Paris: Presses Universitaires de France, 1948.

Chickering, Roger. *Imperial Germany and a World without War: The Peace Movement and German Society, 1892–1914*. Princeton: Princeton University Press, 1975.

Cochenhausen, Friedrich von, ed. *Von Scharnhorst zu Schlieffen, 1806–1906*. Berlin: Mittler, 1933.

Courbis, Jean Charles. *Le comte Schlieffen: Organisateur et stratège*. Paris: Berger-Levrault, 1938.

[257]

Craig, Gordon A. *The Politics of the Prussian Army, 1640–1945.* London: Oxford University Press, 1964.

Ernharth, Ronald L. "The Tragic Alliance: Austro-German Military Cooperation, 1871–1918." Columbia University dissertation, 1970.

Farrar, Lancelot L. *The Short-War Illusion: German Policy, Strategy, and Domestic Affairs.* Santa Barbara: ABC-Clio, 1973.

Fischer, Fritz. *War of Illusions: German Policies from 1911 to 1914.* New York: Norton, 1975.

Foerster, Wolfgang. *Aus der Gedankenwerkstatt des deutschen Generalstabes.* Berlin: Mittler, 1931.

Fornaschon, Wolfgang. "Die politischen Anschauungen des Grafen Alfred von Waldersee und seine Stellungnahme zur deutschen Politik." *Historische Studien* vol. 273. Berlin, 1935.

Gasser, Adolf. "Deutschlands Einschluss zum Präventivkrieg, 1913–14." In *Discordia concors: Festgabe für Edgar Bonjour,* vol. I. Basle and Stuttgart: Helbing & Lichtenhann, 1968.

Gayl, Egon von. *General von Schlichting und sein Lebenswerk.* Berlin: Stilke, 1913.

Germany. Reichsarchiv. *Der Weltkrieg.* 3d ser. *Kriegsrüstung und Kiregswirtschaft.* Berlin: Mittler, 1930.

Glaise von Horstenau, Edmund. *Franz Josephs Weggefährte: Das Leben des Generalstabschefs Grafen Beck.* Zurich and Vienna: Amalthea, 1930.

Goltz, Colmar von der. *The Nation in Arms.* London: Rees, 1914.

Görlitz, Walter, *The German General Staff: Its History and Structure, 1657–1945.* London: Hollis & Carter, 1953.

Groener, Wilhelm. *Commander against His Will: Operative Studies of the World War.* Trans. Martin F. Schmitt. Washington, D.C.: U.S. Army War College Library, 1943.

Groener, Wilhelm. *Lebenserinnerungen.* Gottingen: Vandenhoek & Ruprecht, 1957.

Groener, Wilhelm. *The Testament of Count Schlieffen.* Trans. W. P. Papenforth. Mimeo. Fort Sherman, Kans.: U.S. Army, 1931.

Haeussler, Helmut. *General William Groener and the Imperial German Army.* Madison: State Historical Society of Wisconsin, 1962.

Kluck, Alexander von. *The March on Paris and the Battle of the Marne.* London: Arnold, 1920.

Kuhl, Hermann von. *Der deutsche Generalstab in Vorbereitung und Durchführung des Weltkrieges.* 2d ed. Berlin: Mittler, 1920. Trans. François Douchy as *Le Grand Etatmajor allemand avant et pendant la guerre mondiale.* Paris: Payot, 1922.

Kuhl, Hermann von, and Walter von Bergman. *Movements and Supply of the German First Army during August and September, 1914.* Ft. Leavenworth, Kans.: Command and General Staff School Press, 1929.

Ludendorff, Erich. *The General Staff and Its Problems.* 1920; rpt. Freeport, N.Y.: Books for Libraries, 1971.

Moltke, Helmuth Johannes Ludwig von. *Mémoires, lettres et documents.* Paris: Payot, 1933.

Moltke, Helmuth Karl Bernhard von. *Moltke's Tactical Problems from 1858 to 1882.* Kansas City, Mo. Hudson-Kimberley, 189–.

Moltke, Helmuth. *Die deutschen Aufmarschpläne, 1871–1890.* Ed. Ferdinand von Schmerfeld. Berlin: Mittler, 1929.

Moltke, Helmuth. *Essays, Speeches, and Memoirs.* New York: Harper, 1893.

Moritz, Albrecht. *Das Problem des Präventivkrieges in der deutschen Politik während der ersten Marokkokrise.* Bern and Frankfurt: Lang & Lang, 1974.

Noce, Daniel. *Strategic Demolitions of Railroads in Front of the German Right Wing, August–September 1914.* Occasional Paper no. 72. U.S. Army Engineering School, March 1940.

Rich, Norman R. *Friedrich von Holstein.* Cambridge: Cambridge University Press, 1965.

Ritter, Gerhard. *The Schlieffen Plan: Critique of a Myth.* New York: Praeger, 1958.

Ritter, Gerhard. *The Sword and the Scepter: The Problem of Militarism in Germany.* 3 vols. Coral Gables, Fla.: University of Miami Press, 1969, 1972.

Rohl, John C. G. *Germany without Bismarck.* Berkeley: University of California Press, 1967.

Schlieffen, Alfred von. *Briefe.* Ed. Eberhard Kessel. Gottingen: Vandenhoeck & Ruprecht, 1958.

Schlieffen, Alfred von. *The Schlieffen Problems of 1891, 1896, 1901, 1903, 1904, and 1905.* U.S. Army translation. Ft. Leavenworth, Kans.: Command and General Staff School, 1935–36.

Staabs, Hermann von. *Aufmarsch nach zwei Fronten.* Berlin: Mittler, 1925.

Tunstall, Graydon A. "The Schlieffen Plan: The Diplomacy and Military Strategy of the Central Powers in the East, 1905–1914." Rutgers University dissertation, 1974.

Wallach, Jehuda L. *Das Dogma der Vernichtungsschlacht: Die Lehren von Clausewitz und Schlieffen und ihre Wirkungen in zwei Weltkriegen.* Frankfurt: Bernard & Graefe, 1967.

Wallach, Jehuda L. *Kriegstheorien: Ihre Entwicklung im 19. und 20. Jahrhundert.* Frankfurt: Bernard & Graefe, 1972.

Zoellner, O. von. "Schlieffens Vermächtnis." *Militarwissenschaftliche Rundschau,* supplementary issue, 1938.

RUSSIA

Ageev, A. "Ofitsery russkogo general'nogo shtaba ob opyte russko-iaponskoi voiny 1904–1905 gg." *Voenno-istoricheskii zhurnal* no. 8, 1975, pp. 99–104.

Astaf'ev, I. I. "Potsdamskoe soglashenie 1911g." *Istoricheskie zapiski* no. 85 1970, pp. 112ff.

Barsukov, E. Z. *Artilleriia russkoi armii, 1900–1917.* Moscow: Voenizdat, 1948.

Basily, Nicholas de. *Diplomat of Imperial Russia, 1903–1917: Memoirs.* Stanford: Hoover Institution Press, 1973.

Beloi, A. *Galitsiiskaia bitva.* Moscow: Gosizdat, 1929.

Bestuzhev, I. V. *Bor'ba v Rossii po voprosam vneshnei politiki, 1906–1910.* Moscow: Akademiia Nauk, 1961.

Bestuzhev, I. V. "Bor'ba v Rossii po voprosam vneshnei politiki nakanune pervoi mirovoi voiny (1910–1914 gg.)." *Istoricheskie zapiski* no. 75 (1965).

Borisov, V. E. *Logistika (iskusstvo general'nogo shtaba): Vvedenie v voenno-kriticheskii razbor russko-iaponskoi voiny 1904–1905 gg.* St. Petersburg: Svet, 1912.

Borisov, V. E. *Smelaia napadatel'naia taktika: Russkaia voennaia doktrina.* St. Petersburg: Svet, 1913.

Bovykin, V. I. *Iz istorii vozniknoveniia pervoi mirovoi voiny: Otnosheniia Rossii i Frantsii v 1912–1914 gg.* Moscow: Moskovskii Universitet, 1961.

Brusilov, A. A. *A Soldier's Notebook, 1914–1918.* London: Macmillan, 1930.

Brusilov, A. A. *Moi vospominaniia.* Moscow: Voenizdat, 1963.

Danilov, Iurii Nikiforovich. *Rossiia v mirovoi voine, 1914–1915 gg.* Berlin: Slovo, 1924. Trans. and expanded as *La Russie dans la Guerre Mondiale (1914–1917).* Paris: Payot, 1927.

Danilov, Iruii Nikiforovich. *Velikii Kniaz' Nikolui Nikolaevich.* Paris: Imprimerie de Navarre, 1930. Trans. as *Le Grand-Duc Nicolas.* Paris: Berger-Levrault, 1932.

Denikin, Anton Ivanovich. *The Career of a Tsarist Officer: Memoirs, 1872–1916.* Minneapolis: University of Minnesota Press, 1975.

Dobrorol'skii, Sergei. "La mobilisation de l'armée russe en 1914." *Revue d'histoire de la Guerre Mondiale,* April-June 1923, pp. 144–65.

Emets, V. A. "O roli russkoi armii v pervyi period mirovoi voiny 1914–1918 gg." *Istoricheskie zapiski* no. 77 (1965).

Emets, V. A. *Ocherki vneshnei politiki Rossii v period pervoi mirovoi voiny: Vzaimootnosheniia Rossii c soiuznikami po voprosam vedeniia voiny.* Moscow: Nauka, 1977.

Evseev, N. F. *Avgustskoe srazhenie 2-i russkoi armii v Vostochnoi Prussii (Tannenberg) v 1914 godu.* Moscow: Gosvoenizdat, 1936.

Fuller, William C. "The Russian Empire and Its Potential Enemies, 1909–1914." Colgate University, unpublished manuscript, 1981.

Golovin, N. N. *The Russian Army in the World War.* New Haven: Yale University Press, 1931.

Golovin, N. N. *The Russian Campaign of 1914.* Ft. Leavenworth, Kans.: Command and Staff School Press, 1933.

Hamilton, Ian. *A Staff Officer's Scrap-book during the Russo-Japanese War.* 2 vols. London: Arnold, 1907–1908.

Ignat'ev, A. A. *Piat'desiat let v stroiu.* Moscow: Gosizdat khudozhestvennoi literatury, 1959.

Ignat'ev, A. V. *Russko-angliiskie otnosheniia nakanune pervoi mirovoi voiny (1909–1914 gg.).* Moscow: Izdatel'stvo sotsial'no-ekonomicheskoi literatury, 1962.

Kozlov, N. *Ocherk snabzheniia russkoi armii voenno-tekhnicheskim imuzhestvom v mirovuiu voinu.* Moscow: Gosvoenizdat, 1926.

Lukomskii, A. S. *Vospominaniia.* Berlin: Kirscher, 1922.

Maksheev, F. A. *Voennoe khoziaistvo: Kurs Intendantskoi Akademii.* St. Petersburg: USOV, 1912.

Manikovskii, A. A. *Boevoi snabzhenie russkoi armii, 1914–1918 gg.* Moscow: Voennyi redaktsionnyi sovet, 1923.

Melikov, V. A. *Strategicheskoe razvertyvanie.* Moscow: Voenizdat, 1939.

Mikhnevich, N. P. *Strategiia.* St. Petersburg: Berezovskii, 1911.

Neznamov, A. *Sovremennaia voina.* St. Petersburg: Skachkov, 1911.

Pokrovskii, M. "Tri soveshchaniia." *Vestnik narodnogo komissariata inostrannykh del,* 20 June 1919, pp. 12–44.

Polivanov, A. A. *Iz dnevnikov i vospominanii po dolzhnosti voennogo ministra i ego pomoshchika, 1907–1916 gg.* Moscow: Vyshii voennyi redaktsionnyi sovet, 1924.

Rostunov, I. I. *Russkii front pervoi mirovoi voiny.* Moscow: Nauka, 1976.

Russia. 10-i otdel General'nogo shtaba RKKA. *Vostochno-prusskaia operatsiia: Sbornik dokumentov.* Moscow: Gosvoenizdat, 1939.

Russia. Nachal'nik general'nogo shtaba (Palitsyn) and 1-i ober-kvartirmeister (Alekseev). *Doklad o meropriiatiiakh po oborone Gosudarstva, podlezhashchykh osushchestvleniiu v blizhaishee desiatiletie.* St. Petersburg, n.d.

Russia. *Svod ukazanii dannykh nachal'nikom General'nogo shtaba vo vremia voennoi igry ofitserov General'nogo shtaba v 1907 godu.* St. Petersburg: Voennaia tipografiia, 1908.

Samoilo, A. *Dve zhizni.* Moscow: Voenizdat, 1958.

Savant, Jean. *Epopée russe: Campagne de l'armée Rennenkampf en Prusse-Orientale.* Paris: Calmann-Lévy, 1945.

Sazonov, Sergei. *Fateful Years, 1909–1916.* New York: Stokes, 1928.

Shatsillo, K. F. "Razvitie vooruzhennykh sil Rossii nakanune pervoi mirovoi voiny." Institut Istorii of Moscow dissertation, 1968.

Shatsillo, K. F. *Rossiia pered pervoi mirovoi voinoi: Vooruzhennye sily tsarizma v 1905–1914 gg.* Moscow: Nauka, 1974.

Shatsillo, K. F. *Russkii imperializm i razvitie flota nakanune pervoi mirovoi voiny (1906–1914 gg.)* Moscow: Nauka, 1968.

Stone, Norman. *The Eastern Front, 1914–1917.* New York: Scribner's, 1975.

Strokov, A. A. *Vooruzhennye sily i voennoe iskusstvo v pervoi mirovoi voine.* Moscow: Voenizdat, 1974.

Sukhomlinov, General V. A. *Vospominaniia.* Moscow: Gosizdat, 1926.

Suvorov, A. N. "Voennaia igra starshikh voiskovykh nachal'nikov v aprele 1914 goda." In A. A. Svechin, ed., *Trudy komissii po issledovaniiu i ispol'zovaniiu opyta voiny 1914–1918 gg.* Reprinted from *Voenno-istoricheskii sbornik.* 1919.

Svechin, A. A. "Bol'shaia voennaia programma." *Russkaia mysl'*, bk. 8, pt. 17 (1913), pp. 19–29.

Thaden, Edward C. *Russia and the Balkan Alliance of 1912.* University Park: Pennsylvania State University Press, 1965.

Trutko, I. "Podgotovka tyla iugo-zapadnogo fronta (1914g.)." *Voenno-istoricheskii zhurnal* no. 3 (1939), pp. 92–113.

Ushakov, K. *Podgotovka voennykh soobshchenii Rossii k mirovoi voine.* Moscow: Gosizdat, 1928.

Valentinov, N. [N. V. Vol'skii]. "Voennye soglasheniia Rossii s inostrannymi gosudarstvami do voiny." *Voenno-istoricheskii sbornik* no. 2 (1919).

Vasil'ev, N. *Transport Rossii v voine 1914–1918 gg.* Moscow: Voenizdat, 1939.

Vatsetis, I. I. *Operatsii na vostochnoi granitse Germanii v 1914g. Chast' 1-ia: Vostochno-prusskaia operatsiia.* Moscow: Gosizdat, 1929.

VPO (*Vostochno-prusskaia operatsiia*). See: Russia, 10-i otdel. . . .

Zaionchkovskii, A. M. *Podgotovka Rossii k imperialisticheskoi voine.* Moscow: Gosvoenizdat, 1926.

Zvonar'ev, K. K. *Agenturnaia razvedka.* Vol. I: *Russkaia agenturnaia razvedka vsekh vidov do i vo vremia voiny 1914–1918 gg.* Moscow: Izdanie IV upravleniia shtaba RKKA, 1929.

Index

Cornell Studies In Security Affairs

A Series Edited by

Robert Jervis
Robert J. Art
Stephen M. Walt

LIBRARY OF CONGRESS CATALOGING IN PUBLICATION DATA

Snyder, Jack L.
 The ideology of the offensive.

 (Cornell studies in security affairs)
 Bibliography: p.
 Includes index.
 1. Offensive (Military strategy)—History—20th century. 2. Military planning—
France—History—20th century. 3. Military planning—Germany—History—20th
century. 4. Military planning—Soviet Union—History—20th century. 5. World
War, 1914–1918—Campaigns. I. Title. II. Series.
U162.S58 1984   355.4'3'09034   84–7783
ISBN 0–8014–1657–4 (cloth: alk. paper)
ISBN 0-8014-8244-5 (pbk: alk. paper)